The Book of Isaiah, chronologically arranged: an amended version with historical and critical introductions and explanatory notes

Cheyne, T. K. (Thomas Kelly)

BIBLIOLIFE

THE BOOK OF ISAIAH

CHRONOLOGICALLY ARRANGED

AN AMENDED VERSION

WITH HISTORICAL AND CRITICAL INTRODUCTIONS

AND EXPLANATORY NOTES

By T. K. CHEYNE, M.A.

FELLOW OF BALLIOL COLLEGE, OXFORD

London

MACMILLAN AND CO.

1870

PREFACE.

THE present work is a fragment of a much larger one planned by the editor several years ago. He was induced to abridge his scheme by the urgent necessity which appeared to exist for works of moderate size and accurate information on the most important books of the Old Testament. He trusts, therefore, that teachers of theology may find this attempt a convenient substratum for their own more extended instruction, and at the same time ventures to hope that the independent researches, which have accompanied the writing of every part of it, will recommend it to the attention of professional scholars.

The object of this edition is not in the least connected with the recent movement for a revision of the Authorized Version :—it is simply to restore the probable meaning of Isaiah, so far as this can be expressed in appropriate English. The basis of the version is naturally the revised translation of 1611, but no scruple has been felt in introducing alterations, wherever the true sense of the prophecies appeared to require it. These might indeed have been largely increased, but the affectionate reverence with which the Authorized Version is so justly regarded, appeared to demand that changes should not be made for any but comparatively grave reasons.

The obligations of the editor to German critical works of all schools are too numerous to be expressed. His greatest are those to Ewald, whose work on the Prophets is certainly the most important contribution ever made to the study of this subject. But many other writers, whose names are unfamiliar to the English reader, have suggested ideas, or originated trains of thought, which could hardly have been arrived at without their assistance. To mention a few only would be an injustice to the rest, but the editor would be ungrateful were he not to acknowledge the valuable information he has frequently derived from the notes of Delitzsch. English books on Isaiah have not been neglected, but have scarcely influenced this commentary to any appreciable extent.

The references made in the following pages to the editor's 'Notes and Criticisms on the Hebrew Text of Isaiah' are given for the benefit of the less advanced student. The editor conceives that much of the information in that little work is not accessible to an English reader in any other form, and confidently believes that the method of philological inquiry there adopted is the only one likely to be fruitful of solid results

OXFORD, *May* 2, 1870.

INTRODUCTION.

SECTION I.

The prophetic career of Isaiah.

LITTLE is known of the personal history of Isaiah. A Rab-
binical legend identifies his father with a brother of the
Jewish king, Amaziah, and this, though probably unhistorical, implies a correct appreciation of his character and capacities. The
lofty bearing of the prophet in his intercourse with Ahaz and
Hezekiah, and his statesmanlike interest in the fortunes, not only
of his own, but of other countries, are a sufficient justification of
this instructive story. The scene of his ministry was never shifted
from Jerusalem, and his audience was for the most part confined
to the prosperous and educated classes[1]. It is true that some of
the latter appear to have derided his exhortations[2], but this must
have been owing rather to the monotony of his subject, and his
continual appeals to the conscience, than to any deficiency of
oratorical power. His discourses, at any rate, in the form in
which they are now extant, presuppose in their author a high
degree of literary cultivation, received, as we may not unfairly

[1] Cp. Isa xxix. 11, p 66.   [2] Cp. Isa. xxviii. 10, p. 61.

conjecture, in the 'schools of the prophets.' In this respect we may contrast Isaiah with his gifted predecessor, Amos, who distinctly admits[1] that he was no educated prophet, and no prophet's scholar. But however acquired, there is a classical sense of proportion in Isaiah, which we fail to trace in the same degree in any other prophet, and which implies a systematic training superadded to an original genius. Of Isaiah's literary characteristics we shall speak presently; it will be sufficient to remark here that, like the prophets in general, he devoted a careful study to the ideas and even the phraseology of his predecessors, as a comparison of the following passages, which might easily be added to, will sufficiently prove.

Isa. i. 11, 14. To what purpose is the multitude of your sacrifices unto me? saith Jehovah; I am full of the burnt offerings of rams and the fat of fed calves, and I delight not in the blood of bullocks, or of lambs, or of he-goats. . . . Your new moons and your holy days my soul hateth, they are a trouble unto me, I am weary of bearing.

Comp. Amos v. 21, 22, and Hos. vi. 6. I hate, I despise your feast days, and will not smell a sweet savour in your solemn assemblies. Though ye offer me burnt offerings and your meat offerings, I will not accept them, neither will I regard the thank offerings of your fat beasts.

For I delight in charity, and not in sacrifice; and in the knowledge of God more than in burnt offerings.

Isa. iii. 9. The look of their countenance witnessed against them, and their sin they published as Sodom without disguise; alas for their soul, for they have wrought for themselves evil.

Comp. Hos. v. 5. The pride of Israel doth testify to his face: therefore shall Israel and Ephraim fall for their iniquity.

[1] Amos vii. 14.

Isa. iv. 2. In that day shall the buds of Jehovah be beautiful and glorious, and the fruit of the land a pride and an ornament for them that are escaped of Israel.

Comp. Joel iii. 18; Amos ix. 13; Hos. ii. 21, 22. In that day the mountains shall drop down new wine, and the hills shall flow with milk, and all the rivers of Judah shall flow with water, and a fountain shall come forth of the house of Jehovah, and shall water the valley of Shittim.

Behold, the days come, saith Jehovah, that the ploughman shall overtake the reaper, and the treader of grapes him that soweth seed; and the mountains shall drop new wine, and all the hills shall melt.

In that day I will answer, saith Jehovah, I will answer the heavens, and they shall answer the earth; and the earth shall answer the corn, and the wine, and the oil; and they shall answer Jezreel.

Isa. x. 23 (comp. xxviii. 22). For destruction by a sure decree will Jehovah of Hosts perform in the midst of all the earth.

Comp. Joel iii. 14. Multitudes, multitudes in the valley of the sure decree: for the day of Jehovah is near in the valley of the sure decree.

It is altogether uncertain when the prophetic career of Isaiah began. The superscription of chap. i asserts that he 'saw visions' as early as the reign of Uzziah, but this is probably a mere editorial inference from the first verse of chap. vi (p. 22). We are informed in the latter passage that Isaiah passed through a grave moral and religious crisis, which ended in his attaining the conviction of his Divine mission, in the year of Uzziah's death, B.C. 758, that is, shortly before that event. But there is no ground for ascribing any of the extant prophecies to the reign of Uzziah, nor even (with perhaps one exception, see p. 5) to that of Jotham.

It was the rapid decline of the nation under the feeble sway of Ahaz, and its imminent danger first from Syria and then from Assyria, which aroused the slumbering energies of the impatient prophet. The reign of Ahaz, and the former half of the reign of Hezekiah, may to a great extent be reconstructed from the prophecies of Isaiah.

The latest occasions known to us, on which Isaiah exercised his public functions, are recorded in chaps. xxxvi–xxxix[1]. One of the uncontested prophecies, however, belongs in all probability to a still more recent period. If we are not mistaken in assigning the oracle on the fortunes of Egypt (chap. xix) to the year 700 B.C., he must have been then almost eighty years of age[2]. He had probably long retired from active life, and occupied a part of his leisure in developing the Messianic doctrine, i.e. the ultimate triumph of Jehovah's sovereignty, in relation to the races excluded from the covenant with Israel. The great thought of a personal Messiah is now supplemented by that of the spiritual brotherhood of all nations. Egypt and Assyria, as representatives of the Gentile world, are admitted to a share of the privileges hitherto restricted to the Israelites, a bright and cheering picture not unworthy of the close of a prophetic ministry!

The plan of this work does not allow us to attempt a complete sketch of Isaiah's religious position. With all his originality, our prophet was indebted for his most essential doctrine to Joel, Amos, and Hosea, his predecessors. The claims of Jehovah to undivided allegiance were preached by the latter with a fervid enthusiasm, which

---

[1] See remarks on pp. 101–103

[2] It is just possible, however, that the age of Isaiah has been exaggerated. If we accept the latest account of the Assyrian chronology, the length of his prophetic career would be reduced by about twenty years. See 'The Annals of Tiglath-Pileser II,' by George Smith, in Lepsius's 'Zeitschrift für ägyptische Sprache und Alterthumskunde,' Jan. 1869.

even Isaiah could not surpass, though his capacity for influencing the higher classes of society enabled him to preach the same doctrine with more striking results. Yet these results, imperfect and transitory as they proved to be, are not the highest honours of which Isaiah can boast. His place in the affections of all succeeding generations is due to the fact that he was, perhaps, the first to preach in distinct terms the doctrines of a personal Messiah and of the spiritual brotherhood of all nations. He foresaw that in the awful 'day of Jehovah,' which former prophets had announced, few even of the chosen people should pass the ordeal, and so deep was his conviction of this that he expressed it in the name of one of his sons, Shear Jashub, 'a remnant shall return[1].' But he was too 'bold,' as St. Paul says[2], to terminate his speculations at so early a point. By combining the doctrine of the few that should be saved with that of the necessary triumph of Jehovah's kingdom, he was prepared to receive a new and grand revelation. He saw, in prophetic vision, an exalted personage ascending the throne of David, who should attract the whole world into voluntary submission to his rule. Not that his intuition of this great truth was at all moments equally clear. We shall find reason to suppose that the germ implanted in his mind in the reign of Ahaz only attained its full proportions in his extreme old age[3]. But even from the first there are hints, which we can understand better than Isaiah himself, of the glorious future in which all mankind should participate. And thus to the twofold elementary doctrine of the sole divinity of Jehovah and the awful strictness of the impending judgment a fellow-truth was added, viz. that of the personal Messiah, which developed finally into the crowning doctrine of the spiritual equality of all nations.

[1] Cp. note on Isa. x. 21, 22, p. 83.   [2] Rom. x. 20.
[3] Cp. notes on pp. 31, 87.

SECTION II.

The writings of Isaiah.

A few hints may be offered as to the origin of the Book of Isaiah in its earliest form, i. e. in that which it presented before the addition of chaps. xl–lxvi, and certain other chapters, which we have reason to assign to a later age. It would be natural to a student unfamiliar with the subject to suppose that Isaiah wrote down his prophecies as soon as they were delivered, and thus gradually formed the collection before us. But this is not confirmed by a closer examination. Jeremiah informs us[1] that in the twenty-third year of his ministry he dictated the first summary of his discourses, and though such direct evidence is wanting in the case of Isaiah, there are not many prophecies which can be fairly regarded as representing his original words. The attention, which he evidently bestowed on the form of his prophecies, of itself excludes this idea in the majority of instances, while some, such as those which relate to foreign nations, were of course written down without ever having been delivered at all. With this exception, however, we may reasonably consider the extant prophecies of Isaiah to be reproductions, in a condensed form, of the main outlines of his public teaching. The analyses prefixed to the several groups of prophecies in this edition will further illustrate this, and the case of Jeremiah will prove, if proof be necessary, that the memory of a prophet was strong enough to retain the ideas of a long series of discourses.

In fact, the Book of Isaiah, properly so called, appears to be composed of several smaller books or prophetic collections, the three first of which were published, as internal evidence shews, by

[1] Jer. xxxvi. 2, comp. xxv. 3.

the prophet himself. The chapter which opens the book, in the traditional arrangement, is evidently intended as a general introduction to a large group of prophecies. It is impossible, however, to trace any distinct connection between that chapter and the three following ones, which certainly constitute a single homogeneous prophecy. Equally difficult is it to trace a connection between chap. i and chaps. vi–x. 4; the latter chapters, with the exception of ix. 8–x. 4 (see p. 5), are as distinct and homogeneous as the prophecy already mentioned. But there is a striking resemblance between the historical circumstances implied in chap. i and those in the minor prophecies on foreign nations (see pp. 35–49). All these prophecies appear to have been composed in the beginning of the reign of Hezekiah, when the neighbouring tribes took advantage of the accession of a new sovereign to harass the Jewish territory, and when the shadow of the Assyrian power fell dangerously near the south of Palestine. On the other hand, the prophecy (x. 5–xii. 6), which now precedes the foreign oracles, evidently implies a still further progress of the Assyrian aggressions. We are therefore compelled to admit that it interrupts the original order of the prophecies, and to conjecture that, in a hopeful mood supervening on the accession of Hezekiah, Isaiah published a new and enlarged edition of his works, consisting of the two prophetic writings already in circulation (ii–v, and vi–ix. 7), supplemented by the minor prophecies on foreign nations. On the death or retirement of Isaiah additions may have been made, and the arrangement of the prophecies modified, by his disciples[1], when collecting the fugitive relics of their departed master. Thus, for instance, they seem to have completed the scanty collection of foreign prophecies by the insertion of others of a more recent date. Thus, too, we

---

[1] Cp. Isa. viii. 16, p. 29.

may suppose them to have placed x. 5–xii. 6 in its present position as a parallel to the analogous prophecy of Immanuel. (On ix. 8–x. 4, see pp. 5, 6.) The entire book was concluded by the important group of prophecies on the Assyrian invasion (xxviii–xxxiii), in order, perhaps, to counterbalance the stern admonitions of the opening chapter with the consolatory promises of chaps. xxxii and xxxiii.

The literary characteristics of Isaiah cannot be better described than in the words of Ewald. 'He is distinguished from other prophets by the absence of any special peculiarity. His style is not like that of Joel, Hosea, and Micah, in which some particular aspect, the lyrical, the elegiac, or the oratorical, generally predominates, for he is the perfect master of every kind of style, which the nature of his subject may demand. The habitual tone of his discourse is a lofty and majestic tranquillity, which does not indeed prevent him from now and then expressing a natural excitement or indignation, but which soon reasserts its claim to paramount dominion.' (See ii. 9–iii. 1, xxviii. 11–23, xxix. 9–14[1].) His rhythm is full and vigorous, his imagery natural, his plays upon words not merely arbitrary, but connected with a real antithesis of ideas. Sometimes his love of pregnant conciseness leads him into obscurity, but this is the exception and not the rule, and is probably owing in part to the errors and corruptions of the received text. Not the least of his excellences is his unenvious recognition of the merits of earlier prophets, which induced him on at least two occasions to insert passages from their works, and so to open a new chapter in the history of Hebrew literature[2].

Besides being a prophet, Isaiah was a historian, possibly also a psalmist. The compiler of the Chronicles informs us[3] that

---

[1] 'Die Propheten des alten Bundes,' vol. 1. p. 280

[2] See Isa. ii. 2–4, xv, xvi. 1–12   [3] See 2 Chron. xxvi. 22, xxxii. 32.

there existed in his time an account of 'the acts of Uzziah' by our prophet, and a 'vision of Isaiah the son of Amoz,' which was incorporated in 'the book of the kings of Judah and Israel.' The signification of the latter of these titles is obscure. Was the 'vision of Isaiah' a historical monograph, or a collection of prophecies? Was it composed by Isaiah, or merely a sketch of the prophet's career by some anonymous author, in which one of Isaiah's 'visions' may have been inserted? To neither of these questions can we return a fully satisfactory answer. The idea that Isaiah was a psalmist is due to Hitzig, who thinks that Ps. xlvi-xlviii were composed by the prophet on the destruction of the Assyrian army. A strong resemblance to Isaiah both in phraseology and in ideas cannot fail to strike the reader of these Psalms. Compare the refrain, 'Jehovah is with us,' in Ps. xlvi, with the similar use of Immanuel, 'God is with us,' in Isa. viii. 8, 10, and several verbal parallels in Ps. xlviii, and Isa. xxxiii.

SECTION III.

Rise of the controversy respecting authorship.

The celebrated Jewish commentator Aben Ezra (twelfth century) was the first to suggest the possibility that Isa. xl–lxvi might not be the work of Isaiah, but of some later prophet. His expressions indeed are obscure, but this may be accounted for by the opposition which he conceived to exist between faith and critical inquiry. An ardent lover of truth, he was at the same time sincerely attached to the religion of his forefathers, which might, he feared, be imperilled by undermining the received opinions as to the authorship of the Scriptures. He allows us indeed to infer that various passages in the Pentateuch were added subsequently to the time of Moses, but, he takes care to add, 'the intelligent man will be silent.' This may serve to illustrate his singular remarks on the last twenty-seven chapters of the Book of Isaiah. 'There are passages in this book which refer to the Babylonian exile, spoken in memory of the fact that it was Cyrus who sent back the exiles. . . . And know that the copyists of the Law (the Talmudists) say that Samuel wrote the Book of Samuel, and it is true, (but only) as far as the words, And Samuel died. And the Book of Chronicles proves it[1], for there a succession of generations is given which preceded Zerubbabel. And this passage attests it, Kings shall see and arise, even princes, and shall worship, though it is possible to reply, As soon as they hear the name of the prophet, even though he were dead, they shall worship. The intelligent man will understand.' In other words, Aben Ezra entertained doubts as to Isaiah's authorship of chaps. xl–lxvi, but, in order to avoid offence, supplied a convenient answer to his own objection. In this point, however, the critic was far in advance of his age, and the vague allusions which he dropped as to the authorship of these prophecies met with no 'intelligent man' to discern their value. It was only at the end of the last century that two German scholars, Koppe and Döderlein, revived the theory that the Book of Isaiah was not entirely homogeneous, though the position occupied by them has been greatly modified by later critics. Before proceeding, however, to estimate the arguments adduced on either side, we must remind the reader that the question at issue is not that of the genuineness of certain prophecies, nor even of their authenticity. None of the disputed chapters but chap. xiii claims to be written by Isaiah, and none is deprived of its prophetic character through being assigned to the Babylonian exile. It is

---

[1] Aben Ezra implies that since many generations intervened between Isaiah and Zerubbabel, passages like the following, which he interprets of the reverence paid to the prophetic writer, cannot have been written by Isaiah.

obvious that the question of authorship must be argued apart from any *à priori* canons of a theological or philosophical nature. By the test of language and ideas, and not by the mere occurrence of any single proper name, the Babylonian origin of these prophecies must, if at all, be substantiated.

SECTION IV.

Arguments in favour of the unity of authorship.

We cannot introduce this section better than with the following suggestive remarks of Dr. F. Delitzsch :—'Had we received this book of discourses to the exiles in a separate form, and without the opportunity of comparing it with the prophecies of Isaiah, its contents alone would never have given rise to the idea, that it had for its author a prophet of the time of Hezekiah, or indeed of any period previous to the exile. For there is not a single passage in the book which betrays that the times of the exile are only ideally, and not actually, present to the prophetic writer. The assertion of Hävernick, Keil, Welte, and others, that historical circumstances are frequently alluded to which correspond only to the age of Isaiah, is founded on self-delusion[1].' 'And hence,' as he elsewhere remarks, 'if, as we believe, Isaiah is the author, he has passed entirely out of the actual present, and leads a life in the spirit among the exiles[2].' A hypothesis which appeals so strongly to the imagi-

---

[1] Appendix to Drechsler's Isaiah, vol. iii. p. 386, comp. Delitzsch's Isaiah, p. 385

[2] Delitzsch's Isaiah, p 390. We have selected Delitzsch as the representative of his school in order not to weaken that side of the question by adducing arguments of a less satisfactory nature. Some of this class will be noticed in due course in the commentary. The most ingenious (we regret not to be able to use any other word) recent defence of the unity of authorship is 'De echtheid van het tweede gedeelte van Jesaja,' by Dr A. Rutgers, Leyden, 1866 The silence, not according to us a complete one, which the author of Isa. xl-lxvi

nation, requires surely to be supported by arguments of no ordinary strength. And it is only fair to add that the scholar whose words we have cited, has, up to a certain point, maintained his theory with a candour and ability which leave but little to be desired. His first argument is the correspondence of the traditional view with his own peculiar theory on the arrangement of Isaiah. He points out that a series of prophetic announcements of deliverance from exile is interspersed at regular intervals throughout the first portion of the book, in order to serve as a prelude to the last twenty-seven chapters, which are all composed from the point of view of an exile in Babylon. A brief prophecy of the Babylonian captivity is placed in the very centre of the book as a preparation for the violent transition from the age of Hezekiah to that of Cyrus. But surely such an artificial arrangement is without a parallel in the Old Testament, and presupposes a strange anticipation of modern critical objections. The second argument adduced by Delitzsch is the occurrence of certain favourite expressions of Isaiah in the disputed chapters, e. g. 'the Holy One of Israel,' (a phrase which is only found five times elsewhere,) i. 4, v. 19, 24, &c., comp. xli. 14, 16, 20, xlii. 3, 14, 15, &c.; 'saith Jehovah' (in the imperfect tense), i. 11, 18, comp. xl. 1, 25, xli. 21; 'the Hero of Israel,' i. 24, comp. xlix. 26, lx. 16, 'the Hero of Jacob;' and the use of Jacob as synonymous with Israel, xxix. 23, comp. xl. 27. But a correspondence of isolated phrases, which is not even uniformly exact, is of little value as an argument, and may be counterbalanced by many expressions entirely peculiar to the disputed prophecies, e. g. 'rule' as applied to the true religion, xlii. 1, 3, 4, li. 4; 'righteousness' in the sense of 'grace' or 'salvation,' xli. 2, 10,

maintains in reference to the local characteristics of Babylon, is here exaggerated into an evidence in favour of the Isaianic theory. But the writer forgets that the burden of this prophecy is, 'Depart ye from Babylon' xlv. 8, li. 5, &c.; 'righteous' in that of 'truthful,' xli. 26, comp. lix. 4; the curious word *seghanim*, 'governors,' xli 25, commonly supposed to be of Persian origin; and many other phrases. In fact, the argument from phraseology in Hebrew is merely a subsidiary one. The literature at our command is so narrow in compass, and has, in our opinion, been so often tampered with by unscrupulous editors, that any detailed description of the phases of the language must be attempted with the utmost caution.

The third argument, that from the occurrence of parallel passages, has been applied with great effect to prove that the Book of Job was written before that of Jeremiah. But though it cannot be denied that several passages in Isa. xl–lxvi, parallels to which exist in other prophecies, are marked by great vigour and richness of style, it should be remembered too that so original a genius as our unknown prophet would naturally imitate in a very different manner from the feeble though not ungraceful Jeremiah. Hence the primary character of the passages in Isa. xl–lxvi referred to is much more difficult to substantiate than it would be in a less elevated composition. An unenvious recognition of the beauties of earlier prophecies is a characteristic of the great prophet Isaiah, and why should we be surprised at tracing the same high quality in the work of his noblest successor? It is undeniable that the prophet in Babylon devoted a reverent study to the writings of Isaiah. Not to dwell on the isolated phrases mentioned above, we may refer to lxv. 25, where portions of three successive verses are quoted from Isa. xi, though not without the addition of one striking and original expression. And if our prophet quoted from Isaiah, why should he not also quote the other inspired prophets in the same royal and independent manner?

It is true that this is not the only tenable hypothesis. The passages adduced by Delitzsch from the prophets before the exile may have been interpolated, or, what is still more probable, may have been composed in imitation of some older prophecy, the common source of both the prophecies in question. Considering the large number of prophets who flourished in the regal period, and the probability, not to say the certainty, that Isaiah and other prophets quoted several passages from earlier writings with but little if any alteration, we are of opinion that the latter hypothesis has scarcely received its full share of attention. We subjoin a list of the principal parallel passages in Isa. xl–lxvi and earlier prophecies. Some may also be found in the other disputed chapters, but these will naturally be explained on the analogy of those in the more important prophecy.

Zeph. ii. 15 compared with Isa. xlvii. 8, 10.

,, iii. 10 ,, ,, lxvi 20.

Jer. x. 1–16 ,, ,, xliv. 12–15, xli. 7, xlvi. 7.

,, xxv. 31, 33 ,, ,, lxvi. 16.

,, xxx. 10, xlvi. 27 ,, xli. 14, xliii. 5, xliv. 2.

,, xlviii. 18 ,, ,, xlvii. 1.

,, l. 2 ,, ,, xlvi. 1.

,, li. 54, 56 ,, ,, lxvi. 6.

Ezek. xxiii. 40, 41 ,, ,, lvii. 9.

To the fourth argument, that from tradition, Delitzsch does not appear to attach, or at least to expect his opponents to attach, any great degree of importance. The most ancient testimony adduced for the Isaianic authorship of chaps. xl–lxvi is that of the edict of Cyrus (Ezra i. 2), 'Thus saith Cyrus, king of Persia, Jehovah the God of heaven hath given me all the kingdoms of the earth; and he hath charged me to build him an house at Jerusalem, which is in Judah.' But the utmost which this reference to prophecy can be admitted to prove, is a familiarity with Isa. xl–lxvi on the part of the writer of the edict, not that these chapters are by Isaiah.

Besides, the great historical work in which it occurs, and of which the Books of Chronicles and of Nehemiah also form parts, cannot have been compiled earlier than about 330 B.C., i.e. four centuries later than Isaiah, an interval fraught with vicissitudes, during which a critical estimate of the sacred literature is altogether inconceivable.

Next in order of time is the Septuagint version of Isaiah, in which the disputed prophecies are found, and which may have been produced at some unknown date between 260 and 130 B.C. This is followed by the Greek translation of the book commonly called Ecclesiasticus, which contains a distinct assertion[1] of the unity of authorship. The passage runs as follows :—'He (Esaias) saw by an excellent spirit what should come to pass at the last, and he comforted them that mourned in Zion ; he shewed what should come to pass for ever, and secret things or ever they came.' But the generally accepted date of the composition of Ecclesiasticus is not earlier than 180 B.C.,—and the Greek translation was probably made fifty years later. The statement of these facts is the best answer to assertions of the existence of an unbroken tradition in the Jewish and the Christian church.

SECTION V.

Arguments against the unity of authorship.

The really decisive arguments against the unity of authorship are derived (1) from the historical circumstances implied in the disputed chapters, and (2) from the originality of the ideas, or of the forms in which the ideas are expressed. The point of view occupied throughout these chapters, especially chaps. xl–lxvi, is that of an exile in Babylon. Jerusalem and the temple have long lain in ruins, and the Jews are becoming dispirited at the apparent refusal

---

[1] Ecclus. xlviii 24, 25.

of God to interpose in their behalf. Many of them have given way to the seductions of heathenism, and have learned to scoff at their believing brethren. But God has not cast off his people. Cyrus has already begun his career of victory, and either through his instrumentality, or by a direct miracle, the Jews shall be restored to Palestine. Such a historical position could scarcely have been realized by a prophet living under Hezekiah. For a moment indeed Isaiah and other prophets are apt to forget the melancholy present, and soar into the brighter future, but they soon return to their proper mission of reproving or consoling their contemporaries. But there is not a single verse in all these twenty-seven chapters, in which a definite allusion occurs to the stirring scenes which Isaiah must have witnessed. And the principal passage[1], which has been thought by some to imply the authorship of a resident in Palestine, is given up by Delitzsch as incapable of defence. On the other hand, the prophets between Isaiah and the exile, who ought, according to the traditional theory, to have been familiar with the strange position of affairs so fully described in Isa. xl–lxvi, content themselves for the most part with the vaguest predictions of the impending catastrophe. No allusion can be traced in Habakkuk, Zephaniah, or Jeremiah, to any distinctive statement of Isa. xl–lxvi.

Still more striking is the argument from the new ideas, and forms of representing ideas, in the disputed prophecies, as almost every page of the notes in this volume will shew. The sarcastic descriptions of idolatry, the appeals to the victories of Cyrus in proof of the sole divinity of Jehovah, are unintelligible as proceeding from Isaiah, but are full of beauty and propriety when read in the light of the Babylonian exile. So too these chapters contain the germs of dogmas, which Isaiah was scarcely prepared to under-

[1] Isa. lvi. 9–lvii. 11, pp. 199, 200.

stand, such for instance as the influence of the angelic powers[1], the resurrection of the body[2], and the everlasting punishment of the wicked[3].   And in chap. liii (p. 189) the idea of vicarious atonement is expressed in such vivid language as to produce all the effect of a new revelation.   Indeed the passages which relate to the 'Servant of Jehovah' are so unlike Isaiah that we can hardly avoid ascribing them to some later prophet.   Not that we deny the existence of a certain amount of material common to both writers.   The final establishment of the Divine kingdom on earth is the Gospel of the exiled prophet, as it was that of the prophets of Jerusalem, but the organ through which this is to be effected is no longer the anointed king, but one who bears the lowly name of 'servant.'   Surely this points to a time when the hope of elevating the nation through its king had vanished for ever, and when the ideal of the prophets had grown so spiritual as to find its best expression in a personification of missionary zeal[4].

Perhaps the argument from the omission of any reference to the Messianic king may be fairly regarded as absolutely decisive against the Isaianic theory.   Such an omission can be easily understood, if the Messiah, i. e. the 'anointed' king, be merely a transient form, under which a belief in the ultimate fulfilment of Israel's destinies manifested itself at a particular epoch.   If it be merely a form, then it is not surprising that when the kingdom had fallen, and the house of David had passed into obscurity, some other organ should have been selected for representing the same belief.   Then we can account for the ascription in a secondary sense of the title of Messiah to the Gentile king Cyrus[5], and for the concession of

[1] Isa. xxiv. 21, p 121.   [2] Isa. xxvi. 19, p 127.
[3] Isa. l. 11, p. 183, lxvi. 24, p. 232.
[4] For the meaning of the phrase, 'Servant of Jehovah,' see note on p 154
[5] Isa. xlv. 1, p. 164.

Messianic functions, in the primary sense of the word, i. e. those of realising and propagating the standard of holiness, to the regenerate people of Israel in the person of their representative. So bold a development of the old Messianic idea cannot possibly have proceeded from Isaiah. It presupposes a spirituality of mind, a sympathy with foreign nations, and an indifference to the claims of the house of David, which can only have arisen during a prolonged separation from the soil of Palestine.

SECTION VI.

How came Babylonian prophecies to be inserted in Isaiah?

The question may now be fairly asked, How came the works of five unknown prophets in Babylon to be ascribed to Isaiah, or at any rate inserted in the Book of Isaiah? And, in particular, how came the four groups of Babylonian prophecies which precede Isa. xl–lxvi to be interspersed among the prophecies of Isaiah, instead of being appended to them? It would be in vain to attempt a justification of all the uncritical proceedings of ancient editors. How many of the Psalms are ascribed to David and to Asaph simply on the ground of the celebrity of those great names! Did not the very next century after the Nicene Council see the deputy of a Roman bishop produce two canons of the Synod of Sardica as canons of the Council of Nicæa, 'either from ignorance in himself, almost incredible, or from a bold presumption of ignorance in others, not less inconceivable[1]?' And, to adduce an instance which may be thought still more in point, was not Gregory of Tours misled into ascribing the authority of a Nicene canon to a canon of the Synod of Gangra merely through the copyists' habit of subjoining the decrees of Gangra to those of Nicæa[2]? We will venture,

---

[1] Milman's 'History of Latin Christianity,' vol. i. p. 176.
[2] 'Gregorii Episcopi Turonensis Historia Francorum,' lib. ix. c. 33.

however, to suggest the following reasons for the position accorded to the four Babylonian prophecies in the midst of Isa. i–xxxix. That they were connected with the Book of Isaiah at all, seems to have been caused by a wish to preserve them from the fate of other fugitive compositions. The particular place selected for each prophecy may have been determined by a consideration of its subject. Two of them (xiii–xiv. 23, xxi. 1–10), being concerned exclusively with Babylon, were fitly arranged among the prophecies of Isaiah on foreign nations, whilst the two remaining ones, wider and more comprehensive in their range, were marked out as natural supplements to two important groups of Isaiah's discourses. Chap. xxxv in particular may have been appended as a general conclusion, on account of its consolatory nature, just as, according to David Kimchi, the Book of Isaiah was sometimes placed after Jeremiah and Ezekiel to mitigate the melancholy tone predominant in those prophecies.

The position of Isa. xl–lxvi admits of a still easier explanation. These chapters were evidently added at a later period, and most probably, as Eichhorn[1] suggested, with the object of producing a conveniently large volume, nearly equal in size to those of Jeremiah, Ezekiel, and the Twelve Minor Prophets. In taking this course, the editor might invoke a precedent already familiar to his contemporaries, the Twelve Minor Prophets having been combined into a single volume at some unknown period previous to the composition of the Book of Ecclesiasticus[2].

SECTION VII.

Characteristics of the prophets of the exile.

One of the ablest English apologists of the Isaianic authorship puts

[1] Eichhorn's 'Einleitung in Alte Testament,' Leipzig, 1787, vol. iii. pp. 41, 42.
[2] See Ecclus. xlix. 10, and Fritzsche's note.

the following significant question, 'Has any writer or poet of the first order ever been known to arise in the era of a nation's decadence?' He reminds us that 'the national condition of Israel at this time was the most unfavourable that can be conceived for the production of a writer equal to the creation of such works as these.' . . . It is not only improbable, but we may almost say antecedently impossible, that it should at this time have gathered up its energies, which were historically languid and inert, for the production of any writer of so high a standard[1].' A similar remark was long ago made by J. D. Michaelis, who argues that 'to suppose Isaiah's prophecies respecting Babylon to have been composed in the first year of Cyrus must appear just as improbable as the hypothesis of Harduin, that the most beautiful of the odes of Horace were the production of barbarous monks in the middle ages[2].'

The surprise of these critics would have been diminished had they considered the difference between the excitement of a revolution and the languor by which such periods are succeeded. The news of the advance of Cyrus, and the destruction of the powerful Lydian monarchy, combined with the study of the prophetic records, which limited the duration of the exile to seventy years, may well have animated the most patriotic and religious Jews to an enthusiasm hitherto unknown. The prophecies of Isaiah himself seem to owe their existence to grave national vicissitudes. All, or nearly all of them, are centred in two invasions of the Jewish kingdom, those of the Syrians under Rezin, and the Assyrians under Sennacherib. If the later psalmists of the exile, cheered only by their confidence in the promises of Jehovah, enchant us by a tenderness and spirituality which rivals that of David himself, is it unlikely that, when the prospect of deliverance grew brighter, such minds should

---

[1] Professor Stanley Leathes' 'Witness of the Old Testament to Christ,' pp. 179, 180.   [2] Quoted in Dr. Henderson's Isaiah, p. 111.

have soared to a still higher flight of inspiration? And as for the argument from the contrast between Ezekiel and the author of Isa. xl–lxvi, it should be remembered that the language of the former is exceptionally impure, and is decidedly inferior to that of even the latest portions of the Books of Kings, and that, in general, the style of a writer is the image of his mind, and that the vigour of the unknown prophet's language does but correspond to the fervour of his enthusiasm.

Certainly the five prophets of the exile, whose works have come down to us, are not equally endowed with genius, nor equally spiritual in tone. Their general theme indeed is the same, but the manner in which they unfold their common message is marked by a striking individuality. One prophet[1] is almost unmanned by affection for his adopted home, another[2] longs for vengeance on Israel's enemies; one delights[3] in picturing the happy future of his people, another[4] deals taunts and reproaches to his unprepared countrymen. There is another point, however, besides this subject, in which the five prophecies correspond, viz. their purely literary character. They would seem not to have been delivered in public, like the discourses of Isaiah, but passed on from hand to hand, or from mouth to mouth, among the Jewish patriots. Any other course of action might have drawn down upon the writers the resentment of the Babylonian authorities. And hence they abound in flowing, picturesque descriptions, which are not always devoid of hyperbole, and contrast thereby with the classical sense of proportion conspicuous in Isaiah. Hence, too, their strongly pronounced tendency to pass into lyric poetry, which confirms the idea we ventured to propose just now of the poetic origin of this

---

[1] Isa. xxi. 1–10. pp. 131–134.
[2] Isa. xiii. 2–xiv 23, pp. 134–141.
[3] Isa. xxxiv, xxxv, pp. 112–117.
[4] Isa. lix, pp. 208, 209

prophetic revival[1]. Hence, too, that anonymous character, which has appeared to some so extraordinary a phenomenon. The origin of the earlier prophetic writings was a well-ascertained fact, because the functions of their authors were chiefly exercised in public. That of the Babylonian prophecies, on the other hand, was known to few, if indeed to any but the prophets themselves, because it was not the custom of the Jews to inscribe the name of the author on a mere literary production. This may be seen from the examples of the Pentateuch, the Book of Job, and Ecclesiastes. The Psalms and the Song of Solomon are no instances to the contrary; the authorship of these writings being inferred later from their contents.

The style of the greatest of the Babylonian prophets is thus characterised by Ewald.—'It is somewhat prolix in descriptions, and often rather intricate and clumsy, though this is really occasioned by an exuberant fulness of fresh and original thoughts. Yet in spite of all such symptoms of a declining age, the style of our prophet is unusually forcible, creative, and elevating; and in the more exalted passages, as in chaps. xl and xlii. 1—4. it soars to so clear and bright an elevation, and carries the reader away with so wondrous a charm, that we might easily fancy that we heard the voice of some other prophet, were there not preponderating reasons for believing that it is still the same prophet, only in a different mood[2].'

SECTION VIII

The Hebrew text of Isaiah.

No justification will be required by scholars of the prominence given to conjectural emendation in the present version of Isaiah. The text of the Old Testament, it is well known, is far from being as satisfactorily ascertained as that of the New. There

[1] Cp. Isa. xiv. 4—23, xxv. 1—5, xxvi. 1—13, xxvii. 2—6, xlvii, lx, lxvi. 10, 11.

[2] 'Die Propheten des alten Bundes,' vol. iii. p. 28.

are but few Hebrew MSS. of so early a date as the ninth and tenth
centuries, and even these, so far as they have yet been collated, seem
to throw hardly any light on the most obscure passages. Some
interesting readings have been published by Dr. Pinner[1] from MSS.
formerly at Odessa, and now at St. Petersburg, and by Professor
Chwolson[2] and M. Neubauer[3] from a Firkowitz MS. in the Rus-
sian Imperial Library. An useful summary of the principal various
readings known previous to the discovery of these most ancient
MSS. may be found in Dr. S. Davidson's work, entitled 'The Hebrew Text of the Old Testament revised from Critical Sources,'
London, 1855.

In conjectural emendations of the text we have not been guided
solely by the hazardous desire for originality. We have borrowed
some from Ewald, and others from earlier critics, and have always
been glad to appeal to the authority, when this might be obtained,
of the ancient versions. But the versions themselves are encum-
bered with countless textual errors, and until really critical editions
of the Septuagint and the Targums are produced we shall not be
able to employ them with any confidence as guides to the Hebrew
original. And at the best they give but a doubtful assistance, for,
as Professor Max Müller has well remarked, 'the idea of a faithful
literal translation seems altogether foreign to the Oriental mind[4].'
Safer though less brilliant results may be gained from the best
Arabic-writing Jewish commentators, whose works are still for the
most part unedited.

[1] See 'Prospectus der der Odessäer Gesellschaft . . . gehörenden ältesten
Hebräischen und Rabbinischen Manuscripte,' Odessa, 1845.
[2] See Geiger's 'Jüdische Zeitschrift,' vol. iii. p. 232.
[3] See 'Journal Asiatique,' vol. v. p. 542
[4] 'Chips from a German Workshop,' vol. i. p. 197.

INDEX OF CHAPTERS OF THE AUTHORIZED VERSION.

ORDER OF THE PROPHECIES

in this Edition.

CHRONOLOGY OF EVENTS

Illustrating the first Part of this Volume.

(See 'La Chronologie Biblique fixée par les éclipses des inscriptions cunéiformes, par M. Jules Oppert. Extrait de la Revue Archéologique. Paris, 1868')

B.C.

810 Accession of Uzziah.

744 Accession of Tiglath-Pileser.

742 Accession of Ahaz.

733 Assyrian expedition against Pekah.

727 Accession of Shalmaneser V and of Hezekiah. (Cp. notes on pp. 91, 240.)

724 Commencement of siege of Samaria.

722 Death of Shalmaneser V.

721 Accession of Sargon, and capture of Samaria.

713 Illness of Hezekiah.

704 Accession of Sennacherib.

700 Assyrian expedition against Judah.

698 Accession of Manasseh.

NOTICE.

THE reader is requested to bear in mind that the form Jehovah is not adopted in this book on the supposition of its correctness, but simply in deference to custom. The proper form is Jahveh. He is also requested to refer to the 'Supplementary Notes' at the end of the volume, especially with reference to the Prophecy on Moab, and the name of Sargon.

CORRECTIONS.

Page 9, last line but one, *for* 'become a splendour and honour,' *read* 'be beautiful and glorious.'

„   82, line 1, *for* 'x. 1,' *read* 'x 5.'

„   103, line 1 of translation, *for* 'xxxviii,' *read* xxxvii.'

„   107, line 7, *for* 'eighty-eight,' *read* 'a hundred and eight.'
line 8, *for* 'ten,' *read* 'thirty.'

„   109, last line but three, *for* 'to Egypt,' *read* 'to Israel.'

„   116, last line but two, *add* 'The worship of Lilith, mixed with Persian elements, existed among the Jews of Mesopotamia as late as the seventh century A.D. See remarks of Professor Levy of Breslau on some Chaldee inscriptions in "Journal of the German Oriental Society," vol. ix. pp. 461–491'

„   125, line 4, *for* 'despite,' *read* 'in despite of.'

THE

BOOK OF ISAIAH

CHRONOLOGICALLY ARRANGED.

THE

BOOK OF ISAIAH

CHRONOLOGICALLY ARRANGED.

I. PROSPECTS IN THE REIGN OF AHAZ.

(Isa. ii.–v. 25; ix 8–x. 4; v. 26–30.)

THAT a well-merited judgment must fall on Jerusalem and its inhabitants before it could become the centre of a world-wide spiritual empire,—such was the burden of the first group of prophecies, which Isaiah appears to have collected. The kingdom of Judah was then approaching the end of a long period of prosperity. The successes of Uzziah and Jotham, especially the conquest of Elath, had not only opened up a steady commerce, but produced a general affectation of foreign fashions and superstitions. See ii. 6–18 ; iii. 2, 3, 16–23 ; 2 Kings xiv. 22. Meantime the social condition was altering greatly for the worse; rich men increased their estates by oppression, and obtained false verdicts through bribery, while the new king was a mere youth of a frivolous, effeminate character. See iii. 14; v. 8, 23; iii. 12, note. To the real dangers of the State, both without and within, all but the prophet were blind. The northern kingdom had long become tributary to Assyria, but the prophet was mocked and jeered at when he forewarned the Judæans of still worse calamities. See iii. 26; v. 19, 26–30. The following passages are a summary of these warnings, and perhaps of earlier ones. Taking for his text a popular passage out of some older prophet, Isaiah draws a vivid contrast between the ideal future and the circumstances of the present. The former cannot be realized till a fearful judgment has taken place, the certainty, manner, and causes of which are unsparingly proclaimed, till at last calm returns with a fresh picture, this time an original one, of the Messianic future. (Part I.)

After a pause of days, weeks, or months, during which all that he has said acquires ever greater distinctness, Isaiah takes up the old thread, in order to develope more in detail the close connection of sin with punishment. His text is now the parable of a vineyard. The men of Jerusalem are called in as umpires, but in condemning the vineyard, they condemn themselves : v. 3, comp. Luke xx. 16. Then, as if to prevent a suspicion of unfairness, the prophet counts up one by one the national sins—covetousness, luxury, and depravity; and describes with Dantesque exactness the corresponding punishment. See Part II.

Another pause, and the prophet assumes a fresh standing-point, indicated in the Hebrew by the perfect and imperfect tenses. Judgment, he says, has followed upon judgment, the 'whole people,' north as well as south, have suffered the penalties of sin. A verse of transition describes, in language probably symbolic, the destructiveness of the Divine anger. Then follow four short strophes, each describing a special sin together with its retribution, and each closing with the same refrain. The first three relate exclusively to Israel, whose arrogance, impenitence, and lawlessness, are successively chastised; the fourth chiefly, if not entirely, to Judah, the refined tyranny of whose princes is threatened with a sudden overthrow. The obscure admonition in the last strophe prepares the way for a distinct concluding reference to the dreaded Assyrians.

The restoration of the striking prophecy, ix. 8–x. 4, to its proper place is due to the sagacity of Ewald. It removes, with a completeness to which no other hypothesis can lay claim, the apparent want of naturalness in several passages, as, for instance, in the mention of Syria parallel with 'the warriors of Rezin' (vv. 10, 11), in the recurrence of the refrain, and in the otherwise uncalled-for extension (vv. 26–30) of the elaborate section which precedes.

The date of the prophecy is settled, so far as the undisputed portion is concerned, by the mention of the very three points which characterized the reign of Ahaz—idolatry, love of foreign fashions, and the weak character of the king: comp. 2 Kings xvi. 3, 4, 10. Neither in age nor in character could Uzziah and Jotham fitly be termed children; and although worship at the high places was very general in their time, there is no evidence that it was idolatrous; certainly the kings themselves adhered to the religion of Jehovah. From the absence of all reference to the Syro-Ephraimitish invasion, we should conclude that the prophecy was written before that event, i. e. early in the reign of Ahaz.

Let us now consider by itself the passage we have incorporated, ix. 8–x. 4. It contains notices of five successive events:—1. Comparatively trifling losses, described metaphorically in ver. 10; 2. The hostility of the Syrians under Rezin, of the Philistines, &c., vv. 11, 12; 3. A defeat with considerable loss of life, ver. 14; 4. General anarchy, vv. 19, 20; 5. Plundering raids into Judah, ver. 21. The first of these may perhaps refer to the invasion of Pul, 2 Kings xv. 19, but is too vaguely expressed to be of much consequence; the fourth, to any portion of the period between the kings Zachariah and Hosea: comp. Hosea iv. 1–5, Zech. xi. 6, with 2 Kings xv. 8–30. The second, which is the most important notice, and prescribes the import of the third, obviously points to a period preceding the Syro-Ephraimitish alliance. The fifth may be illustrated by the notice in 2 Kings xv. 37: ‘In those days [apparently at the end of Jotham's reign] began Jehovah to send against Judah Rezin, king of Syria, and Pekah, son of Remaliah,’ for although the incursions here mentioned are probably not identical with those referred to by Isaiah, the temper which produced them had doubtless occasioned others at an earlier date. Hence, contrary to the view held by Ewald, we regard this prophecy as older than the rest of the collection, and assign it to the period preceding the Syrian alliance, i.e. to the reign of Jotham. And this

enables us to account for the position which it occupies in the received arrangement.   Being still remembered as an independent
prophecy, some later editor of Isaiah conceived himself at liberty to
find a new place for it, where the judgments denounced upon
Ephraim and Judah might serve to heighten, by contrast, those
denounced in x. 5–30 upon Assyria.   We may add that the passages
v. 25 and v. 26–30 were, in our opinion, added by the prophet himself
on the formation of this first collection of his works, the former
verse in order to connect the new prophecy with the old, and the
latter to form a suitable close to the whole volume.

[II. 1.]   *The word that Isaiah, son of Amoz, saw concerning*
Judah and Jerusalem.

PART I.

1.

'And in the days to come shall the mountain of the house
of Jehovah be established on the top of the mountains, and exalted
above the hills, and all nations shall flow unto it, and many
peoples shall go and say, Come let us go up to the mountain of
Jehovah, to the house of the God of Jacob, that he may teach us
of his ways, and we may walk in his paths. for out of Zion
shall go forth doctrine, and the word of Jehovah from Jerusalem.
He shall judge between the nations, and give sentence to many
peoples; and they shall beat their swords into ploughshares, and
their spears into pruning-hooks, nation shall not lift up sword
against nation, neither shall they learn war any more.'   O house
of Jacob, come let us walk in the light of Jehovah.

2.

[6.]   Nay, thou hast forsaken thy people, the house of Jacob,
because they were replenished from the East, and were cloud-

observers like the Philistines, and bargained with the children
of aliens; so that their land was filled with silver and gold,
(there was no end of their treasures,) and their land was filled
with horses, (there was no end of their chariots,) and their
land was filled with vain gods, — they worshipped the work
of their hands, that which their fingers had made: therefore
was the man abased, and the lord cast down, and thou durst
not forgive them. Enter into the rock, and hide thee in the
ground, before the terror of Jehovah, and before the splendour
of his majesty. The lofty eyes of man were cast down, and
the haughtiness of lords abased, and Jehovah alone. was exalted
in that day.

3.

[12.] For a day is set by Jehovah of Hosts upon all that is
proud and high, and upon all that is lifted up, that it be cast
down: and upon all cedars of Lebanon, that are high and lifted
up, and upon all the oaks of Bashan, and upon all the high mountains, and upon all the hills that are lifted up, and upon every lofty
tower, and upon every fenced wall, and upon all ships of Tarshish,
and upon all watch-towers of pleasure; so that the loftiness of
man may be abased, and the haughtiness of lords cast down, and
Jehovah alone be exalted in that day.

4.

[18.] But the vain gods shall utterly vanish; and men shall go
into caves of rocks, and into holes of the ground, before the terror
of Jehovah, and before the splendour of his majesty, when he
ariseth to affright the earth. In that day shall a man cast his vain
gods of silver and his vain gods of gold, which were made for
him to worship, to the moles and to the bats, that he may go into
the clefts of the rocks, and into the tops of the ragged rocks,

before the terror of Jehovah, and before the splendour of his majesty, when he ariseth to affright the earth.

Care ye no more for man, in whose nostrils is a breath; for of what account is he?

5.

[III. 1.] For behold, the Lord, Jehovah of Hosts, removeth from Jerusalem and from Judah stay and staff, [all stay of bread and all stay of water,] mighty man, and man of war, judge, and prophet, and soothsayer, elder, captain of fifty, and honourable man, counsellor, and dexterous wizard, and skilled enchanter, and I will make boys their princes, and contumely shall rule over them. The people shall tyrannize, man over man, and neighbour over neighbour; they shall be insolent, the boy towards the old man, and the despised towards him that is honoured. When a man shall lay hold of his brother in his father's house, 'Thou hast a cloak, thou shalt be our ruler, and let this ruin be under thy hand;' he shall cry out in that day, saying, 'I will not be a repairer; for in my house is neither bread nor cloak: ye shall not set me to be ruler of the people.'

6

[8.] For Jerusalem is ruined, and Judah fallen: because their tongue and their doings were against Jehovah, to provoke the eyes of his glory; the look of their face witnessed against them, and their sin they published as Sodom without disguise: alas for their soul, for they have wrought for themselves evil. Say ye, that with the righteous it is well, for they shall eat the fruit of their doings, alas, with the wicked it is ill, for the work of his hands shall be given him. My people's tyrant is a child, and women rule over him. O my people, thy guides lead thee astray, and the way of thy paths have they swallowed up. Jehovah setteth himself to plead, and standeth to judge the peoples. Jehovah will enter into judgment with the elders of his people, and the princes thereof: 'And ye, ye have eaten up the vineyard, the spoil of the suffering is in your houses. What mean ye that ye·beat my people to pieces, and grind the face of the suffering?' It is the utterance of the Lord, Jehovah of Hosts.

7.

[16.] And Jehovah said: Because the daughters of Zion are haughty, and walk with stretched-forth necks and leering eyes, mincing as they walk, and tinkling with their anklets; therefore the Lord will smite with a scab the crown of the head of the daughters of Zion, and Jehovah will discover their secret parts. In that day the Lord will remove the bravery of the anklets, and the little suns and moons, the ear-drops, and the necklaces, and the fine veils, the coronets, and the arm-bands, and the girdles, and the perfume-boxes, and the amulets, the signet-rings, and the nose-rings, the festival-robes, and the tunics, and the mantles, and the pouches, the gauzes, and the fine linen, and the tires, and the long veils; then, instead of sweet smell, there shall be rottenness, and instead of a girdle a rope, and instead of well-set hair baldness, and instead of the breadth of a cloak girding of sackcloth, and branding instead of beauty. Thy men shall fall by the sword, and thy forces in war, and her gates shall lament and mourn, and she being emptied shall sit upon the ground. Seven women shall take hold of one man in that day, saying, We will eat our own bread, and wear our own apparel: only let us be called by thy name, take away our reproach.

8.

[IV. 2.] In that day shall the buds of Jehovah become a splendour and honour, and the fruit of the land a pride and ornament for them that are escaped of Israel. Then shall he that is left in Zion, and remaineth in Jerusalem, be called holy, every one that is enrolled unto life in Jerusalem, when the Lord hath washed away the filth of the daughters of Zion, and purged the blood-shed of Jerusalem from the midst thereof by a breath of judgment and a breath of consumption. And Jehovah shall create upon every place of mount Zion, and upon her assemblies, a cloud by day with smoke, and the shining of a flaming fire by night, yea, over every glory shall be a screen ; and she shall be a booth for shade by day from the heat, and for a refuge and for a covert from storm and from rain.

Par. 1. *Jehovah.* The reader will hardly require to be reminded that Jehovah is an extremely incorrect form, which dates no farther back than the sixteenth century The most eminent Hebraists of all schools, including Delitzsch, who is a recent convert to this view, appear to be agreed on the substitution of Jahveh, or, as English pronunciation obliges us to write it, Yahveh The philological arguments are very strong, and are confirmed by a tradition mentioned by Theodoret and Epiphanius.

The etymology of the word is more uncertain. If it be from *hâvâh=hâyâh,* 'to be,' it should signify 'the Creator, the Giver of being.' But probably the name is of primitive Semitic origin, and its ancient meaning irrecoverable. Its usage, however, is not doubtful, it cannot differ widely from the word with which it is so often coupled, *Kâdosh,* 'the Holy One,' i e. one distinct from the world and from man

The mountain, &c. That is, Mount Zion shall one day be acknowledged as the religious centre of the world See especially Ezek v 5 ; and, for the image, compare Ezek. xl. 2 ; Zech. xiv. 10.

O house of Jacob These abrupt words are merely introduced to connect the first section with the second The main part of the first is admitted to be a quotation from some older prophecy. It occurs, with a few variations of a more original aspect, and one additional verse, in Mic. iv 1-4, but as the prophecy to which it is attached there was delivered under Hezekiah (Jer. xxvi. 18), it is impossible to ascribe the authorship to Micah. The style, as Hitzig first observed, is similar to that of Joel. Possibly the passage may have formed part of some lost oracle by that prophet.

Par 2 Thou hast forsaken Throughout this section the prophet throws himself mentally into the future, and describes the national sins and their punishment as if already past, so certain is he of the issue

Replenished from the East. The Geneva Bible (1560) renders 'full of the East maners'

Horses, chariots. These are not here censured so much as signs of a military spirit, as of luxury comp. 2 Sam. xv. 1; 2 Kings v. 9, 15; Eccl. x 7 (Hitzig). The horse supplanted the ass first under Solomon.

Par. 3. *Jehovah of Hosts*, or, as expanded by later writers, 'Jehovah, the God of Hosts.' The appellation appears to have arisen in time of war (the early wars of David?), and implies the meaning, 'Jehovah, who sendeth his angels to fight for his people.' See Josh. v. 13–15, where 'the captain of the host of Jehovah' is seen by Joshua standing with his sword drawn, as the champion of Israel Others suppose the 'hosts' to mean the stars, either as the dwelling of God, or as subject to his dominion, as a protest against planet-worship. Perhaps the two meanings may have existed side by side, for the Hebrews appear to have connected the stars very closely with the angels, and possibly regarded the latter as the inhabitants of the former. Comp. Gen i , where the stars are reckoned among living beings, Job xxv. 5, xxxviii. 7.

High towers Comp. 2 Chron. xxvii. 4; Hos viii. 14.

Ships of Tarshish. Uzziah had recovered the port of Elath on the Red Sea, 2 Kings xiv. 22

Watch-towers of pleasure. Comp. Ezek. xxvi. 12. 'They shall destroy thy pleasure-houses.' For other renderings, see the author's 'Notes and Criticisms,' pp 4, 5.

Par. 4. *Shall a man cast.* The fugitives pause a moment to wreak their vengeance on the 'unreal gods' (*'elil*) that deluded them. Comp. xxx 22; xxxi. 7.

Par. 5. *All stay of bread, &c.* Probably a gloss from the margin, suggested by the phrase 'stay the heart,' Gen xviii. 5, Ps civ. 15, but against the context.

Par 6. *Is ruined.* Again Isaiah surveys the disorders of the present from a standing-point taken in the future.

The look of their face, i. e their impudent expression.

My people's tyrant is a child, literally, 'his tyrants are a child.' The construction is suddenly broken, as in xlv. 8, and Job xli. 21 (Heb.). We should have expected it to run thus: 'My people's tyrants are a child and women,' i. e. Ahaz in his harem.

The peoples. The prophets of this period have ceased to regard Israel as an isolated nation. She is, however, still the central figure in the expected judgment.

The utterance, literally, 'whisper,' a vestige of the primitive, oracular stage of prophecy.

Par. 8. *The buds of Jehovah,* literally, 'bud,' but here collectively, as in lxi 11. Comp Ps civ. 16: 'The trees of Jehovah are full of sap, even the cedars of Lebanon, which he hath planted.' The passage is designed as a contrast to the previous description. It amounts to saying that the regenerate nation shall return to primitive simplicity, and that the divine beauties of nature shall quite supplant the luxuries of art. Comp. Joel iii 18; Amos ix. 13, Hos ii. 21, 22.

PART II.

1.

[**V. 1.**] Come let me sing of my well-beloved, a song of my beloved, touching his vineyard.

My well-beloved had a vineyard on a very fruitful height; and he digged it up and stoned it, and planted it with the choicest vine, and built a tower in the midst of it, and even hewed out a wine-vat therein, and looked that it should bring forth grapes, but it brought forth wild grapes.

And now, O inhabitants of Jerusalem, and men of Judah, judge, I pray you, betwixt me and my vineyard. What could have been done to my vineyard more than I have done therein? Wherefore, when I looked that it should bring forth grapes, brought it forth wild grapes? [5.] And now, go to, I will tell you what I will do to my vineyard,—I will take away the hedge thereof, that it become a pasture, and break down the wall thereof, that it become a place trodden down; and I will make a full end of it, that it be neither pruned nor digged, but be grown over with briars and thorns; I will also command the clouds that they rain no rain upon it. For the vineyard of Jehovah of Hosts is the house of

Israel, and the men of Judah his cherished planting; and he looked for reason, but behold treason; for right, but behold fright.

2.

[8] Woe unto them that join house to house, that lay field to field, till there is no more room, so that ye must dwell alone in the midst of the land. In mine ears (calleth) Jehovah of Hosts, Of a truth many houses shall become a desolation, even great and fair, without inhabitant. For ten acres of vineyard shall yield but a bath, and the seed of an homer shall yield but an ephah.

3.

[11.] Woe unto them that rise up at dawn to pursue strong drink, that linger in the twilight inflamed with wine, whilst harp and lute, tabret and pipe, and wine, make their feast; but they regard not the work of Jehovah, neither consider the operation of his hands. Therefore was my people exiled unawares, while his nobility was spent with hunger, and his riotous throng dried up with thirst. Therefore the underworld enlarged her craving, and opened her mouth without measure, and down went her splendour, and her throngs, and her songs, and he that was joyous within her. Thus was the man abased, and the lord cast down, and the eyes of the lofty cast down; thus was Jehovah of Hosts exalted through judgment, and God the Holy hallowed through right-eousness; whilst lambs feed as on their pasture, and the waste places of the fat ones kids devour.

4.

[18.] Woe unto them that draw iniquity with cords of naughti-ness, and sin as it were with a cart-rope; that say, Let his work haste, let it speed, that we may see it, and let the purpose of the Holy One of Israel draw nigh and come, that we may know it!

Woe unto them that call evil good, and good evil; that put dark-ness for light, and light for darkness; that put bitter for sweet, and sweet for bitter! Woe unto them that are wise in their own eyes, and in their own judgment men of understanding! Woe unto them that are mighty men for drinking wine, and men of strength for mingling strong drink; which declare righteous the wicked for a bribe, and take away the righteousness of the righteous from him! Therefore as the tongue of fire devoureth stubble, and hay which is a-flame sinketh in, so their root shall be as rottenness, and their blossom shall go up as dust: for they have despised the doctrine of Jehovah of Hosts, and rejected the word of the Holy One of Israel.

Par. 1. *Reason ... treason.* The love of assonance being so characteristic of the style of Isaiah, the translator has endeavoured to mark the most striking examples of it

Par. 2. *Bath* A liquid measure, equal to seven gallons, four pints, English.

Homer. A dry measure, equal to thirty-two pecks, one pint. The tenth part of this was an ephah.

Par. 3. *Was exiled.* The past of prophetic certainty.

Her splendour, i. e that of Jerusalem.

PART III.

1.

[V. 25.] Therefore was the anger of Jehovah kindled against his people, and he stretched forth his hand against them, and smote them, so that the hills trembled, and their carcases were as sweepings in the midst of the streets. For all this his anger turned not away, but his hand was stretched out still.

2.

[IX. 8.] The Lord sent a word into Jacob, and it lighted down in Israel, so that the whole people felt it, Ephraim and the inhabitant of Samaria, in spite of their pride and self-conceit in saying, Are bricks fallen down? then we will build with hewn stones; are sycomores cut down? then we will put cedars in their place. Therefore Jehovah set up the warriors of Rezin against them, and pricked their enemies on, Aram from the East, and the Philistines from the West; and they devoured Israel with open mouth. For all this his anger turned not away, but his hand was stretched out still.

3.

[13.] But the people turned not unto him that smote them, and to Jehovah of Hosts they had no recourse. Therefore did Jehovah cut off from Israel head and tail, palm-branch and rush, in one day; (the elder and the honourable, he is the head; and the prophet that teacheth lies, he is the tail;) and the guides of this people became misleading, and they that were guided of them were swallowed up. For this cause had Jehovah no joy in their young men, and over their fatherless and widows had he no yearning: for every one was unholy and an evil-doer, and every mouth speaking ungodliness. For all this his anger turned not away, but his hand was stretched out still.

4.

[18.] For wickedness burned like fire, devouring briers and thorns, and kindled the thickets of the forest, so that they rolled up in towering smoke. Through the wrath of Jehovah of Hosts was the land stifled, and the people became as fuel of fire, no man sparing his brother; one tore on the right hand, but was hungry, and ate on the left, but was not satisfied, every man eating the flesh of his own arm, — Manasseh, Ephraim, and Ephraim, Manasseh,—both at one against Judah. For all this his anger turned not away, but his hand was stretched out still.

5.

[X. 1.] Woe unto them that prepare unrighteous decrees, and the writers which have so long written mischief, to thrust aside helpless ones from judgment, and to rob of their sentence the sufferers of my people, that widows may be their prey, and that they may spoil the fatherless! But what will ye do in the day of visitation, and in the ruin which shall come from far? to whom will ye flee for help, and whither will ye go and leave your glory? Except they crouch as captives, and fall under the slain? For all this his anger is not turned away, but his hand is stretched out still.

6.

[V. 26.] So he hath lifted up an ensign to the distant nations, and hissed to him (Asshur) to come from the ends of the earth; and, behold, he cometh with speed swiftly: there is none that is weary, and none that stumbleth therein, he slumbereth not and sleepeth not, neither does the girdle of his loins loosen, nor the latchet of his shoes tear: he, whose arrows are sharpened, and all his bows bent, his horses' hoofs counted like flint, and his wheels like the whirlwind: his roar is like the lioness, he roareth like young lions, and murmureth and layeth hold of the prey, and carrieth it away safe with none to deliver. And there shall be a murmuring over it in that day like the murmuring of the sea, and if one look unto the earth, behold troublous darkness, for the light is darkened through the mists thereof.

Par 2. *It lighted down.* Comp Zech. ix. 1, where Damascus is called the 'resting-place' of the word of Jehovah; also Dan iv. 31, 'there *fell* a voice from heaven,' and the expression for revelation in the Koran, *anzala,* 'he hath sent down.'

The warriors of Rezin Auth. Vers. 'the adversaries of Rezin,' i.e. the

Assyrians, but an indirect allusion of this sort is contrary to Isaiah's usual manner. The 'enemies' in the next clause are certainly the enemies of Israel, not of Syria, and the notice or the hostility of the Syrians immediately afterwards leads to the natural inference that Rezin is mentioned, because he was the reigning king. The rendering 'warriors,' or more literally, 'harassing ones,' may be supported by xi. 13, where *sōrerē Yehudah* is translated by Gesenius and Ewald 'the hostile ones of Judah.' Ewald, however, in the passage before us, adopts an easier reading found in many MSS., 'princes' (*sārē* for *sārē*); we have therefore selected a middle word, to suit either explanation. For the mention of the Philistines, comp. 1 Kings xv 27.

Palm-branch and rush, i.e. high and low The words which follow are a gloss; they break the symmetry of the strophe, and seem to be founded on an nseasonable reminiscence of iii. 2.

Par. 6. *Troublous darkness.* Comp. the parallel passage, viii. 22.

APPENDIX.

SYRIA AND EPHRAIM.

(Isa. xvii. 1-11.)

THE following fugitive passage is added, for the sake of comparison with Part III. of the preceding prophecy. The subject may be described as follows:—Damascus shall perish, Ephraim shall lose its fortresses, and Syria its capital. The few survivors of the Syrian host shall share the fate of the proud Ephraimites. This is next described under the image of a harvest-field in the vicinity of the capital, where but few ears would be left for a tardy gleaner. And yet a few would certainly be left, as few as the olive-berries forgotten at the regular gathering, and beaten down with a stick by some casual traveller. An equally scanty remnant of the Ephraimites shall then be convinced of the folly of their idolatry, and shall turn to the true God. But the result of their conversion is left in obscurity. The fortresses on which they now rely will then be as desolate as

C

those of the accursed Canaanites; and the cause of the ruin is, that Ephraim has forgotten her true fortress, and wasted her zeal on the service of foreign gods.

This prophecy transports us to a time when Syria and Ephraim were confederates. The object of this alliance at a later period is described in ch. vii.; it was no less than the reduction of the southern kingdom to a state of vassalage. Since this is passed over here in complete silence, we may venture to infer that it was not yet openly avowed. Hence, in assigning a date to the oracle, our choice will lie between the end of the reign of Jotham, and the beginning of that of Ahaz. We may perhaps advance further by considering the difference of tone between this prophecy and one which we have dated somewhat earlier, ix. 8–x. 4. The latter is one long indignant threat, the former a calm regretful warning. Hence we must allow an interval for the prophet's mood to have softened, i e. the interval between the formation of the Syro-Ephraimitish league and the abortive invasion of Rezin and Pekah, and ascribe the prophecy before us to the early part of the reign of Ahaz. See, for the account of its fulfilment, 2 Kings xvi. 9, xvii. 6.

1.

[**XVII. 1.**] Behold, Damascus shall be removed from being a castle, and be cast low in ruin; the cities of Aroer shall be forsaken, they shall be given up to flocks, which shall lie down, with none to make them afraid. The stronghold shall cease from Ephraim, and the kingdom from Damascus, and the remnant of Aram shall be as the glory of the children of Israel: it is the utterance of Jehovah of Hosts.

2.

[**4.**] Then in that day shall the glory of Jacob be impoverished, and the fatness of his flesh wax lean. And it shall be as when one gathereth standing corn at harvest, while his arm reapeth the ears,

and shall be as he that gleaneth ears in the valley of Rephaim;
and there shall be left thereof but a gleaning, as at the beating of
an olive-tree, two or three berries at the uppermost point, four or
five in the branches of the fruit-tree: it is the utterance of Jehovah,
the God of Israel.

3.

[7.] In that day shall a man look to his Maker, and his eyes
shall have respect to the Holy One of Israel, and he shall not look
to the altars, the work of his hands, neither shall respect that
which his fingers have made, either the Asherim or the figures
of the sun.

4.

[9.] In that day shall his fortress-cities be like the deserted
places in thickets and summits, which men deserted before the
children of Israel, and it shall become a desolation. Because
thou didst forget the God of thy salvation, and wast not mindful
of thy fortress-rock, therefore didst thou plant lovely plantings,
and set them with strange slips; in the day of thy planting
thou didst hedge them in, and in the morning didst bring thy
seed to blossom; but the harvest is flown on a day of sickness
and desperate pain.

Par. 1. *Castle . . cast low.* The assonance corresponds to that in the
original.

The cities of Aroer, i e. the East Jordanic region, through which the Assyrians
passed on their march against Israel. There were two Aroers, one on the
frontier of the Amorites, the other on that of the Ammonites

Par. 2. *Rephaim*, a plain stretching south-west of Jerusalem, towards
Bethlehem

Par 3. *Asherim*, i e the images or emblems of Asherah. The latter was
the goddess of fertility and good fortune, and was worshipped with rites
similar to those of the Babylonian Mylitta (2 Kings xxii. 7). More precise

information cannot be given, owing to the danger of confounding the many local varieties in the Semitic mythology.

The figures of the sun. Comp. 2 Chron. xxxiv. 4, where these figures are mentioned as standing upon the altars of Baal, the Sun-God of the Phœnicians.

Par. 4. *The deserted places*, i. e. the ruins of Canaanitish fortresses.

Lovely plantings, i. e. the sensual rites of heathenism.

II IMMANUEL AND THE SYRIAN INVASION.

(Isa. vi–ix. 7.)

PROLOGUE. (Isa. vi.)

IF 'the year that King Uzziah died' were the date of the composition as well as of the event narrated, this would be decidedly the earliest of all Isaiah's prophecies. Two objections, however, have been urged against this opinion. One is drawn from the supernatural circumstances of the vision, which are regarded by some critics as mere scenic decorations, invented long after the prophet's entrance upon his office, and analogous to the 'Vision' of Burns or the 'Dedication' prefixed to Goethe's Poems. This view is thought to be confirmed by the inaugural visions of Jeremiah and Ezekiel, to which this of Isaiah has evidently served as a model, while to adduce the contrast between the freshness of the original and the pale colours of the imitations no more proves the literal exactness of the former than it would in the parallel case of Burns and Goethe. The objection referred to, however, does not seem to be well-founded. It leaves out of sight the fact that Isaiah, by the admission of all, had a strongly religious genius, and was liable to every experience peculiar to persons so gifted. Now, no phenomena are so familiar in the comparative history of religions as the claim put forward on the part of their leaders to the enjoyment of intercourse with spiritual beings, and the equally earnest faith of these leaders in the form which they report their intercourse to have assumed.

A safer ground for objection is furnished by the despondency of the latter part of the narrative. The sudden transition from the height of enthusiasm to the depth of despair (despair, so far as the present is concerned) is unnatural in the extreme. It is also entirely contrary to analogy. Throughout the Old Testament we detect a gracious proportion between the revelation vouchsafed and the mental state of the person receiving it, as, for instance, in the Messianic prophecies; but what proportion can be observed between the fervid zeal of the novice, breaking forth on the first word of encouragement, and the sudden check which it receives by an untempered disclosure of coming troubles? It is no mere undertone of melancholy which pervades these verses,—that would not in the least have surprised us, for even in the preliminary part of the vision Isaiah is well aware of the low moral condition of his age,—it is an oppressive despair, which may not unfairly be pronounced psychologically impossible.

Our conclusion, therefore, is that the second part of this chapter embodies the revelation of a later period. We may suppose, either that, in recalling the great event of his youth, Isaiah interpreted the doubts which may even then have sobered his confidence, in the light of his subsequent experience, or else that two revelations, that of his prophetic mission, and that of his ill success, are brought together for the purpose of mutual illustration. Observe that vv. 1–8 are quite complete without the revelation which follows.

However this may be, the narrative is evidently intended as the prelude to a fresh group or summary of prophecies, the contents of which cannot be defined with certainty. Ewald's view, however, has no small degree of probability, that the passage vii. 1–ix. 7, formed the chief portion of the summary in question. The object of that important fragment is, in fact, the confirmation of the ideas of this prelude, namely, the obstinacy of the present generation, and the certainty of a glorious future following upon a terrific judgment of purification. We shall shortly find reason for assigning the date to the early part of the reign of Hezekiah.

1.

[**VI. 1.**] In the year that king Uzziah died I saw the Lord

ˑsitting upon a throne, high and lifted up, and his train filling the palace. Seraphim stood above him; each one had six wings, with twain he covered his face, and with twain he covered his feet, and with twain he did fly. And one cried to the other and said, Holy, holy, holy, is Jehovah of Hosts: the whole earth is full of his glory. And the foundations of the threshold shook at the voice of him that cried, and the house became full of smoke. Then said I, Woe is me! for I am undone; because I am a man of unclean lips, and I dwell in the midst of a people of unclean lips, because mine eyes have seen the King, Jehovah of Hosts. Then flew one of the seraphim unto me with a hot stone in his hand, which he had taken with the tongs from off the altar; and he caused it to touch my mouth, and said, Lo, this hath touched thy lips, and thine iniquity is taken away, and thy sin forgiven. And I heard the voice of the Lord, saying, Whom shall I send, and who will go for us? Then said I, Here am I, send me.

2.

[9.] And he said, Go and say to this people, Hear on, but understand not; and see on, but perceive not. Make the heart of this people fat, and their ears heavy, and besmear their eyes; lest they see with their eyes, and hear with their ears, and lest their heart understand, and they return, and be healed. And I said, How long, Lord? And he said, Until the cities be waste without inhabitant, and the houses without men, and the ground be wasted to a desolation, and Jehovah have removed men far away, and the deserted places be many in the midst of the land. And though there should yet be a tenth in it, it must again be burned; (yet) like the terebinth and like the oak, in which at the felling a stock is left, (so) there shall be an holy seed, the stock thereof.

Par. 1. *The palace*, i.e. heaven : comp. Ps. xxix. 9. Jehovah is described as a king, seated on his throne of state, and surrounded by his counsellors. Comp. ver. 8, 'Who will go *for us ?*'

Seraphim. Literally, 'serpents,' such as those which are said to have bitten the Israelites in the desert, Num. xxi. 6. Possibly Isaiah employs the dragons who guarded the treasures of the gods in primeval mythology, as he elsewhere (xiv. 29) employs the fabulous flying serpents of Arabia, as mere poetical machinery. Since, however, the Seraphim are described here as men, though as men of a higher order, symbolized by their wings, and since the divine guards are in Gen. iii. 24 called Cherubim (connected with γρὺψ, 'griffin,' as even Keil admits), it seems better to compare the Arabic *sharif*, 'noble,' and consider Seraphim to signify the nobility of heaven, i. e. the angels. Comp. the vision of Micaiah, 1 Kings xxii 19

Full of smoke. The smoke proceeded from the altar of incense mentioned in ver. 6. The original image of a palace is now qualified by images drawn from the temple.

A hot stone The Law directed that altars should be constructed either of earth or of unhewn stones, Exod xx 25.

Par. 2. *Make the heart of this people fat*, i. e blunt their feelings. Note the delicate irony which pervades this description. A stage in the prophet's career is closed, and when he looks for results, it seems as if he had been destined to render the coarse nature of 'this people' coarser than it was before.

Though there should yet be a tenth. The few who may be spared by the first judgment will be still so far from holiness, that a second will be required. Comp the refrain of Part III. of the preceding group, 'For all this his ange turned not away,' &c.

THE PROPHECY.

(Isa. vii. 1-ix. 7)

THE confederate kings of Damascus and Samaria are on their march to Jerusalem, with the view of conquering the country, and imposing a puppet of their own as king. The dismay of Ahaz is extreme. Isaiah comes forward to reassure him, promising, on the authority of Jehovah, that the enterprize shall fail, and guaranteeing his veracity by the offer of a sign. The king hypocritically declines the offer. Then the prophet, penetrating his diplomatic intentions, announces a sign of mixed import connected with the birth and childhood of a certain Immanuel. The result of his conduct will be, that though the immediate danger shall pass away, it shall be succeeded by a far more terrible one. Assyria and Egypt shall make Judah their battle-field, and destroy every vestige of cultivation. See Pars. 1–3.

On a subsequent occasion two fresh signs are produced; a tablet, with an enigmatical inscription dedicating it to the expected ravager, and the same oracular words converted into a name for the prophet's second son. See Par. 4. The remaining discourse is apparently esoteric. It begins by depicting the Assyrian devastations. These, with regard to the northern branch of the nation, are the just retribution of its sympathy with the profane enterprize of Pekah. The only gleam of hope for Ephraim is the thought that, after all, Ephraim and Judah belong by right to the same king, and will form, when reunited, 'thy land, O Immanuel.' At the sound of that potent name, the prophet rises to a defiant enthusiasm, which, for the sake of his disciples, he further justifies by a special revelation. Reverence for Jehovah, such is its purport, is the true source of intrepidity. Then, after describing his own calm attitude of expectation, he glances at the dark future of the votaries of magic, who reject the true oracles which they will one day desire in vain. He piles, as it were, obscurity on obscurity to convey the extent of their despair, till suddenly the Messianic hope breaks out in a climax of striking ideas and bold, original phraseology.

The whole passage is an epitome of the discourses delivered at this great national crisis, i. e. about B.C. 740. The epitome itself apparently belongs to the beginning of the reign of Hezekiah, before the piety of the king had exerted much influence on the people. This we gather (1) from the expression 'it came to pass in the reign of Ahaz,' which would be unnatural, if Ahaz were still alive, (2) from the Messianic description, which, by its vividness, implies a reign of more than ordinary promise.

1.

[**VII. 1.**] And it came to pass in the days of Ahaz, son of Jotham, son of Uzziah, king of Judah, that Rezin, king of Aram, with Pekah, son of Remaliah, king of Israel, went up against Jerusalem to assault it, (but he was not able to assault it). And it was told the house of David, saying, Aram resteth on Ephraim, and his heart trembled, and the heart of his people, as the trees of the forest tremble before the wind. Then said Jehovah unto Isaiah, Go forth now to meet Ahaz, thou, and Shear-Jashub thy son, at the end of the conduit of the upper pool, on the highway of the fuller's field, and say unto him, Take heed, and be quiet ; fear not, neither be faint-hearted for these two stumps of smoking fire-brands, for the burning anger of Rezin, and Aram, and the son of Remaliah. [**5.**] Because Aram hath taken evil counsel against thee, with Ephraim and the son of Remaliah, saying, 'Let us go up against Judah and vex it, and burst it open for us, and set the son of Tabel as king in the midst of it:' thus saith the Lord Jehovah, It shall not stand, neither shall it come to pass. For the head of Aram is Damascus, and the head of Damascus is Rezin, [and within threescore and five years shall Ephraim be broken that it be not a people,] and the head of Ephraim is Samaria, and the head of Samaria is Remaliah's son. If ye hold not fast, verily ye shall not stand fast.

2.

[**10.**] And Jehovah spake further to Ahaz, saying, Ask thee a sign of Jehovah thy God, going deep down to the abyss, or far up to the height. But Ahaz said, I will not ask, neither will I tempt Jehovah. And he said, Hear ye now, O house of David ; is it too little for you to weary men, that ye weary my God also ? Therefore the Lord himself shall give you a sign ; behold, the damsel shall conceive, and bear a son, and call his name God-with-us. Cream and honey shall he eat, when he shall know to refuse the evil and choose the good. For before the boy shall know to refuse the evil and choose the good, the land, before whose two kings thou shrinkest, shall become a desert. Jehovah shall bring upon thee, and upon thy people, and upon thy father's house, days such as have not come since the day that Ephraim departed from Judah, [the king of Assyria].

3.

[18.] And in that day shall Jehovah hiss to the flies that are in the uttermost part of the streams of Egypt, and to the bees that are in the land of Assyria, and they shall come and rest in the valleys of the steep hills, and in the clefts of the rocks, and in all the thorn-bushes, and in all the pastures. In that day shall the Lord shave with the razor that is hired beyond the river, [with the king of Assyria,] the head, and the hair of the feet, and it shall also consume the beard. And in that day shall a man nourish a young cow and two sheep; and because of the abundant yielding of milk he shall eat cream, for cream and honey shall every one eat that is left in the land. And in that day shall every place, where there are a thousand vines at a thousand silverlings, it shall even be for briars and thorns; with arrows and with bow shall men come thither, for all the land shall become briars and thorns. And as for all the mountains that are digged with the mattock, thou shalt not come thither for fear of briars and thorns; but it shall be a place for the sending forth of oxen, and for the treading of sheep.

4.

[VIII. 1.] And Jehovah said to me, Take thee a large tablet, and write upon it with the style of the people, To

Spoil-swiftly Rob-quickly, and I will take to me, as faithful witnesses, Uriah the priest, and Zechariah son of Jeberechiah. Then I went near to the prophetess; and she conceived, and bare a son. And Jehovah said to me, Call his name Spoil-swiftly Rob-quickly; for before the boy shall have knowledge to cry, My father, and my mother, men shall carry away the riches of Damascus and the spoil of Samaria before the king of Assyria.

5.

[5.] And Jehovah spake yet again unto me, saying, Forasmuch as this people insulteth the waters of Shiloah that flow softly, and exulteth in fellowship with Rezin and the son of Remaliah, therefore, behold, the Lord bringeth upon them the waters of the river, mighty and great, [the king of Assyria and all his glory;] and it shall come over all his channels, and go over all his banks, and shall glide into Judah, overflowing and passing over, and reaching even to the neck, and the stretching out of his wings shall fill the breadth of thy land, O God-with-us. Vex yourselves, ye peoples, and ye shall utterly fail, and give ear, all ye of far countries; gird yourselves, and ye shall utterly fail, gird yourselves, and ye shall utterly fail; form a purpose, and it shall come to nought, speak a word, and it shall not stand: for God is with us. For Jehovah spake thus to me, when his hand was mighty, and warned me not to walk in the way of this people, saying, Call ye not everything a conspiracy, which this people calleth a conspiracy, neither fear ye their fear, nor count it worthy of dread. Jehovah of Hosts, him shall ye hallow, and let him be your fear, and let him be your dread. Then shall he be for a sanctuary, but for a stone of stumbling and for a rock of offence to both the houses of Israel, for a gin and for a snare to the inhabitants of Jerusalem; and many among them shall stumble, and shall fall, and be broken, and be snared, and be taken.

6.

[16.] 'Bind up the admonition, seal the doctrine among my disciples.' And I wait for Jehovah, though he hideth his face from the house of Jacob, and I hope in him; behold, I and the children whom Jehovah hath given me are for signs and for portents in Israel from Jehovah of Hosts, which dwelleth in mount Zion. And when they say unto you, 'Consult the ghost-seers and the wizards, that chirp and that mutter! Should not people consult their gods, even the dead on behalf of the living?' To the doctrine and the admonition! They surely shall speak according to this word, for whom there is no daybreak; and they shall pass along, hardly bestead and hungry; and then, when they are hungry, they shall fret themselves, and curse by their king and god, and shall look upwards. And they shall look unto the earth, but behold distress and darkness, the dimness of trouble, and they are driven into gloom.

7.

[IX. 1.] Nay, though the land was troubled, it is no longer dark; as the former time brought shame to the land of Zebulon and the land of Naphtali, so the latter hath brought unto it honour, unto the way by the sea, the other side of Jordan, the district of the nations. The people that walked in darkness have seen a great light; they that dwelt in the land of obscurity, upon them hath the light gleamed. Thou hast multiplied the nation, even unto them hast thou given great joy: they joy before thee according to the joy in harvest, as men exult when they divide the spoil. For the yoke of his burden, and the staff of his shoulder, the rod of his tyrant, thou hast broken, as in the day of Midian; yea, every shoe of him that tramped with clatter, and the cloak rolled in bloodshed, was for burning, fuel of fire. For a child has been born unto us, a son has been given unto us, and the government was laid upon his shoulder; and one called his name, Wonderful-Counsellor Mighty-God Everlasting-Father Prince-of-Peace: for the increase of the government and for peace without end upon the throne of David and over his kingdom, to establish it and to support it through right and justice from henceforth even for ever. The zeal of Jehovah of Hosts will perform this.

Par. 1. *Resteth.* Comp ver 19, where the swarming warriors are said to 'rest' or settle in the valleys

Shear-Jashub, i e. 'a remnant shall return,' or, be converted, one of Isaiah's principal doctrines. Comp x. 20–22

The highway of the fuller's field, i e the road to Joppa, which began outside the western gate. Ahaz had doubtless gone thither to prepare for a siege by securing the reservoir of Gihon, on which the inhabitants of Jerusalem depended for much of their supply of water. In the neighbourhood of this reservoir was the fuller's field.

The son of Tabel, evidently a Syrian, the meaning of the name in Chaldee being 'God is good.'

Within threescore and five years. These words are inclosed as a gloss, (1) because they interrupt the context, (2) because the effect of the passage consists in the quick succession of short, equal clauses. If we omit them, the connection is clear 'Rezin is prince of Damascus, and Remaliah's son prince of Samaria, both of whom are feeble mortals; but the prince of Jerusalem is Jehovah, who is pledged to deliver you.' Yet, with a play upon words, the prophet concludes, 'if ye do not hold fast by him, ye shall not stand fast,' i e. ye shall not preserve your national independence. But what was the event referred to by the writer of the gloss? Not the fall of Samaria, for that took place only twenty years after the accession of Ahaz. Perhaps it was the colonization ascribed to Esar-haddon in Ezra iv 2 · comp 2 Chron. xxxiii. 11, an event which the writer had not improbably witnessed.

Par. 2. *A sign.* A sign is an omen that the announcements of a prophet will be fulfilled. It may consist (1) in some ordinary phenomenon, as in 1 Sam. x 2–9, Isa viii 18, xix. 20, xxxvii 30; (2) in some wonderful event, entirely contrary to experience, as in Exod. vii 3, 9.

Deep down to the abyss, perhaps with an allusion to Ahaz's fondness for necromancy.

Neither will I tempt Jehovah. Probably Ahaz had already projected an alliance with Assyria, and knew that Isaiah was disinclined to it. Hence his pretended reluctance to 'tempt Jehovah.'

The damsel, Heb. *bā'almah*. So far as the etymology of this word is concerned (see 'Notes and Criticisms,' pp. 7, 8) there is nothing to prevent us from interpreting it of the wife of the prophet. We know that Isaiah's sons received symbolical names, and in viii 18 they are actually called 'signs to the house of Israel' Since, however, the word is limited by its usage in the Old Testament to the unmarried woman, it is perhaps better to choose some other explanation. The most probable seems to be that which refers the passage to the mother of the Messiah, whose advent was placed by Isaiah in connection with the Assyrian invasion (see ix., xi). The objection to it is that the Davidic origin and royal dignity of the child are passed over here without notice, which may be answered by recalling the circumstance that this is the earliest prophecy of Isaiah in which, on our hypothesis, the Messiah is mentioned. Even in the passage ix 6, 7, written apparently at a somewhat later time, there is no allusion to the descent of the Messiah from David; and considering the length of time required for the evolution of the doctrine of the Messiah from the vague faith in the establishment of God's kingdom, there is nothing to surprise us in its comparatively slow development in the mind of Isaiah himself. The revelation of the Davidic descent is first made in xi 1 We may confirm the explanation given above by Micah v. 3–5, in which the Messianic descriptions of Isa. vii. and ix are condensed.—Observe that the sign given to Ahaz consisted not in the manner of the child's birth, but in his name and fortunes. 'Behold,' cries the prophet, 'the damsel destined for so high an honour shall soon bear a son, whose name she shall call, God-on-our-side. Do you ask the reason of this strange name? It is that, between the birth of the child and his arrival at years of discretion, Syria and Israel shall cease to be formidable. This has, from the first, been the Divine intention. But now, as a punishment for your want of faith, the promise is qualified. At the time when the child shall have reached the years of discretion, he shall feed, not on corn and wine, but on cream and honey, for his native land will have been desolated by an Assyrian army.' In viii. 8 we seem to be on the verge of a still further disclosure, preparing the way for ix. 4.

Shall conceive, or, 'is with child,' thus bringing the fulfilment a little nearer the time of the prediction.

Cream and honey. This is a feature, not of fruitfulness, but of desolation, as appears from the next paragraph (ver. 22), and from the parallel clause in the explanation of the sign, ' Jehovah shall bring upon thee,' &c.

When he shall know to refuse, &c. A period intentionally made rather indefinite Comp. viii 4, in which the prospect of fulfilment has grown more distinct.

Shall become a desert. See, for the fulfilment, 2 Kings xv. 29, xvi. 9.

The king of Assyria. These words, which are repeated in the 3rd and 5th paragraphs, are probably a gloss They certainly weaken the force of the passage.

Par. 3. *Egypt and Assyria* These great and rival powers are to meet in Judah, and make it their battle-field

A thousand vines at a thousand silverlings, i e. each vine was worth a silver shekel, about 2s. 3d. In modern Syria, a vine is said to be valued at a piastre, about 3d.

As for all the mountains. Cultivation shall be broken off on account of the hopeless desolation. Note the tautology of the style, a mark of the despondency of the writer.

Par. 4 *The style of the people,* i.e. in large and legible characters.

Par 5. *Insulteth . . . exulteth.* See ' Notes and Criticisms,' pp 8, 9.

Shiloah = gushing; comp John ix. 7. This was a fountain in the south-east of Jerusalem, and is here employed as an image of the mild government of the house of David

Thy land, O God-with-us This passage supplies a point of connection between vii. 14 and ix. 1. Isaiah recollects the promise of the wonderful child, and seems to feel that it is not exhausted by the overthrow of the Syrians and Ephraimites; he already sees dimly the triumph of the Messiah over Assyria. This seems to be involved in the ejaculation of ver. 8, and the challenge of vv 9, 10, both of which are founded upon the word ' God-with-us.'

When his hand was mighty, i. e. in a moment of a specially strong prophetic impulse.

Call ye not everything a conspiracy, i.e do not give way to panic. Conspiracy is too serious a name for the enterprize of Rezin and Pekah, for it implies an attainable object. Comp. vii, 4

A stone of stumbling Comp note on xxviii 16.

Par. 6. *Bind up the admonition* A speech of Jehovah The revelation contained in the previous paragraph is to be committed to the guardianship of ' God's disciples.' Comp. liv. 13.

And I wait for Jehovah, i.e. I retain my faith in the future regeneration of God's people.

And when they say unto you. The prophet, in his excitement, has omitted the apodosis of this passage. It would naturally be, ' Hearken not unto them.'

The ghost-seers Well rendered by Lxx ἐγγαστρίμυθοι, 'ventriloquists,' which is confirmed not only by the proper meaning of 'ōb, 'a hollow,' but also by the expression, 'that chirp and that mutter,' i. e that imitate the 'squeaking and gibbering' of ghosts; comp. xxix. 4. Necromancy and magic arts were still prevalent in the period of Isaiah Many, but not all, their varieties are collected in Deut xviii. 10, 11, the force of which passage will be heightened, if we accept the late date of Deuteronomy A vivid picture of a necromantic consultation is given in 1 Sam. xxviii. 1–20 See, for a discussion of the passage before us, ' Notes and Criticisms,' pp. 9–11.

Their gods, i e the spirits of the departed national heroes. Comp. 1 Sam. xxviii 13, where the witch of Endor says, speaking of Samuel, ' I saw Elohim ascending out of the earth '

They surely shall speak, i. e they shall cry out for the true revelations, as opposed to the oracles of the necromancers, when it will be too late : comp. xxviii 19, Amos viii. 12. ' Daybreak'=a favourable turn of events

Par. 7. *The way by the sea,* i. e. the tract of land on the west of the Sea of Galilee. The districts here specified were the first to be depopulated by the Assyrians, 2 Kings xv. 29

Have seen. The events anticipated are settled in the Divine purpose, and therefore ideally past

Unto him. This is the marginal reading in the Hebrew, as well as in Auth Ver. The pronoun is placed first for emphasis, as in Ps. xvii. 14 (Heb.).

The day of Midian. See Judges vii ' Day' stands for ' battle,' as commonly in Arabic

Wonderful-counsellor, &c. The length of this name is to express, in Oriental manner, the dignity of its bearer. It consists of two pairs of compound names united, describing the character of the Messiah, first from within, and then from without Taking the names singly, the first (lit. ' wonder of a counsellor,' comp Gen xvi. 12, Heb.) describes the king's political sagacity. The second, ' God the Mighty' (*El gibbōr*), is applied to Jehovah in x 21, but also to godlike heroes, Ezekiel xxxii 12. A word even more expressive of divinity, Elohim, is frequently applied in the early books to those who filled the sacred office of judge. See, among other passages, Exod xxi. 6; Judges v. 8; 1 Sam ii. 25, and comp. Ps xlv. 6, where Elohim, if a vocative, is certainly addressed to the theocratic king; and Zech xii. 8, ' the house of David shall be as Elohim.'   Similarly, the Israelitish king is said in 1 Chron. xxix. 23 to 'sit upon the throne of Jehovah,' and in Ps. cx. to 'sit on the Lord's right hand' All these expressions denote that the officers in the theocracy are appointed by, and derive their power from, Jehovah   Observe that none of them are ever styled Jehovah; this, to a prophet contending for monotheism, would have seemed a blasphemy.   The meaning of the third, 'everlasting Father' depends to some extent on the interpretation of ver. 7, 'from henceforth even for ever' 'Father' is applied to the king's minister or representative in xxii. 21; Gen. xlv 8 The fourth, 'Prince of Peace,' describes the Messiah in his relation to foreign nations   Comp. Micah v. 5, and note the contrast evidently intended between the two claimants of universal dominion the Messiah and the king of Assyria

The government, i e that of God's kingdom

From henceforth even for ever, i.e either the Messiah shall be immortal, comp xxv 8, a Babylonian prophecy, or, more probably, that nothing shall interrupt the regular succession of the kings of his house, comp. 2 Sam. vii 13

III PROSPECTS ON THE ACCESSION OF HEZEKIAH.

(Isa. i., xiv. 28–32, xv., xvi., xxi. 11–17.)

PROLOGUE. (Isa. i.)

THE general character of the contents of this prophecy mark it out as being composed for a prologue. Its place in the traditional arrangement is best accounted for by Ewald, who regards it as the introduction, not only to the prophecies on foreign nations, but also to Isaiah's two previous collections, or, in fact, as the prologue to a new and enlarged edition of the prophet's works.

The opening of the prophecy is dramatic. Jehovah himself is introduced complaining pathetically of his unfilial people. Then the prophet, who seems to act the part of a Greek chorus, remonstrates with his countrymen on their madness; they do but invite a renewal of their chastisement. Already the whole body politic is disorganized. The land of which Jehovah is the patron is almost as completely ruined as Sodom of old, or, to speak more plainly, bands of foreigners have overrun the country, and penetrated to the very gates of Jerusalem. At this point a transition is made to the rulers and the people, no longer of Zion, but of the second Sodom. Their punctual observance of the ceremonial law is declared by God Himself to be odiously hypocritical. A rigorous self-reformation will be the first step to prosperity. (See Pars. 1 and 2.)

Hitherto Jehovah has spoken in anger; he now changes his tone, and offers a judicial trial, with the prospect of pardon and peace, on condition of obedience for the future. But the prophet, struck by the contrast of present circumstances, breaks in upon this offer with a strain of elegy. 'Therefore,' the chance being so small that Jehovah's conditions will be accepted, he announces that he will apply the last remedy, and after a terrible judgment on the idolatrous and profane, will restore Zion to its pristine state of security. (See Pars. 3–5.)

There is a wide divergence of opinion as to the date of this prophecy, owing to the paucity of historical references. Gesenius assigns it to the Syro-Ephraimitish war in the reign of Ahaz. But this is improbable, because that war was carried on rather against the Davidic dynasty than against the people of Judah, and there is no evidence that it involved such general devastation. Hitzig therefore refers it to the invasion of Sennacherib, but at that great crisis, as we know from chaps. xxxiii. and xxxvii., Isaiah's tone was sympathetic and encouraging. We doubt whether the description in ver. 7 will answer to a regular invasion; it seems to point rather to a succession of plundering inroads. The prophecies on the small neighbouring tribes which follow may perhaps have been caused by molestations of this kind. In fact, we know from 2 Chron. xxviii. 17, 18, that the Philistines and Edomites harassed the south of Judah in the reign of Ahaz, and from 2 Kings xviii. 8, that the former were reduced to submission by Hezekiah. If the prophecy has any historical foundation at all, it should be assigned to the early years of Hezekiah's reign, not long subsequent to Isaiah's previous collection.

1.

[I. 2.] Hear, O heavens, and give ear, O earth; for Jehovah speaketh · I have reared and brought up sons, and they have rebelled against me! An ox knoweth his owner, and an ass his master's crib Israel doth not know, my people doth not consider! Ah sinful nation, a people laden with iniquity, a seed of evil-doers, sons that act corruptly · they have forsaken Jehovah, they have reviled the Holy One of Israel, they are gone away backward. Why will ye still be smitten, revolting more and more? The whole head is sickly, and the whole heart faint; from the sole of the foot even unto the head there is no soundness in it, but wounds, and bruises, and festering sores: they have not been pressed, neither bound up, neither mollified with oil. Your country is desolate, your cities are burned with fire, your land, strangers devour it in your presence, and it is desolate, as overthrown by strangers; and the daughter of Zion is left as a booth in a vine-yard, as an hammock in a field of cucumbers, as a besieged city. Except Jehovah of Hosts had left us a very small remnant, we should have been as Sodom, and we should have been like unto Gomorrah.

2.

[10.] Hear the word of Jehovah, ye rulers of Sodom; give ear unto the doctrine of our God, ye people of Gomorrah. To what purpose is the multitude of your sacrifices unto me? saith Jehovah; I am full of the burnt offerings of rams and the fat of fed calves, and I delight not in the blood of bullocks, or of lambs, or of he-goats. When ye come to behold my face, who hath required this at your hands, the trampling of my courts? Bring no more vain oblations; incense is an abomination unto me; the new moon, and the sabbath, and the calling of assemblies, the feast that is kept with hypocrisy, I cannot endure. Your new moons and your holy days my soul hateth, they are a trouble unto me, I am weary of bearing. And when ye spread forth your hands, I hide mine eyes from you; yea, though ye pray much, I do not hear! your hands are full of blood. Wash ye, make you clean, put away the evil of your doings from before mine eyes, cease to do evil, learn to do well, seek right, reclaim the violent, judge the fatherless, plead for the widow.

3.

[18.] Come now, and let us dispute together, saith Jehovah: though your sins be as scarlet, they shall be white as snow; though they be red like crimson, they shall be as wool. If ye be willing and hearken, the good of the land shall ye eat; but if ye refuse and rebel, by the sword shall ye be eaten: for the mouth of Jehovah hath spoken it.

4.

[21.] How is she become an harlot, the faithful city, she that was full of right, in whom justice was wont to lodge, but now murderers! Thy silver is become dross, thy wine weakened with water: thy rulers are unruly and companions of thieves, every one loveth bribes, and pursueth rewards; they judge not the fatherless, neither doth the cause of the widow come unto them.

5.

[24.] Therefore this is the utterance of the Lord, Jehovah of Hosts, the Hero of Israel: Ah, let me ease myself of mine adversaries, and avenge me of mine enemies, and let me turn mine hand upon thee, purging as with lie thy dross, and take away all thine alloys, and restore thy judges as at the first, and thy counsellors as at the beginning: afterward thou shalt be called, Town of justice, Faithful city; Zion shall be redeemed through right, and her converts through justice. But renegades and sinners shall be ruined together, and they that forsake Jehovah shall be consumed. For ye shall be ashamed of the oaks which ye desired, and ye shall blush for the gardens which ye chose; yea, ye shall be as an oak whose leaf fadeth, and as a garden that hath no water. And the powerful one shall become tow, and his work a spark, and they shall both burn together with none to quench them.

Par. 1. *Hear, O heavens*, &c. A poetic expression for the great idea of the prophetic period, viz. that the God of Israel is also the God of the universe. Comp. Deut. xxxii. 1; Hab. ii. 20; Zech. ii. 13.

As overthrown by strangers. As far as the eye can reach, there is nothing but ruin—a ruin so complete, that for the moment one seems to miss the one point of light and hope. It is as if the marauding bands had effaced every vestige of cultivation; but it is only 'as if,' the comparison is not entirely perfect. Jerusalem is still left, though she be as forlorn as a watchman's hammock, as solitary as if already under siege. See 'Notes and Criticisms,' p. 2.

Booth . . . hammock. Comp. xxiv. 20; Job xxvii. 18. The 'hammock' was for the watchman's security from wild beasts.

As a besieged city. Lit. 'like a fortress that is watched,' either in a good sense by the garrison, or in a bad by the besiegers. The latter sense harmonizes best with the context.

Par. 2. *To what purpose*, &c. Isaiah, like his fellow-prophets, Amos, Hosea, and Micah, depreciates the ceremonial in comparison with the moral law. That he did not, however, go so far as to deny all religious value to the former is probable from the earnest reforms in the temple-service carried out by Hezekiah, who can hardly be supposed to have acted in opposition to the prophet.

To behold my face. Auth. Ver. 'to appear before me,' which is based on the traditional vowel-points, but seems, on grammatical grounds, hardly defensible. In two passages only, where some variety of the Hebrew for this phrase is found, is the rendering 'to appear before God' indisputable (Exod. xxiii. 17; 1 Sam. i. 22), in four passages doubtful (Exod. xxxiv. 23, 24; Deut. xvi. 16, xxxi. 11); in four others, extremely improbable, not to say impossible (Exod. xxiii. 15, xxxiv. 20; Ps. xlii. 2, where the Syriac renders 'to see God,' and the passage on which we are commenting). The scruple which influenced the Jewish editors to affix the vowels of another conjugation may be illustrated by the rendering of the Lxx in Exod. xxiv. 11 (Auth. Ver. 'they saw God'), ὤφθησαν ἐν τῷ τόπῳ τοῦ Θεοῦ, and by the controversies of the Moslem sects as to the anthropomorphic expressions in the Koran.—The phrase 'to behold the face of God' is connected with the view of the special efficacy of prayer in the sanctuary. Jehovah was said symbolically (1 Sam. iv. 4, &c.) to 'dwell under the cherubim' of the mercy-seat, so that wherever the ark was, there the worshipper stood 'before God,' Joshua xviii. 10, xix. 51, &c. And so great was Jehovah's love for his earthly dwelling that, as one of the prophetic historians writes, 'His eyes were open toward this house night and day to hearken unto the prayer which his servant should make toward this place,' 1 Kings viii. 29 Compare the entire prayer of Solomon—one of the most exquisite monuments of the prophetic period.

The trampling of my courts, i e your devotions are as destitute of religious value as the movements of the victims driven in to be sacrificed.

Reclaim the violent, i. e. keep him within bounds by inflicting the due punishment. Delitzsch remarks here on the political tone of Isaiah's admonitions, as distinguished from the ethical tone of Micah's.

Par 3 *They shall be white as snow.* The condition of this promise is contained in the next verse.—' If ye be obedient for the future '

Par. 4. *Thy rulers are unruly,* i. e those who should be the patterns of their people in observing the law of God are the foremost in breaking it This is expressed, as usual, by a paronomasia.

Par. 5. *Zion shall be redeemed through right* This must be interpreted by ix 7, where ' right' and ' justice' are said to form the basis of the government of the Messiah

Renegades, from which Coverdale's word ' runagates' is corrupted, is a stronger word than ' sinners,' and means those who have renounced the religion of Jehovah

The oaks. Most modern interpreters render ' terebinths,' but the names for this tree and for the oak are not always distinguished by the Hebrew writers The terebinth is not common in Palestine, and is neither shady nor evergreen, qualities which are both presupposed by the passage before us. Dense, evergreen oaks, on the other hand, may be found in every village and on every hill-side, and are still regarded as the abodes of Genii See ' The Land and the Book,' by Dr. Thomson, pp 242-244; and comp Isa lvii 5; 2 Kings xvi. 4.

His work as a spark, i e. his idol is the germ of his ruin.

I. ON PHILISTIA.

(Isa xiv. 28-32.)

THE burden of the prophecy may be described as follows. The revolt of the Philistines from the house of David has indeed been crowned with success, but their exultation is premature, for the mild yoke which they have shaken off will be succeeded by one of far greater severity. The fate in store for them is nothing less than the depopulation of the whole country. Meantime the Jews, who now appear so helpless, will enjoy their own land in peace Rather should Philistia lament, for already the prophet can descry on the horizon the smoke of the advancing hosts of Assyrians. Vain will it be to sue humbly for the alliance of Judah. 'Zion is safe under the protection of her God,' will be the only answer vouchsafed.

The title, 'In the year that king Ahaz died was this prophecy,' is to be rejected for two reasons :—(1) The employment of the word *massā*, 'oracle' or 'prophecy,' which occurs elsewhere only in the unauthentic titles of xiii.–xxiii., and xxx. 6; (2) The indignation expressed at the revolt of the Philistines, which seems to imply that it was still recent. According to 2 Chron. xxviii. 18, the Philistian inroads began much earlier than the death of Ahaz, so that although the prophecy may be assigned to the reign of that king, the precise date of its composition must be uncertain. The source of the error in the title is not difficult to find. It was most likely produced by fancying an allusion in the 'basilisk' of the first verse to Hezekiah. Comp. 1 Kings xviii. 8.

1.

Rejoice not so entirely, O Philistia, that the rod which smote thee is broken, for out of the serpent's root shall come forth a basilisk, and his fruit is a flying dragon. The firstborn of the helpless shall feed, and the needy shall lie down securely, but I will kill thy root with famine, and thy remnant shall be slain.

2.

Wail, O gate; cry, O city; faint entirely, O Philistia: for out of the north a smoke cometh, and none walketh singly in their troops. What shall one then answer the messengers of the nation? That Jehovah hath founded Zion, and the sufferers of his people seek refuge in her.

Par 1. *Basilisk.* The basilisk, or *vipera cerastes,* is common in Egypt and the desert. Comp. 1 Kings xii 11.

A flying dragon. The only mention of a fabulous creature in the genuine Isaiah. Herodotus (ii 75) speaks of winged serpents in Egypt and Arabia, but this is not confirmed by the Egyptian sculptures

The firstborn of the helpless. Comp Job xviii. 13, 'The firstborn of death,' i e. a most terrible death

Par. 2. *None walketh singly,* i.e. none fall behind from weariness: comp. ver. 27.

II. ON MOAB.

(Isa. xv., xvi.)

THE prophecy consists of three strophes followed by an epilogue. The connection in the first and third of these is so simple, and in the second so obscure, that we forbear to prefix an analysis. Compare throughout Jeremiah's amplification (ch. xlviii.), and contrast the tone of Isaiah's ode on Tyre (ch. xxiii.).

The epilogue is admitted by all critics to be from the pen of Isaiah. It contains the ratification of an earlier prophecy, 'This is the word that Jehovah spake long since.' Now, does Isaiah mean by this that xv.–xvi. 12 is the work of an earlier prophet, and is only quoted by himself in order to connect it with its fulfilment, or that it is an early production of his own? The philological and historical *data* induce us to decide for the former alternative. Not to mention a large number of other un-Isaian expressions, the monotonous recurrence of *ki,* 'for,' 'yea,' 'when,' and *'al-kén, lākén,* 'therefore,' is without a parallel in the undisputed prophecies. Only in xvi. 4*b*, 5 can we trace a similarity to Isaiah, which may either be explained as an interpolation due to the prophet's fondness for Hezekiah, or as having served Isaiah as a model for imitation. If the former be the case, we have (1) no *data* at all for fixing the age of the prophecy, and (2) the words 'long since' are deprived of their full meaning. If the latter, then we may confidently refer the prophecy to the beginning of the reign of Uzziah, whose good and prosperous reign stands in sharp contrast with the troublous time of his father Amaziah, 2 Kings. xiv., xv.; 2 Chron. xxv., xxvi. Thus the expressions of ch. xvi. 4, 5 become distinct and natural.

A slightly different hypothesis has been proposed by Ewald in the second edition of his great work on the prophets. The peculiar style of xvi. 4 b, 5, combined with the interruption caused by the contextual words, have induced him to assign xvi. 1–6 to a third writer, who lived in Judah about fifty years previously to Isaiah, and incorporated it in the work of an old Israelitish prophet. We regret to be unable to adopt this attractive addition to Jewish literary history. True, that vv. 1–6 appear at first sight to interrupt the elegy. Let it be weighed, on the other hand, (1) that the first gush of lamentation is already brought to a natural close in xv. 9, and that its renewal in xvi. 7 requires a fresh motive; (2) that there are three interruptions hardly less serious in the passage xvi. 1–6 itself, since vv. 1–4 a do not cohere with vv. 4 b, 5 (which are unintelligible as an utterance of the Moabites), and vv. 1–5 do not cohere with ver. 6, which is unintelligible as the answer of Zion to Moab, and is simply the prophet's own statement of the historical characteristics of the Moabitish nation. If therefore we are to argue from the mere fact of an interruption to a difference of authors, we must infer the existence not of a single fresh hand only, but of three.

The unity of the three strophes being conceded, let us sum up briefly their contents. The author is apparently a native of the northern kingdom. This is rendered probable (1) by his deep and tender interest in Moab, (2) by his minute acquaintance with Moabitish topography. He is, however, at heart, like his countryman Hosea (iii. 5, viii. 4), an adherent of the Davidic rights, and regards the extorted independence of the Moabites, no less than their previous submission to the Ten Tribes, to be among the causes of their impending calamities. Of these calamities, which are only past in prophetic imagination, he draws an ideal sketch (comp. note on x. 28–32). He seems to see the whole territory of the Moabites devastated, and the only remedy which he can find is the immediate renewal of their allegiance to the Davidic sovereign. The character of the latter, and the peace which he has restored to his realm after long and grave disorders, will be the best guarantee of Moab's security. The prophet, however, foresees that such advice would be offered in vain. Moab's hereditary pride is but too likely to prevent its adoption, although this consequence is rather implied than expressed. Pride at any rate is the source of these calamities, and an obscure hint is even dropped by the way of yet more severe judgments (xv. 9), which will lead to the complete extinction of the Moabitish race.

At which of the neighbouring tribes, hostile to the Moabites, the original prophecy was directed, it is impossible to say. Since the fugitives proceed in a southerly direction (xv. 5–8), the foes must have been expected from the north. Our choice will lie between the Arabs and the Israelites on the east of the Jordan. The 'lion' alluded to in xv. 9 was doubtless interpreted by Isaiah of the king of Assyria, but whether of Sargon or Sennacherib does not appear.

1.

[**XV. 1.**] Yea, in the night Ar-Moab was laid waste, and brought to silence, yea, in the night Kir-Moab was laid waste, and brought to silence. Baith and Dibon are gone up the high places to weep: on Nebo and on Medeba Moab waileth; on all their heads is baldness, and every beard cut off. In their streets they have girded themselves with sackcloth; on the tops of their houses, and in their broad places, the whole people waileth, running down in weeping. And Heshbon crieth out, and Elealeh; even unto Jahaz their voice is heard; therefore the valiant ones of . Moab shriek, his soul shrinketh within him. My heart crieth out for Moab, whose fugitives fled unto Zoar, unto the third Eglath . for the mounting up of Luhith they ascend with weeping; for in the way of Horonaim they raise up a cry of destruction. For the

clear waters of Nimrim will be desolate: for the grass is dried
up, the young herb at an end, there is no more green. Therefore
the abundance which they have gotten, and that which they have
laid up, they carry away over the torrent of the willows; for the
cry hath gone round the border of Moab, their wailing hath
reached unto Eglaim, and their wailing unto Beer-Elim; for the
waters of Dimon are full of blood, yea, I will bring yet more
upon Dimon, a lion unto them that escape of Moab, and unto the
remnant of the land.

2

[XVI. 1.] 'Send ye the lambs of the ruler of the land from
Sela toward the wilderness, unto the mount of the daughter of
Zion.' Then will the daughters of Moab at the fords of Arnon
become like wandering birds, like scattered nestlings. 'Bring
counsel, frame a decision, make thy shadow as the night in the
midst of the noon-day, cover the outcasts, bewray not him that
wandereth. Let the outcasts of Moab sojourn with thee, be thou
a covert to them from the face of the spoiler.' For the oppression
hath ceased, the spoiling is at an end, they that trode down have
vanished out of the land, and through kindness hath the throne
been established; and there sitteth upon it in faithfulness in the
tent of David a judge that seeketh right, and is ready in justice.

3.

[6.] We have heard of the haughtiness of Moab, the very
haughty; his high mind, and his haughtiness, and his fury, the
falsehood of his babbling. Therefore let Moab wail for Moab,
altogether wail, for the raisins of Kir-Hareseth shall ye mourn,
sorely afflicted. For the fields of Heshbon languish, and the vine
of Sibmah, whose branches overcame the lords of nations, and

reached unto Jazer, and strayed into the wilderness, whose shoots
did stretch out, and passed over the sea.   Therefore I will weep
with the weeping of Jazer for the vine of Sibmah: I will water
thee with my tears, O Heshbon and Elealeh, for upon thy fruitage
and upon thy vintage a strange cheer hath fallen; and joy is taken
and exultation from the plentiful field, and in the vineyards there
is no singing, neither is there shouting, the treader treadeth out
no wine in the presses; I have made the vintage cheering to cease.
Wherefore mine affections are stirred like an harp for Moab, and
mine inward parts for Kir-Heres.   Yet when Moab spendeth his
strength in vain on the high place, and cometh to his sanctuary to
pray, but prevaileth not, [then shall he turn to Jehovah].

4.

[13.] This is the word that Jehovah spake concerning Moab
long since.   But now Jehovah speaketh, saying, Within three
years, as the years of an hireling, shall the glory of Moab be
brought to shame, with all his great multitude, and the remnant
shall be very small and feeble.

Par. 1. *In the night*   Two other renderings may be mentioned —(1) That
of Ewald (2nd edition), 'In the night when Ar-Moab was stormed, it was
desolated,' which is tautological; (2) That of Hitzig, 'In the night when
Ar-Moab was stormed and laid waste, Baith and Dibon went up,' &c., which
is too lengthy for a passage so full of excited feeling   Hence we must either
read *belail*, or regard *lêl* as a collateral form, comparing *shêsh* and *shaish*, *bêk*
(*haik*), *'êd* (*'aid*).
   Ar-Moab   The capital of Moab, situated probably at the confluence of two
arms of the Arnon, comp Josh xiii 9, 16
   Kir-Moab   The chief fortress of Moab, some distance to the south of the
capital, called in the third strophe *Kir-Hareseth* and Kir-Heres, and still called
Kerak, or 'castle'
   Baith.   Probably the same as Beth-Diblathaim, Jer. xlviii 22.

The third Eglath. Eglath, or slightly different forms of that word, was a common name in this region. See 'Notes and Criticisms,' p. 19

Nimrim. Note the allusion to the meaning of the name, which is cognate with the Arabic *namîr*, 'limpid.'

Torrent of the willows. Identified by Delitzsch with the Wâdy Sufsâf, or 'torrent of the willows,' near the frontier of Moab and Edom.

Dimon. This is the same as Dibon, mentioned earlier in the strophe. The name is altered in order to create an assonance to *dâm*, 'blood,' as if it meant 'the place of blood.'

Par. 2. *Send ye the lambs.* One chance of escape is left for the Moabites— the renewal of their long-suspended tribute to the house of David. (Comp. 2 Kings iii 4.) The north end of the Dead Sea being blocked up by the enemy, the fugitives must choose the southern route passing by Sela through the desert.

The daughters of Moab The inhabitants of the various districts of Moab (comp. Ps xlviii 11) will collect irresolutely at the fords of Arnon.

Bring counsel, frame a decision That is, the speakers resign the decision of their fate to the Jews, or rather, the prophet urges the Moabites to do so, and confirms his advice by describing the character of the Davidic king. He foresees, however, that the counsel 'would be offered in vain, which furnishes a motive for a fresh burst of lamentation. See Introduction to the prophecy.

Par. 3. *The raisins* The word occurs in four other places, and, it would seem, always with this meaning. Auth Ver renders here 'foundations,' which is defensible, but unnecessary, elsewhere (e.g. Cant ii 5), 'flagons,' which is a mere guess of the Rabbis.

Overcame Literally, 'struck down ' comp xxviii. 1. Ewald renders, 'The lords of the nations have struck down her branches,' but less naturally

With the weeping of Jazer That is, 'Let me mingle my tears with those of Jazer.

A strange cheer The word *hêdâd* is used in a double sense, of the cheer or song of the vintage, and of the battle-cry.

But prevaileth not. All translators except Ewald render, 'He shall not prevail,' taking the *vâv* as a mark of the apodosis But Ewald's rendering develops the parallelism better, and the idea that Moab should finally turn to Jehovah is in keeping with the rest of the prophecy, and makes a noble conclusion. The loss of a clause, or even of a whole verse, may easily be paralleled from other parts of the Hebrew Bible.

III. DUMAH.

(Isa. xxi. 11, 12.)

THE prophet upon his watch-tower hears, or seems to hear, the unspoken question of the Edomites, then beginning to suffer from Assyrian invasions, how long their night of trouble should continue. But he has no tidings of good, and returns a gentle but evasive answer. The title, 'Prophecy of Dumah,' seems at first sight a misnomer, for though Yakut, the Arabic geographer, notices several places called Dumah, none of them belong to the mountains of Seir. Hence Ewald interprets the word as a witty allusion to the vagueness of the prophetic reply. More probably it is a transformation of the name Edom, expressing the silence which was so soon to reign over the desolated region.

One calleth to me out of Seir, Watchman, what hour of the night? Watchman, what hour of the night? The watchman saith, The morning came, and now also the night. If ye will inquire, inquire ye. come again.

The morning came. 'Your time of prosperity came and passed, and has given place to troubles, from which there is no immediate prospect of deliverance.'

IV. ARABIA.

(Isa xxi. 13-17.)

AT the time of this prophecy, the caravans of the Dedanites, a powerful Arabian tribe, were threatened with destruction. They were compelled to hide themselves in the low, thorny bushes of the desert, and beg their bread of the friendly tribes of Tema (Job vi. 19). But within a year the proud and warlike tribes of Arabia should all share the same fate. The conquerors alluded to are evidently the Assyrians. Both Sargon and Sennacherib have recorded the subjection of Arabian tribes on the Assyrian monuments, and the latter is called by Herodotus (ii. 141) 'king of the Arabians and the Assyrians.'

In the bushes must ye lodge at evening, O travelling companies of Dedanites. Bring ye water to meet the thirsty, O inhabitants of the land of Tema, meet with his bread him that fleeth. For they have fled before the swords, before the drawn sword, and before the bent bow, and before the grievousness of war. For thus said Jehovah unto me, Within a year, as the years of an hireling, all the glory of Kedar shall fail; and the number of bows that is left 'of the mighty sons of Kedar shall be small, for Jehovah, the God of Israel, hath spoken it.

At evening. The Authorised Version, following the vowel-points, renders 'in Arabia;' but this is extremely unnatural, since the persons addressed were themselves Arabs. Hence we must alter the points with the Lxx and the Targum, and render as above. When Meier accuses this of tautology, he forgets Ps. xxx. 6: *Lūn* in Hifil is not merely 'to pass the night,' but also 'to take a lodging.' The words 'at evening' were adopted by the editor of Isaiah's prophecies as a title.

Kedar. A general name for the nomade tribes between Arabia Petræa and the plain to the east of Haurân.

IV. WARNINGS OF INVASION.

(Isa. xxii.)

I. THE VALLEY OF VISION. (Isa. xxii. 1–14.)

THE prophet assumes the attitude of a stranger, and inquires the cause of the crowd assembled on the roofs. This is no time, he urges, for boisterous merriment. The Jewish warriors have all surrendered or fled, the enemy is at the gates, and nothing short of destruction is to be anticipated. Hasty measures of defence have indeed been taken, but not the only effectual one, a serious repentance. In vain do the citizens try to drown care in sensual pleasure; they only draw down upon themselves the more quickly an irrevocable doom.

The description of the siege in this prophecy is not to be interpreted literally, as if it corresponded to events of which the writer was an eyewitness. The only siege of Jerusalem during the period of Isaiah is the one commemorated in the famous inscription of Sennacherib (see Rawlinson or Lenormant), but this does not appear to have lasted long enough for such gloomy apprehensions, as those expressed in vv. 4 and 5, to have arisen. We know, too, that Isaiah's tone during great national crises was one of sympathy and encouragement, that when at a later time the danger from Assyria became terribly urgent, the prophet was full of confidence that the capital would be delivered, and we have in x. 28–32 a picture of an invasion which even Delitzsch does not consider to be historical. On all these grounds we regard this prophecy as an imaginative description of a possible catastrophe, composed with the view of alarming the Jews out of their moral and spiritual torpor, but at a period when the actual danger from Assyria was not so great as it became afterwards.

1.

[**XXII. 1.**] What aileth thee now, that thou art wholly gone up to the house-tops, thou that art full of stirs, a tumultuous city, a joyous town? Thy slain men are not slain with the sword, nor dead in battle. All thy captains fled together from the bow, they were bound; all that were found of thee were bound together; they fled far away. Therefore say I, Look away from me, I would weep bitterly; press not to comfort me for the spoiling of the daughter of my people. For a day of tumult, and of treading down, and of perplexity is set by the Lord, Jehovah of Hosts, in the valley of vision; the wall shall be unwalled, and the crying shall sound unto the mountains.

2.

[**6.**] Elam carried the quiver in troops of horsemen, and Kir made bare the shield; and already thy choicest valleys were full of troops, and the horsemen set themselves in array towards the gate, and he uncovered the curtain of Judah, and then didst thou look to the armour of the forest-house, and ye saw that the breaches of the city of David were many, and ye gathered together the waters of the lower pool, and ye numbered the houses of Jerusalem, and brake down the houses to fortify the wall, and ye made a basin between the two walls for the water of the old pool, but ye looked not unto the maker thereof, neither had respect unto him that fashioned it long ago.

3.

[**12.**] In that day did the Lord, Jehovah of Hosts, call to weeping and to mourning, and to baldness, and to girding with sackcloth. But behold joy and gladness, slaying oxen and killing sheep, eating flesh and drinking wine, eating and drinking, for 'to-morrow we shall die.' But Jehovah of Hosts hath revealed himself in mine ears; surely this iniquity shall not be purged from you till ye die, saith the Lord, Jehovah of Hosts.

Par. 1. *On the house-tops.* The crowds were attracted to the roofs, not by curiosity, but by a morbid appetite for pleasure, produced by despair: see ver. 13. The roof was a place of concourse on festivals (Judges xvi. 27; Neh. viii. 6).

From the bow; or, following the Hebrew accents, 'without the bow they were bound.'

All that were found of thee, i.e. the rank and file of the troops, as well as their captains.

The valley of vision, i.e. the place where the prophets received their revelations. The phrase is singular, for the hills in the neighbourhood of Jerusalem do not convey the impression of great height, and the city itself is divided between hill and dale (comp. ver. 7) Still, the sacred poets delighted to magnify their trifling highlands, apparently with the object of symbolising the Divine protection which Jerusalem enjoyed. Comp. Deut. xxxiii. 12; Ps. cxxv. 2.

The wall shall be unwalled. These words and those that follow are obscure, but some paronomasia is evidently intended. Luzzatto, a modern Hebrew critic of great acuteness, followed by Ewald (2nd edition), takes Kir ('wall') and Shoa ('cry') as the names of tribes in the Assyrian army, 'Kir breaketh down, and Shoa is at the mount (Zion).'

Par. 2. *Kir.* An Assyrian province or tribe, situated by the river Cyrus, and corresponding to the modern Georgia.

Troops Heb. *rekeb,* in the sense of the Arabic *rakb,* 'a troop of riders.' Comp xxi. 7, 9.

Made bare, i.e. took away the leathern coverings of the shields.

He uncovered the curtain of Judah, i.e. God permitted the enemy to see the utter weakness of the State.

The armour of the forest-house. The armoury built by Solomon on mount Zion was called 'the house of the forest of Lebanon,' from its being raised on four rows of cedar pillars (1 Kings vii. 2, x. 17).

And brake down the houses. See the account of Hezekiah's preparations for a siege, 2 Chron. xxxii. 2, 5.

II. SHEBNA.

(Isa xxii. 15-25)

SHEBNA, the ambitious prime minister of Hezekiah, is threatened with dismission and exile, and Eliakim, a man of purer religion and milder character (comp. the phrases 'my servant,' 'a father') is nominated to succeed him. The numerous dependents of the former, adds the prophet, shall share his fate.

The vagueness with which the Assyrians are indicated, and the easy explanation of the position held by Shebna from the well-known foreign sympathies of Ahaz, lead us to assign the prophecy to the early years of Hezekiah's reign. As an invective against an individual, it stands alone in Isaiah, and in fact reminds one rather of the politicians among the prophets, Elijah and Elisha.

1.

[XXII. 15.] Thus saith the Lord, Jehovah of Hosts, Go, get thee unto this favourite, even unto Shebna, which is over the house, (and say unto him,) What hast thou here, and whom hast thou here, that thou hewest thee out a sepulchre here, hewing thee out thy sepulchre on high, graving an habitation for thyself in the rock? Behold, Jehovah will hurl thee violently, thou mighty man, and lay a firm hold on thee; he will roll thee tightly into a ball, (and toss thee) into a large country; thither shalt thou go to die, and thither shall go thy glorious chariots, thou shame of the house of thy lord! And I will push thee from thy station, and from thy place shall he (God) pull thee down.

2.

[20.] And in that day will I call my servant Eliakim, the son of Hilkiah, and clothe him with thy robe, and bind him with thy

girdle, and will lay thy government in his hand, and he shall
be a father to the inhabitants of Jerusalem and to the house of
Judah; and I will lay the key of the house of David upon his
shoulder, and he shall open, and none shall shut, and shut, and
none shall open.   And I will strike him as a nail into a sure place,
and he shall be for a throne of honour to his father's house; and
all the honour of his father's house shall be hung upon him, the
offspring and the offshoots, all the vessels of small quantity, from
the vessels of bowls to all the vessels of flagons.

3.

[25.] In that day (it is the utterance of Jehovah of Hosts) shall
the nail that is struck into a sure place give way; it shall be cut
down, and fall, and the burden that is upon it shall be destroyed,
for Jehovah hath spoken it.

Par. 1. *Shebna*   Shebna is shewn by its termination to be a Syriac name.
Thus Isaiah might fairly ask in the next verse, What hereditary right, or what
family, hast thou here?   Probably Shebna belonged to the Egyptian party,
which is so strongly denounced by the prophet in chaps. xxix.–xxxi.

Over the house.   The office of steward of the palace was instituted by Solomon,
1 Kings iv 6.   Its importance is shewn by the fact that it was once held
by a king's son, 2 Chron. xxvi 21.

On high   That is, probably, on mount Zion, which was reserved for the
sepulchres of the kings, 1 Kings ii. 10.

Par. 2 *Eliakim.*   In ch xxxvi. we find Eliakim occupying the post of
steward, and Shebna, not indeed banished, but in the lower rank of secretary.

All the honour, &c.   The members of Eliakim's family shall all, in their
various degrees, derive honour from him.

Par 3 *The burden that is upon it*   Not only Shebna, but his numerous
dependents (foreigners, probably, like himself) should fall.

V. TYRE.

(Isa. xxiii.)

THIS is a prophetic ode on the fall of Tyre, in three strophes, followed by an epilogue. The first of these pictures the ruin of Tyre's commerce; the second, that of her aristocratic pride; the third, that of her foreign empire. All who are connected with Tyre—the ships returning from Tartessus, the Tyrian islanders, the whole Phœnician people, and the Egyptian corn-growers—are successively invited to join the mourners. The Tyrians themselves are advised to flee to their Spanish colony, and if a curious stranger should inquire after the cause of these strange events, the prophet will inform him that it is the Divine anger at human presumption. Next, Isaiah congratulates the colonies, which Tyre had governed so harshly, on their emancipation, specifying Tartessus as their representative, threatens the Tyrian fugitives in Cyprus with pursuit, and points sarcastically to the land without a people, abandoned to wild beasts, strewn with the fragments of ruined towers and palaces. Then, with the refrain, ' Wail, ye ships of Tarshish,' he concludes his elegy. The epilogue continues in another strain. Seventy years shall be spent by Tyre in complete oblivion, each year so like the last that it might seem like the reign of a single king. Then shall the merchant-city resume her traffic, no longer, indeed, for self-aggrandizement, but to supply the pressing wants of the people of Jerusalem.

The settlement of the date has caused much perplexity to commentators. Many of them have failed to see that the preliminary question is one, not of exegesis, but of criticism. The date of the ode obviously depends on that of the siege of which it prophecies, and this again depends primarily on the genuineness of the word ' Chaldeans ' in ver. 13 (see note). If we admit the genuineness of this word, we must assign the ode to the years preceding the siege of Nebuchadnezzar (shortly after 588), for though it is possible that Chaldean soldiers were engaged in the siege of Shalmaneser, it is at least improbable that they played a conspicuous part in it, since the contemporary description of an Assyrian army in Isa. xxii. omits all mention of them. If, on the other hand, as the author is inclined to do, we deny the genuineness of the word, the supporters of the later date are driven to a secondary argument, viz. that the seventy years assigned to the Chaldean sovereignty in the epilogue are borrowed from Jeremiah (xxix. 10, xxv. 11, 12). This argument, however, seems highly precarious; for (1) the Isaian authorship of the epilogue is not entirely free from suspicion. The ideas expressed in it point rather to the beginning of the Persian dominion, when, as the prophecies of Haggai and Zechariah shew, the restored Jews were in a state of great penury, while Tyre had, presumably, shewn evident traces of reviving prosperity. It may be added that the epilogue throws the glorification of the Jewish state, i. e. the Messianic period, into a greater distance than is usual with Isaiah. (See note on xxxii. 9.) This, in fact, appears to the author decisive. But (2) even if we reject this hypothesis, Jeremiah, whose proneness to imitation is acknowledged, may quite conceivably have borrowed the 'seventy years' from a prophecy of Isaiah. In this case, the poverty of Jerusalem referred to in ver. 18 may be an allusion to the distresses produced by the last great judgment, which, as Isaiah repeatedly foretold, should precede the Messianic period: comp. iv. 1

It is remarkable that neither the siege of Shalmaneser, nor even that of Nebuchadnezzar, fulfilled the predictions of Isaiah. The former, says Menander, quoted by Josephus (Archæol ix. 14, 2), 'lasted five years, and still the Tyrians held out, and drank of the water they had out of the wells they dug.' But, as Grote has shewn, it is in the highest degree improbable that the siege of Nebuchadnezzar was more successful (History of Greece, vol. iii. p. 445, note). And thus the only permanent interests of the prophecy will be the poetical one, based on the exquisite form in which it is clothed, and the ethical one, based on Isaiah's sublime confidence, that selfishness and violence prepare their own ruin.

[XXIII 1.]   1.

Wail, ye ships of Tarshish,
    For it is laid waste, so that there is no house, no entering in!
    From the land of the Kittim this is revealed to them.
Be dumb, ye inhabitants of the isle,
    Which the merchants of Zidon that pass over the sea re-
        plenished,
    And whose revenue was the seed of the Nile, the harvest of
        the River on the great waters,
    So that she became a mart of nations
Be thou ashamed, O Zidon, for the sea, the stronghold of the
        sea, speaketh, saying,
    I have not travailed, nor brought forth, neither nourished
        young men, nor brought up virgins.
When the report cometh to Egypt, they shall shudder at the
        report of Tyre

[6]   2.

Pass ye over to Tarshish;
    Wail, ye inhabitants of the isle!
'Is this your joyous city, whose origin is of ancient days,
    Whose feet were ever carrying her far away to sojourn?
Who hath taken this counsel against Tyre, the distributer of
        crowns,
    Whose merchants were princes, whose traffickers were the
        honourable of the earth?'
Jehovah of Hosts hath taken it,
    To profane the pride of all splendour, to bring to shame all
        the honourable of the earth.

[10.]   3.

Overflow thy land, as the Nile,
　　O daughter of Tarshish, the bridle is gone.
He stretched out his hand over the sea, he made kingdoms to
　　　tremble;
　　Jehovah of Hosts gave commandment concerning Canaan, to
　　　destroy the strongholds thereof;
And he said, Thou shalt no more exult, O thou subdued virgin-
　　　daughter of Zidon;
　　Arise, pass over to the Kittim; there also thou shalt have no
　　　rest!
Behold the land of the Canaanites!
　　Yonder people is no more; Asshur hath appointed it for
　　　wild beasts;
　　They set up their towers, they raised their palaces,
　　He (Asshur) hath made it an heap of ruins.
Wail, ye ships of Tarshish,
　　For your stronghold is laid waste!

                              4.

[15] And in that day shall Tyre be forgotten seventy years,
as the days of one king; at the end of seventy years Tyre shall
fare as in the song of the harlot:—

　　'Take the harp, go about the city, thou forgotten harlot!
　　　Make sweet melody, sing many songs, that thou mayest
　　　　be remembered.'

For at the end of seventy years Jehovah shall visit Tyre, and she
shall turn to her hire, and play the harlot with all kingdoms of
the earth on the face of the ground.　But her winnings and her
hire shall be consecrated to Jehovah: they shall not be treasured,

nor laid up; but her winnings shall be for them that dwell before Jehovah, to eat sufficiently, and for stately clothing.

Par. 1. *From the land of the Kittim.* The merchant-ships are supposed to touch at Cyprus (Kittim = Citium) on their homeward voyage, and thus to learn the news of the destruction of Tyre.

Ye inhabitants of the isle, i.e. of the insular Tyre, which was the real emporium The old Tyre on the mainland had submitted to Shalmaneser. See Josephus, Archæol. ix. 14, 2.

The merchants of Zidon, i.e. the Phœnician merchants. Comp. 1 Kings xvi. 31, and the use of Σιδόνιος in Homer.

Par. 2. *Of ancient days.* The priests of Hercules boasted to Herodotus that their temple and city were 2300 years old (Herod. ii. 44), while Josephus asserts that it was built 240 years before Solomon's temple (Archæol. viii. 3, 1).

Whose feet were ever carrying her. Hitzig and others render, ' Whose feet bear them,' understanding the passage of the journey of the Tyrians to their place of exile. But the expression answers best to spontaneous motion, as in Prov vii. 11, 'Her feet abide not in her house.'

To profane the pride, &c. The same idea is developed in ii. 12-17.

Par 3 *Thou shalt have no rest,* i.e thou shalt be pursued by the foe. Delitzsch, however, explains the words less naturally, as it would seem, of the unfriendly reception accorded to the fugitives by the Cyprian colonists.

Behold the land of the Canaanites. Authorised Version, following the received text, renders ' Chaldeans,' which Ewald was the first to correct into ' Canaanites.' See the author's ' Notes and Criticisms,' pp. 22-26, and the note of Delitzsch, who allows that Ewald's conjecture is highly plausible, but himself proposes the following impossible rendering, ' Behold the land of the Chaldeans, this people that was not [understand, " formerly of any importance, but which now,"] as for Assyria, hath appointed it for wild beasts' The corruption ' Chaldeans' is probably due to some early editor or copyist, who thought, by creating this point of transition, to harmonize the ode with the epilogue.

Par 4 *As the days of one king,* i. e. as though they were but a single reign, monotonous and unchanging. Comp. Gen. xxix. 20.

The song of the harlot, i e. a well-known taunting song, a fragment of which follows. Note that in the ode, which is certainly by Isaiah, Tyre is represented not under the dubious symbol of a ' harlot,' but as the ' violated virgin.'

Them that dwell before Jehovah, i. e. the people of Jerusalem, not necessarily the priests. See Ps. xxvii. 4.

VI. GROWING APPREHENSIONS OF INVASION.

(Isa. xxviii.-xxxiii.)

I. THE SCOFFERS AND THEIR FATE. (Isa. xxviii.)

EPHRAIM, with its gay and careless capital, is now so near its end, that, after a few sympathetic words, the prophet passes on to the fate of his own people. On the day of Samaria's fall will the promise of the ideal future begin to be realized. At this point, as on a similar previous occasion (ii. 6), the melancholy contrast of the present forces itself on the attention. The Ephraimitish vice of drunkenness is rife in Jerusalem itself, and is indulged in the most sacred offices; a profanity which is aggravated by incredulous scoffs at the revelations of Isaiah. But retribution is at hand. God will return scoff with scoff, till the unbelievers meet their destruction. Those indeed who believe the prophet's announcement respecting 'Zion's foundation-stone' may be undismayed, but the rest, in spite of their vaunted skill in politics, shall suffer blow upon blow, and find the revelation which they venture to satirize only too intelligible. Then follows a last appeal to the common sense of the audience, more especially of Isaiah's disciples. 'Does not the countryman obey the rules which God has taught him, and perform his different operations at the right moment and with discrimination? See in this a parable of the Divine method, which is applied alike to the pious and the profane, in mercy to the one, in judgment to the other.'

The date of this portion of the prophecy is determined by the threat of the fall of Samaria. Probably it was delivered in substance in the first year of the siege of that city by Shalmaneser, or, more correctly, Sargon, i.e. B.C. 722.

1.

[XXVIII. 1.] Woe to the proud crown of the drunkards of Ephraim, and the fading flower of his glorious adorning, which is on the head of the fat valley of them that are overcome with wine. Behold, the Lord hath a strong and powerful one, who, like a tempest of hail, and a destroying storm, like a tempest of mighty waters overflowing, shall cast down to the earth with violence. It shall be trodden down with the feet, the proud crown of the drunkards of Ephraim; and the fading flower of his glorious adorning, which is on the head of the fat valley, shall become as an early fig before the fruitage, which one seeth, and while it is yet in his hand he swalloweth. In that day shall Jehovah of Hosts be for a crown of adorning and a diadem of glory unto the remnant of his people, and for a spirit of judgment to him that sitteth on the judgment-seat, and of might to them that drive back war to the gate.

2.

[7.] But even yonder they reel with wine and stagger with strong drink; the priest and the prophet reel with strong drink, they are swallowed up of wine, they stagger with strong drink; they reel in vision, they totter in giving judgment. Yea, all tables are full of filthy.vomiting, so that there is no place clean. 'Whom will he teach knowledge? and whom will he cause to understand revelation? Them that are weaned from the milk, and drawn from the breasts? For (he is for ever saying), 'Correct, correct, correct, correct; direct, direct, direct, direct; a little here, and a little there.' Yea, with stammering speech and with another tongue will he speak to this people; he, who said to them, Here is your rest, cause ye the weary to rest, and here is refreshment, but they would not hear; therefore the word of Jehovah shall be unto them (indeed), 'Correct, correct, correct, correct; direct, direct, direct, direct; a little here, and a little there,' in order that they may go, and fall backward, and be broken, and be snared, and taken.

3.

[14] Wherefore hear the word of Jehovah, ye scornful men, that rule this people which is in Jerusalem. Because ye have said, We have made a covenant with death, and with the underworld are we at agreement; the overflowing scourge, when it passeth through, shall not come unto us, for we have made a lie our refuge, and under falsehood have we hid ourselves; therefore, thus saith the Lord Jehovah, Behold, I have founded in Zion a stone, a tried and precious corner-stone of assured foundation; he that believeth shall not hasten away. And I will appoint right for a line, and justice for a plummet, and the hail shall sweep away the refuge of a lie, and the waters shall overflow the hiding-place of falsehood, and your covenant with death shall be wiped out, and your agreement with the underworld shall not stand; when the overflowing scourge passeth through, ye shall be trodden down by it; as often as it passeth through, it shall take you: for morning by morning shall it pass through, by day and by night; and it shall be unmingled terror to understand the revelation. Truly, too short is the bed to stretch oneself on it, and the covering too narrow, when one wrappeth oneself in it. For Jehovah shall rise up as on mount Perazim, he shall be wroth as in the valley of Gibeon, that he may do his work, his strange work, and bring to pass his act, his marvellous act. Now therefore be ye not mockers, lest your bands become strong, for I have

heard from the Lord, Jehovah of Hosts, of destruction by a sure decree, which hangeth over all the earth.

4.

[23] Give ye ear, and hear my voice; attend, and hear my speech. Is the ploughman always ploughing that he may sow, and opening and breaking the clods of his ground? When he hath made plain the face thereof, doth he not cast abroad dill, and scatter cummin, and set in wheat by rows, and barley in the place described, and spelt in the border thereof? For one instructed him in the right way, even his God taught him. Surely dill is not threshed with a sledge, neither is a cart-wheel turned about upon cummin, but dill is beaten out with a staff, and cummin with a rod. Bread-corn is threshed; yet he is not for ever threshing it, nor driving the wheel of his cart and of his horses; he doth not crush it to pieces. This also cometh from Jehovah of Hosts; he hath wonderful counsel, and excellent wisdom!

Par. 1. *The proud crown,* i e. Samaria, which was built on a terraced hill rising out of a deep and broad valley. It was 'a mere growth of pleasure and convenience' (Stanley), and took the tone of its manners from the court. For the prevalence of drunkenness, comp. Amos iv. 1, vi. 6.

An early fig. The summer fig of Syria ripens in August; an 'early fig,' therefore, will be one that is ripe in June or July. Comp. Hosea ix. 10; Micah vii 1; Mark xi 13

The remnant. 'Judgment' and 'remnant' in Isaiah are relative terms. The fall of Samaria was, as it were, the first act of the tragedy, which was to end in the destruction of the ungodly inhabitants of Jerusalem. The 'remnant' will therefore mean here the surviving Ephraimites together with the people of the southern kingdom.

To the gate, i. e. the gate of the hostile city, as in 2 Sam. xi. 23.

Par. 2. *Yonder,* i. e. in Jerusalem, in the very sight of the prophet. Comp. Micah ii 11.

In vision, i. e. while in the act of prophesying. Comp xxii 5, 'The valley of vision.'

In giving judgment. Comp. Deut. xvii 9, 'Thou shalt come unto the priests, ... and they shall shew thee the sentence of judgment.'

Whom will he teach? 'Isaiah is too much like a pedantic school-master, always and everywhere finding something to carp at.' Such is the style in which the priests and prophets mimic him over their cups.

Correct, correct, direct, direct. Heb. ṣav lāsav kav lākav, words evidently chosen for the sake of their assonance, to represent the stammer of a drunkard. See 'Notes and Criticisms,' pp. 29, 30.

Yea, with stammering speech. The stammer of the mockers will be met by the stammer of the Assyrian invaders, who, within certain prescribed limits, are God's representatives. Comp. xxix. 3, '*I* will lay siege against thee.' 'Stammering' means 'barbarous, unintelligible.' The language employed by the educated classes throughout Syria and Assyria appears to have been Aramaic (see xxxvi. 11), and Isaiah cannot be expected to have known, what the cuneiform decipherers have proved, that Assyrian was closely allied to his own language.

Your rest. The State had become thoroughly disorganized owing to the disasters of the reign of Ahaz, and needed a period of 'rest,' i. e. of unresisting obedience to Assyria, to recover its strength.

Par. 3 *A lie . . falsehood*, i e. the breach of faith towards Assyria involved in a revolt

A stone. An allusion, probably, to the veneration of sacred stones, which was once general among the Semitic tribes, and lingered among the Jews of this or even of a later period (lvii 6) One of these stones would naturally be the rock on which the temple was founded, and from which a Mosque near that of Omar derives the name *Es-Sachrā*, 'the place of the stone.' The prophet, however, tacitly discountenances this relic of heathenism, by adopting the foundation-stone of the temple as a symbol of the faithfulness of its Divine patron. comp viii 14, xxx. 29 (Heb). That the reference is not to a person, e g the Messiah, is shewn by the following clause, ' He that believeth,' &c., not ' He that believeth on him, or, on it.'

Unmingled terror. Previously the Jews had refused to be 'made to understand revelation' (Par. 2), but soon their terrible experience should force its meaning upon them. comp. viii 20. The passage which follows is a popular, metaphorical description of a state of great distress.

Perazim . . . Gibeon At both places the Philistines were defeated by David : see 2 Sam. v. 20, 1 Chron xiv. 16 The 'strange act' consists in the desolation of the Divine property by Jehovah himself.

Lest your bands become strong, i e. lest ye exchange the mild ties of allegiance for the hard yoke of captivity.

Destruction by a sure decree. The same expression occurs in x. 23, where see note.

Par. 4. *Is the ploughman,* &c. The wise conduct of the countryman is a reflection of the method of his Divine teacher. God, in like manner, will dispense judgment with measure and discrimination.

By rows . . . in the place described. The obscure words of the Hebrew are possibly corrupt.

II. THE RIDDLE OF GOD'S-LION (ARIEL).

(Isa xxix.)

THE purport of this prophecy is as follows. Within a year the 'invincible' city shall be in great peril of capture, but its prophetic title, 'God's-lion,' shall even then prove to be accurate. A storm sent by Jehovah shall shatter the besiegers, so that they pass away like a dream. At this announcement the unsusceptible audience stare in amazement, and the discourse makes a sudden transition to invective. The stupidity and hypocrisy of all classes, both learned and unlearned, shall not escape punishment, though the nature of the penalty is at present merely described as being extraordinary and stultifying. Then, after a slight pause, the prophet denounces plainly the foolish attempt of the politicians at secrecy, as if by any subtlety they could elude the resentment of the all-wise Creator. Woe unto them! for a great crisis is at hand; the nation shall be regenerated inwardly, and all its corrupt members shall be cut off. See, for the date of this, and the succeeding prophecies, the introductory remarks to Section VI.

1.

[**XXIX. 1.**] Ah, God's-lion, God's-lion, city where David camped! Add year to year, and let the feasts go round; then will I distress God's-lion, and wailing shall arise and bewailing, but then shall she be to me God's-lion indeed. For I will camp in a circle about thee, and lay siege against thee with a mound, and set up engines against thee; and thou shalt speak in abase-

F

ment from the ground, and thy speech shall be low from the dust,
and thy voice shall come, as that of a ghost, from the ground, and
thy speech shall chirp from the dust. Yet the multitude of thy
foes shall become like small dust, and the multitude of the terrible
ones as vanishing chaff, and it shall happen at an instant suddenly.
There shall be a visitation of Jehovah of Hosts with thunder, and
with earthquake, and great noise, with whirlwind, and storm, and
the flame of devouring fire; and they shall be as a dream, a vision
of the night, even the multitude of all the nations that fight against
God's-lion; yea, all that fight against her and her munition, and
they that beleaguer her. And as when a hungry man dreameth,
and behold he eateth, but he awaketh, and his soul is empty; and
as when a thirsty man dreameth, and behold he drinketh, but he
awaketh, and behold he is faint, and his soul hath appetite: so
shall the multitude of all the nations be, that fight against mount
Zion.

2.

[9.] Linger now, but then shall ye wonder; blind yourselves
now, but then shall ye be blind indeed! They are drunken, but
not with wine; they stagger, but not with strong drink! For
Jehovah hath poured out upon you a spirit of deep sleep, and hath
closed your eyes [the prophets], and your heads [the seers] hath
he covered, so that everything in the prophecy is become unto
you as the words of a book that is sealed, which men deliver
to one that is learned, saying, Read this, I pray, but he saith,
I cannot, for it is sealed; and if one deliver the book to him that
is not learned, saying, Read this, I pray, he saith, I am not learned.

3.

[13.] And the Lord said, Forasmuch as this people draw near
with their mouth, and with their lips do honour me, but their

heart is far from me, so that their fear toward me is a statute of men which they have learned: therefore, behold, I will go on dealing wonderfully with this people, so that the wisdom of their wise men shall perish, and the understanding of their sagacious men shall be hid.

4.

[15.] Woe unto them that hide their counsel deeply from Jehovah, so that their doings are in a dark place, and they say, Who seeth us, and who knoweth us? Out on your perverseness! Is the potter to be esteemed as the clay, that the work should say of him that made it, He made me not? and the thing framed say of him that framed it, He had no understanding? Is it not yet a very little while before Lebanon shall be turned into fruitful land, and fruitful land esteemed for a forest? and before the deaf hear the words of a book, and the eyes of the blind see out of obscurity and out of darkness, and the meek have fresh joy in Jehovah, and the poor among men exult in the Holy One of Israel, because the terrible one is brought to nought, and the scorner is consumed, and all that wake for iniquity are cut off, that declare men to be sinners for a word, and lay a snare for him that reproveth in the gate, and thrust aside the just for a thing of nought.

5.

[22.] Therefore thus saith Jehovah of the house of Jacob, even he who redeemed Abraham: Jacob shall not now be ashamed, neither shall his face now wax pale; for when his children see the work of my hands in their midst, they shall hallow my name, and shall hallow the Holy One of Jacob, and reverence the God of Israel; and they that erred in spirit shall come to understanding, and they that murmured shall receive instruction.

Par. 1. *God's-lion.* A symbolical name for Jerusalem = 'the invincible.' The rendering 'hearth of God,' adopted by Delitzsch and others, is unnecessary, and results from a misunderstanding of Ezek. xliii. 15, 16. See 'Notes and Criticisms,' p. 31.

Add year to year, &c.; that is, the siege of Jerusalem shall take place as soon as the year just entered upon shall be concluded. The mention of the feasts implies that the theocratic year is intended, which began in the passover-month.

Thy speech shall chirp, &c. ; that is, the inhabitants shall seat themselves on the ground, and 'chirp' or moan for despair. Comp. vii. 19, note.

As a dream; that is, as suddenly as a dream. In the next verse, however, dreaming is used as an image of disappointment.

Par. 2 *Linger now,* &c. 'Hesitate, if you will, to believe the revelation ; when the fulfilment comes, your stupefaction shall be involuntary.'

[*The prophets*] . . . [*the seers*]. Erroneous glosses, contrary to the connection, which denounces the people, not the prophets, as unsusceptible of warning. The two similes which follow describe first the educated and then the uneducated classes. The former were the chief subjects of Isaiah's admonitions ; they alone had the intellect necessary for understanding them even in the letter, though the spiritual meaning was 'sealed' even to them.

Par. 4 *That hide their counsel deeply* Isaiah perceives the court-party to be brooding in secret over some political project, which, between this and the next chapter, is matured into negotiations with Egypt.

Is it not yet a very little while? The following passage describes the material and spiritual changes consequent on the fall of the 'terrible' Assyrians, and the 'scorners' or unbelievers in Israel.

For a word, i. e. for a word of reproof.

A thing of nought, i. e. a trivial pretext

Par. 5 *Jacob.* A personification of the people under the name of the patriarch Comp Jer. xxxi 15, 'Rachel weeping for her children.'

When his children see Literally, 'When he, (namely,) his children, see.' For the apposition, comp. Job xxix. 3 The construction was probably chosen to give transparency to the personification.

III. THE EGYPTIAN ALLIANCE.

(Isa. xxx.)

THE warning of the foregoing prophecy was in vain, and the real purpose of the politicians of the court-party was first discovered by the prophet, when it was already in course of accomplishment. A burst of indignation was the consequence. The prophet, with the eye of imagination, descries the Jewish embassy appearing at the court of Pharaoh, and its abortive results. Poets had given Egypt the surname of 'Arrogant' (Rahab); Isaiah mocks it with the disgraceful augmentation, 'Arrogant-and-slothful,' meaning that none of the grandiloquent promises of the Egyptians to their Jewish suppliants would be carried into effect. At this point Isaiah ceases; oratory has been tried to the uttermost; he seems to hear a Divine whisper bidding him withdraw, and write this contemptuous title on a public tablet. Then in seclusion he proceeds to develope what he had intended to have added, and may afterwards have uttered openly. 'Such wilful rejection of the prophetic word in favour of a crooked, worldly-minded policy is like a rent in a high wall, which grows larger and larger, till the whole structure falls.' But on a sudden, as we so often find, an irresistible longing to impart consolation constrains Isaiah to alter his tone. So grievous is the extremity, he says, that Jehovah himself yearns to interpose, and is only waiting for the fitting moment. Higher and higher rises the ideal description, till the apparently casual mention of the breach bound up, and the wound healed, gives a fresh turn to the discourse. The power of Assyria, so the prophecy concludes, shall certainly be broken; the funeral pile is prepared already, and the victim will not be long wanting.

1.

[**XXX. 1.**] Woe to the rebellious sons, saith Jehovah, which seek to form a counsel apart from me, and to weave a web without my spirit, that they may add sin to sin; that journey to go down into Egypt, without having asked at my mouth, to flee unto the stronghold of Pharaoh, and to take refuge in the shadow of Egypt. Therefore did the stronghold of Pharaoh become your shame, and the refuge in the shadow of Egypt your confusion. When his princes were in Zoan, and his ambassadors arrived at Hanes, they were all ashamed of people that could not profit them, that served not for help, nor for profit, but for shame, and also for reproach.

2.

[6.] Through a land of distress and anguish, from whence come the lioness and the lion, the viper and the flying dragon, they carry their riches upon the shoulders of young asses, and upon the bunches of camels their treasures, to people that shall not profit them. For the help of Egypt is idle and in vain, therefore do I call her name 'Arrogant-and-slothful.'

3.

[8.] Now go, write it on a table before them, and note it in a book, that it may serve to a time to come for a testimony for ever. For they are a revolting people, lying sons, sons that will not hear the doctrine of Jehovah, which say to the seers, See not, and to the prophets, Prophesy not unto us right things, speak unto us smooth things, prophesy delusions, get you out of the way, turn aside out of the path, cause the Holy One of Israel to cease from before us. Wherefore thus saith the Holy One of Israel, Because ye reject this word, and trust in extortion and cunning, and stay thereon, therefore this iniquity shall be to you as a rent that falleth in, swelling out in a lofty wall, whose breaking cometh suddenly at an instant; and one breaketh it as the breaking of a bottle, shivering it without pity, and not a sherd is found in the shivers thereof to take fire from the hearth, and to draw water from the cistern. For thus saith the Lord Jehovah, the Holy One of Israel, In calmness and rest shall ye be delivered, in quietness and in confidence shall be your strength, but ye would not; and ye said, No, but on horses will we fly; therefore shall ye flee: and, On the swift will we ride; therefore shall they that pursue you be swift. One thousand for the rebuke of one, for the rebuke of five shall ye flee, till ye be left but as a beacon on the top of a mountain, and as an ensign on a hill. But therefore will Jehovah long to be gracious unto you, and therefore will he wait in stillness to have mercy upon you, for Jehovah is a God of justice; happy are all they that long for him.

4.

[19.] Yea, O thou people that dwellest in Zion, even in Jerusalem, thou shalt weep no more: he will be very gracious unto thee at the voice of thy cry, as soon as he heareth it, he hath answered thee. And though the Lord give you bread which is distress, and water which is affliction, yet shall not thy teachers withdraw any more into a corner, but thine eyes shall continually see thy teachers, and thine ears shall hear words behind thee, saying, This is the way, walk ye in it, when ye turn to the right hand, and when ye turn to the left. And thou shalt defile the covering of thy graven images of silver, and the coating of thy molten images of gold; thou shalt scatter them as a loathsome thing; thou shalt say unto it, Get thee hence. Then shall he give rain for thy seed, with which thou sowest the ground, and the bread of the increase of the ground shall be fat and juicy; thy cattle shall feed in that day in a large pasture; and the oxen and the young asses that till the ground shall eat savoury provender, which hath been winnowed with the shovel and with the fan. And on every high mountain and on every lofty hill shall be streams that run with water, in the day of the great slaughter, when the towers fall. Then shall the light of the moon be as the light of the sun, and the light of the sun shall be sevenfold, as the light of seven days, in the day that Jehovah bindeth up the breach of his people, and healeth the stroke of their wound.

5.

[27.] Behold, the name of Jehovah cometh from far, with burning anger, and thick and towering smoke; his lips are full of indignation, and his tongue as devouring fire; while his breath is like an overflowing torrent, which divideth even to the neck, to swing nations in the fan of destruction; and a bridle that leadeth astray is upon the cheeks of the peoples. But your song shall rise as in the night when the feast is kept, and joy of heart, as when one walketh to the pipe to come into the mountain of Jehovah, to the Rock of Israel. And Jehovah shall cause his glorious voice to be heard, and shall shew the lighting down of his arm, in the fervour of anger, and the flame of devouring fire, with the bursting of clouds, and a storm of rain, and hail-stones. Yea, at the voice of Jehovah shall Assyria be broken down, when he shall smite her with the rod; and every stroke of the staff of doom, which Jehovah shall let down upon her from above, shall be greeted with tabrets and with pipes, and with battles of swinging will he fight against them. Yea, a Topheth is set in order already; it also is prepared for the king, and made both deep and large; the pile thereof is fire and much wood: the breath of Jehovah, like a torrent of brimstone, shall kindle it.

Par. 1. *Zoan . . . Hanes* Tanis, on one of the arms of the Nile, and Anusis, on an island of the Nile in Middle Egypt, were the two royal residences The dynasty at the time of the prophecy was the Tanitic, which preceded the Ethiopian. Comp. note on xx. 3.

Did the stronghold become. The past tenses in this paragraph are prophetic. In the next paragraph Isaiah returns to the present, and describes the journey of the ambassadors through the wilderness on the borders of Egypt.

Par. 2. *Arrogant-and-slothful.* Literally, 'Arrogance (Rahab), they are indolence,' the plural being used because Rahab refers to a nation. Rahab was the symbolic name of Egypt in Hebrew poetry. See Isa. li. 9; Job xxvi. 12; Ps. lxxxvii 4, lxxxix 10. Isaiah sarcastically modifies it.

Par. 3. *Write it on a tablet,* i e. the enigmatical name just mentioned. Comp. viii 1.

Speak unto us smooth things. The primary distinction between true and false prophets is that the former never announce prosperity and peace unconditionally. The promise of the Messianic future is always coupled with a stern exhortation to repentance Comp Jer xxiii 21, 22, 'I have not sent these prophets, yet they ran; I have not spoken unto them, yet they prophesied But if they had stood in my counsel, and had caused my people to hear my words, then they should have turned them from their evil way, and from the evil of their doings.'

Extortion, i e. the heavy taxation necessary for warlike enterprizes, like the revolt from Assyria.

Therefore will Jehovah long, i. e. because of the extremity of your need. Comp x 23, 24, and see 'Notes and Criticisms,' p 32. *Hākāh,* with the preposition *le,* never has the meaning of 'tarrying' ascribed to it by some, while *yārūm* does not satisfy the parallelism. The former means here, as it does always, 'to expect with longing,' and the latter must be corrected, with two MSS., into *yiddom.* Comp. Ps. xxxvii 7.

Par. 4. *Slaughter .. towers* The former expression refers to the destruction of the enemies of Israel, the latter to the fall of every object of irreligious confidence. Comp. ii. 12.

Par. 5. *The name of Jehovah,* i e. the manifestation of his righteous character. Comp. xxvi. 8.

The fan of destruction. Comp xxix 5, 'The multitude of thy foes shall be as vanishing chaff.'

As in the night when the feast is kept The Passover had, probably, just been celebrated. See note on the words 'Add year to year,' in Par. 1 of the foregoing prophecy.

The staff of doom, i e. the punishment ordained by God's decree.

Battles of swinging, i.e. those in which the hand of Jehovah is incessantly dealing blows to his enemies. Meantime the Jews are supposed to be looking on, and celebrating the ruin of their foes with triumphal music.

A Topheth For the various theories as to the meaning of this word, see Smith's ' Dictionary of the Bible,' s. v., and comp. Jer. vii 31, ' They have built the high places of Topheth, which is in the valley of the son of Hinnom, to burn their sons and daughters in the fire.' The most probable meaning of the obscure words of Isaiah is that proposed by Luzzatto, in his Hebrew commentary, who considers the point of the passage to be a witty allusion to the double meaning of *Melek*, either king of Assyria or king of heaven (Moloch). A Topheth-like altar, says the prophet, shall be erected, which, like the altars of the valley of Hinnom, is destined ' for the king,' not, indeed, to pay honour to Moloch, but to receive the king of Assyria as a victim. Comp. notes on xix 18, xxxii 12.

Deep and large. This implies that the carcases of the whole Assyrian army were to be burned with that of Sennacherib. Comp. xxxiii. 12, xxxiv. 6.

IV. THE DESCENT OF JEHOVAH.

(Isa. xxxi.)

THE connection of ideas in this brief prophecy is closely similar to that in the preceding passage. Beginning with the Egyptian alliance, and the disastrous end of both the parties concerned in it, it closes with the destruction of the Assyrians. The peculiarity is in the middle portion. The assistance of Egypt is said to be unnecessary for the protection of Jerusalem, for Jehovah himself has promised to descend on mount Zion, and fight like a lion against the enemy. Return ye forthwith, cries the prophet, to your offended God, for, when these great events take place, the folly of your idolatry will be manifest. If the Assyrians are to be overcome, as overcome they must be, the sword by which they shall fall is no other than that of Jehovah.

1.

[XXXI. 1] Woe unto them that go down to Egypt for help, and stay upon horses; and that trust in chariots because they are many, and in horsemen because they are a great host, but that look not unto the Holy One of Israel, neither seek Jehovah, (though he is also wise,) therefore he will bring evil, and will not call back his words, but will arise against the house of evil-doers, and against the help of them that work iniquity. Now the Egyptians are men, and not God, and their horses flesh, and not spirit; and when Jehovah shall stretch forth his hand, he that helpeth shall stumble, and he that is helped shall fall, and they all shall be consumed together.

2.

[4.] For thus hath Jehovah said to me, Like as the lion with the young lion, against whom a multitude of shepherds are called, murmureth over his prey,—he is not affrighted at their cry, nor submitteth himself at the noise of them,—so shall Jehovah of Hosts come down to fight on mount Zion and on the hill thereof. Like fluttering birds, so shall Jehovah of Hosts shelter Jerusalem, sheltering and rescuing it, passing over and setting it free. Turn ye unto him, from whom ye have so deeply revolted, O children of Israel.

3.

[7.] For in that day shall ye all reject your idols of silver and your idols of gold, which your hands made you for a sin; and Asshur shall fall by the sword, not of a mighty man, and the sword, not of a man, shall devour him; he shall take his flight from the sword, and his young men shall be for task-service; and his rock shall vanish for terror, and his princes shall be frighted from the standard: it is the utterance of Jehovah, who hath a fire in Zion, and a furnace in Jerusalem.

Par. 1. *He will bring evil.* The tense in the original, throughout this passage, is the prophetic past.

Par. 2. *Like as the lion.* Note the Homeric clearness of the metaphor. Comp. Iliad xviii. 161, &c., xii. 299, &c. (Delitzsch.)

Passing over. An allusion to the typical redemption of the Passover of the Exodus.

Par. 3. *His rock.* This is to be taken collectively, as is shewn by the 'princes' in the parallel clause. Comp. xix. 13, 'the corner-stone,' which is also used collectively of the princes. Ewald renders otherwise, 'He shall overpass his rock, i.e. his castle, for terror;' but the expression seems forced, and unlike Isaiah.

Fire .. furnace. Isaiah means the light of the Divine presence, which consumes the enemies of Jerusalem. (Delitzsch.)

V. HOPES OF THE FUTURE OF HEZEKIAH.

(Isa. xxxii. 1–8.)

'AFTER the destruction of the Assyrians, a new era shall begin for the monarchy. Both king and princes shall realize their ideals; the spiritual dulness of their subjects shall cease; names shall correspond to characters, and characters to names.' The description, eloquent as it is, cannot be strictly called Messianic. It seems as if the pious character of Hezekiah had, for the moment, rendered the preaching of the Messiah unnecessary. As in the times of David and Solomon, the ideal of the theocracy appeared to the sacred poets to be sufficiently realized, so Isaiah would seem, when he wrote this prophecy, to have anticipated a second golden age under Hezekiah. He did not, it is true, remain long in this conviction. See note on xi. 1.

[XXXII. 1.] Behold, the king shall reign after justice, and the princes shall rule after right, and they shall every one be like an hiding-place from the wind, and a covert from the tempest, as streams of water in a drought, as the shadow of a great rock in a gasping land. And the eyes of them that see shall not be dim, and the ears of them that hear shall hearken, and the heart of the headlong shall come to understanding, and the tongue of the stammerers be ready to speak plainly. The vile person shall no more be called noble, nor the malicious surnamed gentle; for the vile person speaketh villany, and his heart worketh iniquity, to work unholiness, and to utter error touching Jehovah, to make empty the soul of the hungry, and cause the drink of the thirsty to fail; and the arts of the malicious are evil, he deviseth wicked plots, to destroy the suffering with lying words, even when the poor is telling his right; but the noble deviseth noble things, and to noble things shall he stand.

After justice, i e after the rule or principles of justice

The princes. The preposition in *lesārim* seems to be a clerical error, produced by the *le* of the following word. Comp. Perowne's note on Ps. lxxiv. 14.

The headlong, i. e. those whose conduct is violent and unprincipled.

The stammerers, i e those who utter incorrect opinions on religious or moral matters. Comp. afterward, 'to utter error touching Jehovah.'

VI. ADDRESS TO THE WOMEN, &c.

(Isa. xxxii. 9–20.)

THIS passage forms a parallel to the address in iii. 16–24. There the subject of rebuke was the love of dress; here it is rather the sensual security, from which the women of Jerusalem come to receive so rude an awakening. The address passes into a description of the coming judgment, particularly as it should affect the capital.

The date of this and of the four preceding prophecies may be easily ascertained. The negotiations with Egypt were obviously caused by Hezekiah's revolt from Assyria, which took place about 715. The synchronism is confirmed by the announcement in xxix. 1, that within a year Jerusalem should be besieged. In fact, Sennacherib, according to the current chronology, 'took all the fenced cities of Judah' (2 Kings xviii. 13; Isa. xxxvi. 1) in 714. The five prophecies must have occupied several months in the course of their delivery, for in the first of them the precise nature of the policy promoted by the court-party is, still a' secret, whilst in the second and third the embassy has been already despatched to Egypt. This trifling variation may be illustrated by the slight difference in the terms fixed by the prophet in xxix. 1, xxxii. 10.

[**XXXII. 9.**] Rise up, and hear my voice, ye women that are at ease; ye careless daughters, give ear unto my speech. When the year is older, ye shall be troubled, ye careless ones, because the vintage hath been consumed, and the gathering shall not come. Tremble, ye that are at ease; be troubled, ye careless ones: strip you, and make you bare, and gird sackcloth upon your loins. Men shall smite upon their breast for the pleasant fields, for the fruitful vine. Upon the land of my people shall come up thorns and briars; yea, upon all houses of delight in the joyous town. For the palace shall be forsaken; the tumult of the city shall become a desert; the hill and the watchtower shall be for caves for ever, the delight of wild asses, the pasture of flocks; until the spirit be poured upon us from on high, so that the wilderness shall become a fruitful land, and the fruitful land be counted for a forest, and right shall inhabit the wilderness, and justice dwell in the fruitful land, and the work of justice shall be peace, and the effect of righteousness quietness and carelessness for ever, and my people shall inhabit the home of peace, careless dwellings, and easy resting-places, but it shall hail, when the forest cometh down, and the city shall be deeply abased. Happy are ye that shall sow beside all waters, that shall let loose the feet of the ox and the ass!

Men shall smite upon their breast. Or, preserving the paronomasia of the Hebrew, 'Men shall smite upon their bosom for the sweet bosom of the fields.'

The palace shall be forsaken, &c. This passage stands alone in Isaiah. Elsewhere (see xxix 5, xxx 19, xxxi. 4) the prophet expresses his confidence that Jerusalem shall be delivered from the Assyrians, but here he looks forward to its being destroyed, and remaining for a long time in ruins The consequence of this is that the Messianic era is thrown into the distant future, instead of taking place immediately on the fall of the Assyrians.

The hill, i e the south-east portion of mount Zion

The watch-tower, i e perhaps, the 'tower of the flock,' mentioned in Mic iv 8, in connection with 'the hill' (Auth Vers. wrongly, 'stronghold').

For ever, i e for a very long period. Comp. Deut. xv. 17; 1 Sam. i 22, &c.

The forest, here mentioned as a symbol of all that is high and noble Comp. ii 13

Happy are ye, &c. Isaiah congratulates those who outlive the impending troubles, and witness the fulfilment of his promises.

VII. CONFIDENCE IN THE FALL OF ASSYRIA.

(Isa x. 5—xii. 6)

THE historical circumstances connected with this prophecy are somewhat different from those of the preceding one. The apprehension of a protracted siege of Jerusalem has entirely passed away, and the excesses, to which the Assyrians have proceeded, have excited in Isaiah the confidence that a swift and terrible Nemesis will not be wanting. Discontented with moderate achievements, and unconscious that he is but an instrument in the hand of Jehovah, the Assyrian king is planning the complete extinction of all the surrounding nations. In fact, if we may expand his meaning by the help of the deciphered inscriptions (see note on the expression 'vain gods,' vv. 10, 11), he regards himself as the missionary of the supreme God, and scorns to admit that a deity like Jehovah, whose weakness is mirrored in that of his worshippers, can prove a serious antagonist. Nay, he himself is more like a god than a man (see note on the phrase 'a hero,' x. 13); he is the dethroner of kings, and the 'bird-nester' of their treasures. Then, with biting sarcasm, the prophet exposes the absurdity of these wild assumptions. (See Pars. 1 and 2.)

The third paragraph describes the punishment of the Assyrians under the images of consumption and fire, and the confidence with which the purified remnant of Israel should rely on God the Mighty One,—a remnant indeed, small and feeble, for, in the words of a recent prophecy, the decree of righteous vengeance is irrepealable. (Par. 3.) Still the immediate prospect is one of consolation. (Par. 4.) The Divine anger shall soon pass over from Israel to the Assyrians, and the wonders of the Red Sea shall be repeated. (Observe, however, that the description given in Pars. 5, 6, of an invasion proceeding from the north-east does not correspond to any event recorded in Jewish history, and is probably an imaginative representation of the hostile projects mentioned in vv. 10–12.)

After this great catastrophe, when Assyria and a great part of Israel have been destroyed, the Messianic period shall begin. (Par. 7.) Low as the house of David has now fallen, it shall then revive in the person of a mighty monarch, wise, just, and God-fearing, full of the Spirit of Jehovah in all its various manifestations. The gulf between the standards of king and people shall then be filled up. The national acceptance of the Divine rule shall be so complete, as to convert the land of Israel into a second Eden. And equally great will be the influence of this transformation on the nations outside the covenant. (Par. 8.) Jerusalem shall become the cynosure of all eyes; Jew and Gentile, but especially the scattered members of Israel, shall gather round the centre of a religious unity. (Comp. ii. 2, 3.) The tribes of the north and the south shall forget their ancient rivalry, and combine in a victorious attack on the races which owed allegiance to David. The exiles shall triumph over all obstacles, and shall express their gratitude in hymns of praise. (Par. 9.)

The date is determined by the notices in x. 9, 27, xi. 11, from a comparison of which we infer that Samaria had already been destroyed, and the people of the northern kingdom carried into exile, but that Judah was still tributary to Assyria. Hence the latest possible date is 715, for in 714 Sennacherib invaded Judah in displeasure at the rebellion of Hezekiah. But the vivid expressions here used of the fall of Samaria point rather to the months immediately following that catastrophe, i. e. 722–721, when the Assyrian army might naturally have been supposed to entertain hostile designs against Judah, such as are alluded to in x. 11, 12. This date is confirmed by the encouraging tone of the prophecy, which commonly in Isaiah indicates a grave national crisis, by the coincidences of language between this prophecy and ch. xxviii. (comp. x. 12 with xxviii. 21; x. 22 with xxviii. 22; x. 26 with xxviii. 18), and by the absence of any mention of the negotiations with Egypt referred to in xxx, xxxi.

1.

[**X. 1.**] Woe unto Assyria, the rod of mine anger; as a staff in whose hand is mine indignation! Against an unholy nation was I wont to send him, and to give him a charge against the people of my wrath, to take the spoil, and to gather the prey, and to tread it down like the mire of the streets. Howbeit he meaneth not so, neither doth his heart think so; but it is in his heart to destroy, and cut off nations not a few. For he saith, 'Are not my princes altogether kings? Is not Calno as Carchemish? or is not Hamath as Arpad? or is not Samaria as Damascus? As my hand hath reached the kingdoms of the vain gods (yet their graven images did exceed those of Samaria and Damascus), shall I not, as I have done to Samaria and her vain gods, so do to Jerusalem and her images?'

2.

[**12.**] But when the Lord shall finish all his work upon mount Zion, and on Jerusalem, I will visit the fruit of the insolence of the king of Assyria, and the vainglory of his haughty looks, because he hath said, 'By the strength of mine hand have I performed it, and by my wisdom, for I am sagacious; I removed the boundaries of peoples, and robbed their treasures, and brought down like an hero them that were enthroned; and mine hand reached as a nest the riches of the peoples, and as one gathereth forsaken eggs, have I gathered all the earth, while there was none that moved the wing, or that opened the mouth and chirped!' Doth the axe boast itself against him that heweth therewith? or the saw shew insolence towards him that swingeth it? As if a rod should swing him that lifteth it up! as if a staff should lift up that which is no wood!

3.

[**14.**] Therefore shall the Lord, the Lord of Hosts, send into his fat parts leanness; and under his glory shall be kindled a burning, like the burning of fire; and the light of Israel shall be for a fire, and his Holy One for a flame; and it shall burn and devour his thorns and his briars in one day; and the glory of his forest and of his fruitful land shall it consume, both soul and body; and it shall be like the sinking of strength in sickness; and the rest of the trees of his forest shall be few, that a boy may write them. In that day shall the remnant of Israel, and such as are escaped of the house of Jacob, no longer stay upon him that smote them, but stay upon Jehovah, the Holy One of Israel, with faithfulness. The remnant shall return, even the remnant of Jacob to God the Mighty One. For though thy people, O Israel, were as the sand of the sea, but a remnant of them shall return: a destruction is decreed, overflowing with righteousness. For destruction by a sure decree will Jehovah of Hosts perform in the midst of all the earth.

4.

[24] Therefore thus saith the Lord, Jehovah of Hosts, Fear not, O my people that dwellest in Zion, because of Assyria; though he smiteth thee with the rod, and lifteth up his staff against thee after the manner of Egypt. For yet a very little while, and the indignation shall cease, and the task of mine anger shall be to waste them away. And Jehovah of Hosts shall brandish a scourge over him, according to the slaughter of Midian at the rock of Oreb, and shall lift up his rod over the sea after the manner of Egypt. And in that day shall his burden depart from off thy shoulder, and his yoke from off thy neck; and the yoke shall burst because of fat.

5.

[28.] He hath come upon Aiath, he hath passed through

Migron; at Michmash he hath laid up his baggage; they, have gone through the passage, they have taken up their lodging at Geba; Ramah hath trembled, Gibeah of Saul hath fled. Cry aloud, O daughter of Gallim; hearken, Laishah; answer her, Anathoth! Madmenah wandereth; the inhabitants of Gebim gather their goods to flee. He will remain at Nob yet to-day, swinging his hand at the mount of the daughter of Zion, the hill' of Jerusalem.

6.

[33] Behold, the Lord, Jehovah of Hosts, shall lop the boughs with violence; and the high ones of stature shall be hewn down, and the lofty shall be humbled; and the thickets of the forest shall be cut down with iron, and Lebanon shall fall by a Majestical One.

7.

[XI. 1.] But there shall come forth a rod from the stock of Jesse, and a branch shall grow out of his roots; and the spirit of Jehovah shall rest upon him, a spirit of wisdom and under-standing, a spirit of counsel and might, a spirit of knowledge and of the fear of Jehovah; and he shall smell a sweet savour in the fear of Jehovah, and shall not judge after the sight of his eyes, nor give sentence after the hearing of his ears, but with justice shall he judge the helpless, and give sentence with equity to the meek of the land, and he shall smite the land with the rod of his mouth, and with the breath of his lips shall he slay the wicked; and justice shall be the girdle of his loins, and faithfulness the girdle of his reins. Then shall the wolf lodge with the lamb, and the leopard lie down with the kid, and the calf and the young lion and the fatling together, and a little child shall lead them; and the cow and the bear shall feed, their young ones shall lie down together, and the lion shall eat straw like the ox; and the sucking child shall stroke the hole of the asp, and the weaned child shall stretch his hand upon the ball of the basilisk's eye. They shall not hurt nor destroy in all my holy mountain, for the land shall be full of the knowledge of Jehovah, as the waters cover the sea.

8.

[10.] Then shall the nations seek after the root of Jesse, which shall stand for the ensign of the peoples, and his resting-place shall be glorious. Then shall the Lord put out his hand yet a second time to recover the remnant of his people from Assyria and from Egypt, and from Pathros and from Cush, and from Elam and from Shinar, and from Hamath and from the coasts of the sea. And he shall lift up an ensign for the nations, and assemble the outcasts of Judah, and gather together the dispersed of Judah from the four skirts of the earth; and the envy of Ephraim shall depart, and the unquiet ones of Judah shall be cut off: Ephraim shall not envy Judah, and Judah shall not disquiet Ephraim. And they shall fly upon the shoulder of the Philistines toward the sea; they shall spoil the sons of the east together; they shall lay their hand upon Edom and Moab, and the sons of Ammon shall obey them. And Jehovah shall curse the tongue of the Egyptian sea, and swing his hand over the river with the violence of his blast, and smite it into seven brooks, and make men go over dryshod; and so shall an highway arise for the remnant of his people out of Assyria, like as there arose to Israel in the day that he came up out of the land of Egypt.

9.

[XII. 1.] And in that day thou shalt say:

Jehovah! I will thank thee, for thou wast angry with me;
　　But thy wrath turneth away, and thou comfortest me.
Behold, the God of my salvation!
　　I will trust and will not tremble,
For Jah Jehovah is my boast and my song;
　　He also became my salvation.

And ye shall draw water with delight out of the wells of salvation.　And in that day ye shall say:

Give thanks unto Jehovah, proclaim his name,
　　Declare his doings among the peoples,
　　Make mention that his name is exalted.
Chant ye unto Jehovah, for he hath done excellent things;
　　This shall be known in all the earth.
Cry aloud and shout, thou inhabitress of Zion,
　　For great is the Holy One of Israel in the midst of thee.

Par. 1. *An unholy nation*　Most commentators explain this and the phrase in the parallel clause of the kingdom of the ten tribes, or of that kingdom and that of Judah together.　But this seems unnecessary, for each of the heathen nations subdued by Assyria might be so designated by a prophet with equal justice

Calno, or Calneh, is identified by tradition with Ctesiphon, on the east bank of the Tigris

Carchemish.　This city is the same as Circesium, at the junction of the Chaboras with the Euphrates.　See 2 Chron. xxxv 20, Jer xlvi 2

Arpad . . . Hamath　Two Syrian cities, the latter (= Epiphania) situated on the Orontes.

The vain gods.　We must apparently admit a certain degree of exaggeration in this description of a heathen king's religious position　For with all the devotion of the Assyrians to their national gods, they can hardly be supposed to have gone to the same length as Isaiah in denying the existence of all gods but their own　That their military ardour, however, was inflamed by a religious enthusiasm, is beyond all question, and the destruction of weaker nationalities appeared to them to involve the destruction of as many rival deities, and consequently the exaltation of their own god, Asshur. In other words, Isaiah regarded the so-called gods of other nations as never having had any existence at all,—Sargon considered it to be his mission to destroy the feeble existence they had previously enjoyed.

Par. 2. His work upon mount Zion, i. e. the destruction of the ungodly part of the inhabitants of Jerusalem. Comp. xxviii. 21, xxix. 14.

Like an hero; perhaps, as in Ps. lxxviii. 25, with the sense of 'a superhuman being.'

Par. 3. His thorns and his briars, i. e. the Assyrian warriors, who are as worthless and impotent as thorns and briars.

His forest and his fruitful land, i. e. the masses of splendidly appointed troops.

Both soul and body. As if the Assyrian army were but one living being.

Like the sinking of strength in sickness. The assonance is too prominent to be omitted.

Overflowing with righteousness, i. e. righteousness under both its aspects,— wrath for the many, mercy for the few.

In the midst of all the earth. That is, Jerusalem shall be the central point of an universal judgment. Comp. xxviii. 22.

Par. 4. To waste them away, i. e. the Assyrian invaders.

The yoke shall burst. This seems, at first sight, to be opposed to Par. 6, where the catastrophe is ascribed to Jehovah. But compare the variation in the opening words of the prophecy, where Assyria is called, first, God's staff, and then the wielder of the staff.

Par. 5 He hath come upon Aiath. The march of the invaders is from the north-east. Their object is to fall upon Jerusalem within three days, and hence the baggage is deposited at Michmash, before entering the famous pass, where Jonathan surprised the garrison of the Philistines, 1 Sam. xiv. Nob is within an hour's march northward from Jerusalem.

Answer her, Anathoth. Or, following the received vowel-points, 'Unfortunate is Anathoth.' In either case there is a play upon words.

Par. 6. A Majestical One, i. e. Jehovah, as in xxxiii. 21.

Par. 7 There shall come forth a rod. This description is remarkable in two respects: (1) because it is the first passage (comp. Mic. v. 2) in which the Messiah is described as descending from David; (2) because of the emphasis which it lays on the moral and religious side of the Messiah's character. We may here pause to inquire, Had Isaiah any definite person in his eye as the Messiah? In vii. 14–16, ix. 6, 7, the vagueness of the language employed induces us to answer confidently in the negative. But even the prophecy on which we are commenting scarcely warrants a very different conclusion. It supplies, no doubt, an additional *datum* of great importance, viz. that the Messiah was to belong to the family of David. But this family was a large one. David, according to 2 Sam v 14-16, had no less than eleven sons born in Jerusalem, and in Zech xii 12, a sort of secondary royal family is mentioned, co-ordinately with 'the house of David,' viz. 'the house of Nathan' The most natural inference from ix. 6, 7, and xi 1, is that the Messiah should rise to his great position suddenly out of deep obscurity Isaiah might well be uncertain which of the numerous princes who were descended from David was the one chosen by God to be the national regenerator. Hezekiah is entirely out of the question. The passages where he is obviously referred to as the inaugurator of a new era (xxxii 1, xxxiii 17) are, however grand, essentially different from the strictly Messianic passages. Besides, Isaiah had already seen too much of the darker side of Hezekiah's character, to apply so severe a test to the king's not excessive humility.

He shall smell a sweet savour Heb *hariho*, an expression apparently suggested by the four times repeated *ruah*. (Hitzig) Comp Lev xxvi 31 ; Amos v. 21.

With the breath of his lips, i. e by his judicial sentences, which involve life and death.

Par. 8 *His resting-place*, i. e. where he (the Messiah) sitteth enthroned. Comp. Ps. cxxxii 8, 14

Pathros, i. e. Upper Egypt, from a Coptic word meaning 'southern.'

The unquiet ones of Judah. Or, as Delitzsch, 'They that vex Judah,' but this, though grammatically easier, is contradicted by the parallelism of the latter part of the verse

The river, i. e. the Euphrates, the symbol of the Assyrian power, as in viii. 7.

Violence. Luzzatto's reading *'osem* seems a necessary correction. See 'Notes and Criticisms,' p. 17

Par 9. *My boast and my song* A reminiscence of Exod. xv. 2 (comp. Ps cxviii 14), which harmonizes beautifully with the references in the preceding paragraph to the history of the Exodus So, immediately afterwards, the 'wells of salvation' are an allusion to the miraculous supplies of water in the desert.

Inhabitress. Comp. the expression 'daughter of Zion.'

APPENDIX.

(Isa. xiv. 24-27)

THIS short prophecy manifestly refers to the preceding one, from which it is only separated by the non-Isaian passage, xiii. 2—xiv. 23. The historical circumstances are the same. The Assyrian oppression continued, probably with additional intensity, and the prophet took occasion to encourage his countrymen by a solemn repetition of his former announcement. Comp. x. 12 with xiv. 25; x. 23 with xiv. 26; and x. 27 with xiv. 25.

[**XIV. 24.**] Jehovah of Hosts hath sworn, saying, Surely as I have thought, so shall it come to pass; and as I have purposed, so shall it stand, that I will break Assyria in my land, and upon my mountains tread him under foot, so that his yoke depart from off them, and his burden depart from off their shoulders. This is the purpose that is purposed concerning the whole earth; and this is the hand that is stretched out upon all the nations. For Jehovah of Hosts hath purposed, and who can disannul it? and the hand that is stretched out is his, and who can turn it back?

VIII. A SIGN FOR EGYPT AND ETHIOPIA.

(Isa. xx.)

SARGON, king of Assyria, had sent an expedition against Ashdod, a fortified town of Philistia. Isaiah, by a symbolic action, intimated that the Assyrians would not only conquer Ashdod, but also subdue Egypt and Ethiopia, upon which the Egyptian party among the Jews should be filled with apprehensions for their own fate.

The position of this prophecy is determined by the allusion in the last verse to the existence of Egyptian sympathies at Jerusalem. The brevity, however, with which the prophet denounces these proves that the party which entertained them was no longer dangerous, and therefore that the prophecy was pronounced subsequently to ch. xxx, xxxi. The siege of Ashdod referred to is doubtless one of the two commemorated by Sargon among the inscriptions translated by M. Oppert. 'Ashdod had probably submitted after the battle of Raphia, and had been allowed to retain its native prince Azuri. This prince, after a while, revolted, withheld his tribute, and proceeded to foment rebellion against Assyria among the neighbouring tribes; wherefore Sargon deposed him, and made his brother Akhimit king in his place.' (Rawlinson, 'Five Great Monarchies,' vol. ii. p. 416.) The Ashdodites, however, rejected the Assyrian nominee, and a second siege by Sargon was the consequence, which ended in the transportation of the inhabitants to a distant region. The easy capture of this important frontier-fortress appears to have so terrified Shebek, the Ethopian ruler of Egypt, that he sent an embassy to Sargon imploring peace, if at least we may trust the interpretation of an unusually difficult passage.

[**XX. 1.**] In the year that Tartan came to Ashdod, being sent by

Sargon, king of Assyria (he assaulted Ashdod, and took it), at that time spake Jehovah by Isaiah, son of Amoz, saying, Go and loose thy sackcloth from off thy loins, and draw off thy shoe from thy foot. And he did so, walking naked and barefoot. Then said Jehovah, Like as my servant Isaiah hath walked naked and barefoot three years for a sign and a portent against Egypt and against Ethiopia, so shall the king of Assyria lead away the captives of Egypt and the exiles of Ethiopia, young men and old, naked and barefoot and with buttocks uncovered, to the shame of Egypt. And they shall be afrighted and ashamed of Ethiopia their expectation, and of Egypt their pride. And the inhabitant of this coast shall say in that day, Behold, so fareth our hope, whither we fled for help to be delivered from the king of Assyria; and how shall we escape?

Tartan. The same name is given in 2 Kings xviii. 17, to the principal general in the army of Sennacherib. According to M. Oppert, it is an official designation.

Sargon. This is the name given in the Assyrian inscriptions to the king who conquered Samaria. In 2 Kings xviii. 9, 10, however, the name of the king who besieged and (as most readers will infer) conquered that city, is given as Shalmaneser. Hence Sir Henry Rawlinson and M. Oppert have conjectured that Sargon reigned at Nineveh immediately after Shalmaneser and before Sennacherib, and, as no Shalmaneser has been found on the inscriptions of this period, they suppose further that Sargon was a successful usurper, who destroyed all the records of his predecessors. Both hypotheses are, we venture to think, highly improbable. Even granting that Sargon was an usurper, why should he adopt this unparalleled mode of signalising his victory? But the notion of his usurpation seems to be quite unsupported by evidence, for few Semitic scholars will be found to admit, with M. Oppert, that the Assyrian form of Sargon, Sar-kin, is derived from *sar*, 'king,' and *kin*, 'to establish,' and means 'the king *de facto*.' The latest inquiries have elicited that Sargon is called in some inscriptions 'Sargon the later,' to distinguish him from another king, who reigned in Babylonia several centuries earlier. (See 'Assyrian History,' by Mr. G. Smith, of the British Museum, in Lepsius's *Zeitschrift,*

1869.) If so, the etymology of the name will be 'Turanian,' and not Semitic

The probability is that the Shalmaneser of the Second Book of Kings is a mistake of the annalist for Sargon. In fact, Shalmaneser was not an uncommon name for an Assyrian king, and was probably more familiar to Jewish writers than Sargon. (See an able paper by Professor Riehm, of Halle, in the *Theologische Studien und Kritiken*, 1868, pp. 683-698.)

Naked, i. e. without the prophetic tunic of hair-cloth. Comp. 2 Kings i. 8; Zech. xiii. 4.

Then said Jehovah. That is, at the end of the three years, during which Isaiah appeared in public in the manner described. Whether the siege of Ashdod lasted as long as three years, is not expressly stated.

This coast, i. e. Palestine in general, but more particularly, as the context shews, Judah.

Ethiopia. Egypt was at this time subject to an Ethiopian dynasty, founded, according to Manetho, by Sabako, who was succeeded by Sebichos (=So, 2 Kings xvii. 4), and Tarakos (=Tirhakah, 2 Kings xix. 9). Sargon, in the inscription referred to above by Rawlinson, boasts of having defeated Shebek at Raphia.

IX. FURTHER PROPHECIES ON THE FALL OF ASSYRIA.

(Isa. xvii 12—xviii. 7.)

I. THE SUDDENNESS OF THE JUDGMENT.

(Isa. xvii. 12-14.)

THIS brief prophecy foretells the sudden destruction of the Assyrian army, as appears from its similarity to xxix. 5, xxxi. 8, 9, xxxiii. 1, 3, where the reference to the Assyrians is unquestionable. Many commentators regard it as forming the introductory strophe to the next prophecy, by which it must at any rate be illustrated; but the concluding words, 'This is the portion of them that spoil us,' &c. appear to us to mark the completion of a distinct work.

Ha, the murmuring of many peoples, which murmur like the murmuring of the seas, and the rushing of nations, which rush like the rushing of mighty waters! The nations rush like the rushing of mighty waters; but he hath rebuked him, and he hath fled afar off, and is chased as the chaff of the mountains before the wind, and as whirling dust before a storm. At evening-tide, behold terror! before morning, he is not! This is the portion of them that spoil us, and the lot of them that rob us.

He hath rebuked him. The prophet considers the destruction of the Assyrians ('him,' because they are directed by a single will) as certain as if it were an event of the past.

II. THE PROSPECTS OF ETHIOPIA.

(Isa. xviii.)

THE subject of this prophecy is the influence of the destruction of the Assyrians on the fortunes of Ethiopia. The latter had already been deeply humbled by Sargon, and now Sennacherib was preparing another expedition to consolidate the work of his father. (Comp. Herod. ii. 141.) He seems to have intended to conquer and annex Judah on his way partly as a punishment to Hezekiah for refusing the tribute paid by Ahaz, and partly no doubt to cover his march homeward from Egypt. On hearing of the Assyrian preparations, the Ethiopian empire would naturally be thrown into great agitation ('Ha, land of resounding wings'). Heralds would be despatched in the light papyrus-vessels suited to the Nile (the βάριες of Herod. ii. 96), to convey the news to the distant provinces, and collect all the available troops. But these very heralds are now commanded by the prophet to return home, and announce the coming of that Divine judgment which so strongly contrasts by its long-suffering calmness with the excitement of the Ethiopians. However famous and enterprising these may be, how feeble are they compared with Jehovah! The crown of all their honourable qualities (comp. Homer's 'Blameless Ethiopians') is this, that, when the great deliverance is accomplished, they will offer homage to its almighty author, the God of Jerusalem.

1.

[XVIII. 1] Ha, land of resounding wings, which art beyond the rivers of Ethiopia, which sendest heralds by the sea, even in vessels of paper-reed on the face of the waters! Go, ye light-footed messengers, to the nation tall and swift, to the people terrible from their beginning hitherto, the nation of great strength and victories, whose land the rivers divide. 'All ye inhabitants of the world, and dwellers on the earth, when one lifteth up an ensign on the mountains, look ye, and when one bloweth a trumpet, 'hear ye.'

2.

[4.] For thus said Jehovah unto me: I will look calmly on in my dwelling-place, while there is the clear heat in the sunshine, while there is the cloud of dew in the heat of the vintage. For before the vintage, when the blossom is over, and the bud becometh a ripening grape, he shall cut off the shoots with pruning-hooks, and remove with a stroke the tendrils. They shall be left together to the ravenous birds of the mountains, and to the beasts of the land; and the ravenous birds shall summer upon them, and every beast of the land shall winter upon them.

3.

[7.] At that time shall a present be brought unto Jehovah of Hosts from the people tall and swift, and from the people terrible from their beginning hitherto, the nation of great strength and victories, whose land the rivers divide, to the place of the name of Jehovah of Hosts, the mount Zion.

Par. 1. *Land of resounding wings.* The prophet compares the tumult of the Ethiopian hosts to the buzz of swarms of insects, such, for instance, as the formidable tsetse-fly with which the interior of Africa abounds. Comp. vii. 18, 'The flies of Egypt and the bees of Assyria.' The Lxx. and Targ., whose versions of this chapter are full of wild guesses, render 'ships,' which Ewald supports by two exceptionally precarious comparisons with the Arabic and Ethiopic. See further, 'Notes and Criticisms,' p. 20, where, in line 23, read 'year' for 'day.'

Which art beyond the rivers of Ethiopia, i. e. which extendest even beyond the rivers, an intentionally vague expression for the unknown region to the south of Seba. Comp. Ps. lxxii. 10, comp. 8, where Seba itself is described as 'the ends of the earth.' Seba (see Gen x 7) is the Meroe of the Greeks, and the

Sennaar of modern geographers. It embraces the whole country to the south of Khartoom, bounded on the east and west by the Blue and White Nile, and though called an island, in reality joins on to Abyssinia at the south base of the triangle.

Victories. Tirhakah, who was the Ethiopian monarch contemporary with Sennacherib, is represented as a great conqueror on several bas-reliefs described by Lepsius (Delitzsch.) Comp. Megasthenes in Strabo xv. 1, 6, who mentions Tearko in company with Sesostris and Nebuchadnezzar.

All ye inhabitants of the world. This is the message supposed to be carried by the heralds. Comp. xiii. 2, xi 12

Par. 2. *I will look calmly on* Jehovah will wait till the Assyrians are ripe for vengeance, till they have well-nigh reached the climax of their oppression.

Par. 3. *Shall a present be brought* Contrast the relation between Israel and the heathen world expressed in xix 24, 25. Here the Ethiopians are described as occupying much the same position with reference to the Jews, as the latter had previously occupied with reference to the Assyrians. Of admission to a share in religious privileges, no trace appears.

X. LAST WORDS AGAINST THE ASSYRIANS.

(Isa. xxxiii.)

BY this time the dreaded invasion has actually come to pass, and the hordes of barbarian soldiery are sweeping the land far and wide. No refuge remains but prayer; yet the prophet is morally convinced from the very first that such unprovoked aggression will meet with a well-deserved retribution. A few fervent ejaculations enable him to realize that the destruction of the Assyrians is as certain as if it belonged to the past. Not only is Jehovah secure from human violence, but so also, through the revival of spiritual religion within its walls, is Jerusalem itself. (See Par. 1.)

In the next paragraph Isaiah describes the scene of mourning at Jerusalem. The baffled ambassadors of Hezekiah have returned, and report that, though Sennacherib has accepted their presents, he has given no pledge that he will desist from hostilities. The high-roads are blocked up with the enemy; fortress after fortress has fallen; and Jerusalem itself is in danger of capture. Yet this is the very moment for which all pious Jews have been longing—the moment when Jehovah must and will manifest his righteousness, and by so manifesting it extort the reverence of the most distant nations. (See Par. 2.)

Now, too, the long neglected admonitions of Isaiah begin to assert an influence over the most unbelieving minds. Many an unquiet conscience dictates the question, Which of us is destined to be tormented with the Assyrians? But the prophet has no answer of peace to give. The righteous, on the other hand, may rely confidently on the protection of Jehovah. They shall yet behold their king, their country, and their temple in their ancient glory, and their recent hair-breadth escape shall become the theme of rapturous meditation. The injured vessel of the state shall yet be repaired; or, to leave the language of metaphor, the very lame and sick shall share in the plunder of the Assyrians; the discouragement of a guilty conscience will be unknown, for the unholy, whether Jews or Gentiles, will all have perished in the great catastrophe. (See Pars. 3 and 4.)

The circumstances here described agree with those mentioned in 2 Kings xviii. 13–16, where the fourteenth year of Hezekiah (714 B.C.) is specified as the date of Sennacherib's invasion. The prophecy seems to have been composed in the autumn, when the falling leaves of Bashan and Carmel appeared to sympathise with the declining fortunes of the state. Compare, with caution, Rawlinson's 'Five Great Monarchies,' vol. ii. pp. 433, 434.

1.

[XXXIII 1] Woe unto thee that spoilest, though thyself not spoiled, and thou that injurest, though not injured by any! When thou shalt cease to spoil, thou shalt be spoiled; when thou shalt make an end of injuring, men shall injure thee. O Jehovah! be gracious unto us; we have waited for thee: be thou our arm every morning, our salvation also in the time of trouble. At the noise of a thundering, the peoples have fled; at the lifting up of thyself are the nations scattered; and their spoil is gathered like the gathering of the caterpillar, as the running to and fro of locusts each one runneth upon it. Jehovah is exalted, for he dwelleth on high; he hath filled Zion with right and justice; and there shall be stability in thy times, even a full store of salvation, of wisdom and knowledge: the fear of Jehovah, that is their treasure.

2.

[7.] 'Behold, the heroes cry without, the ambassadors of peace weep bitterly. The highways lie waste; the wayfaring man ceaseth: he (the enemy) hath broken covenants, he hath despised cities, he regardeth no man. The land fadeth and faileth; Lebanon is ashamed and pineth away; Sharon is like the desert; and Bashan and Carmel shake off their leaves. Now will I rise, saith Jehovah; now will I exalt myself; now will I lift up myself. Ye conceive hay, and ye shall bring forth stubble; your own blast is the fire that shall devour you, so that peoples are as it were burned to lime, as thorns cut off, that are kindled with fire.

3.

[13.] Hear, ye that are far off, what I have done; and, ye that are near, acknowledge my might. The sinners quake in Zion; a shuddering surpriseth the unholy: 'Oh, who will abide in the devouring fire? oh, who will abide in the perpetual burnings?' He that in full measure walketh righteously and speaketh uprightly; he that despiseth the gain of oppressions, that shaketh his hands from holding of bribes, that stoppeth his ear from hearing of bloodshed, and closeth his eyes from looking on evil; he shall dwell on high, with munitions of rock for his shelter; his bread shall be given him, his water shall be sure.

4.

[17.] Thine eyes shall view the king in his beauty; they shall see a land that reacheth afar off. Thine heart shall muse on the terror: 'Where is he that rated? where is he that weighed? where is he that counted the towers?' Thou shalt no more see the fierce people, the people of a deep speech that cannot be heard, of a stammering tongue that one cannot understand. Thou shalt view Zion, the city of our solemnities: thine eyes shall see Jerusalem an easy habitation, a tent that wandereth not, whose nails are never drawn out, neither are any of the cords thereof rent, but where a Majestical One, Jehovah, shall be for us,—a place of broad rivers and streams, whereon shall go no galley with oars, neither shall stately ship pass thereby. For Jehovah is our judge, Jehovah is our lawgiver, Jehovah is our king; he will save us. Thy tacklings hang loosely, they will not hold the socket of their mast, they spread not out the ensign; but then shall the spoils be shared abundantly, even the lame shall take a prey; and no inhabitant shall say, I am sick: the people that dwell therein shall be forgiven their iniquity.

Par. 1. *When thou shalt make an end.* For *kanneloth* read *kekhalloth*, with Cappell, Lowth, and Ewald.

Their spoil is gathered The oppressed nations are represented as retaliating on the Assyrians.

The peoples have fled The tense here employed is the prophetic past.

Thy times, i e. thy fortunes, as in Ps xxxi 15, ' My times are in thy hand.' The pronoun refers to the people of Judah.

Par 2. *The heroes* See ' Notes and Criticisms,' pp 31, 32. Sennacherib, as appears from 2 Kings xviii 14, was laying siege to Lachish, a frontier town of Judah. While so engaged, he received an embassy sent by Hezekiah with tribute, but though he accepted this, he refused to desist from the siege, or to restore the districts which he had conquered from Judah. (See the inscription of Sennacherib quoted in Lenormant's ' Manual of Ancient History.') Hence the lamentation of the ambassadors, which is described as being ' without,' in the open street, as they approach the palace of Hezekiah.

The highways lie waste Comp. the parallel in Judges v. 6.

Sharon, i e. the plain between Cæsarea and Joppa, which was remarkable for its luxuriant vegetation.

Shake off their leaves, as if in sympathy with the troubles of the country. See introductory remarks.

Your own blast, &c. The ' ambition that o'erleaps itself' is the cause of the ruin of the Assyrians.

Par 3. *Oh, who will abide* Literally, ' who to us,' but *lanū,* as *lakhem* in ii 22, simply expresses intensity of feeling. But, it may be asked, why should these Jews apprehend the same fate as the Assyrians (xxx 33)? They probably remembered the warnings of the prophet, to the effect that the impending judgment should extend to the unholy Israelites. Comp. xxviii. 18–21.

From holding of bribes, i e. so as not to hold bribes. The Auth Vers however is too rhythmical to be disturbed.

Par 4. *The king in his beauty*, i e. in his robes of state, which had been laid aside during the siege for a dress of mourning.

Where is he that rated? The three offices referred to in this passage are: (1) that of proportioning the amount of tribute to the population; (2) that of weighing it when it had been paid; (3) that of making a recognizance of the besieged city.

A stammering tongue. See note on xxviii. 11.

A place of broad rivers. That is, Jerusalem shall be like a city, such as Nineveh or Babylon, secured against besiegers by its position on a river. Not even a 'majestic' (it is the word applied above to Jehovah) ship of war shall venture on those charmed waters. The particle of comparison is omitted, as in the previous metaphor of the tent. Comp. Ps. xlvi. 5 (written, possibly by Isaiah himself, after the overthrow of Sennacherib), 'The streams of a river make glad the city of God,' that is, not the fountain of Shiloah, but the gracious influences of the Divine presence.

No inhabitant shall say, I am sick. That is, a good conscience shall inspirit even the lame and the sick to take part in the work of plundering the Assyrians.

APPENDIX.

(Isa xxxvii. 22-35.)

THIS prophecy is one of striking interest, and both in form and matter is stamped with the mark of Isaiah. It describes the blasphemous self-confidence of the king of Assyria, and the final anathema pronounced against him by Jehovah, all expressed in a much less elaborate form than the prophecy to which it forms an appendix. The narrative, however, in which it lies imbedded, cannot have received its present position in the Book of Isaiah from the prophet himself. For, although two passages in the historical style occur in the preceding groups of prophecies (see ch. vii. and xx.), they are both subordinate to the prophecies which they introduce. Here, on the contrary, the preliminary narrative, or, at any rate, the greater part of it, fails entirely to serve the purpose of an introduction.

Still the question may reasonably be asked, Might not the narrative, even if transferred from some other work, have been composed originally by Isaiah, especially as we know from 2 Chron. xxxii. 32 (comp. ix. 29) that the prophet wrote one, if not more than one, historical monograph, from which this might be an extract? The answer is that, while the bare possibility cannot be denied that the existing narrative may be founded on a production of Isaiah's, the form and contents of the latter have, at any rate, been profoundly modified. This is shewn (1) by the variations with which the narrative is repeated in 2 Kings xviii. 13–xx. 19, and which are, generally speaking, very peculiar, and therefore probably more authentic. See especially Isa. xxxviii, noticing the abbreviation of vv. 4 and 5, the addition of the Psalm of Hezekiah, and the wrong position given to v. 21. (2) By the circumstance that the style of Isa. xxxvi and xxxvii (2 Kings xviii. 13–xix. 37) contains nothing to distinguish it from that of many other portions of the two Books of Kings, which are evidently extracted from the royal chronicles, and that the style of Isa. xxxviii (excluding the Psalm) and xxxix closely resembles that of the final editor of the historical books (Genesis—2 Kings), who is apparently also the author of the main part of the Book of Deuteronomy. Comp. Isa. xxxviii. 3, 'a perfect heart,' with 1 Kings viii. 61, xi. 4, xv. 3, 14; Isa. xxxviii. 3, 'I have done that which is good in thy sight,' with 2 Kings xxi. 2, xxii. 3, xxiii. 32, &c.; Isa. xxxix. 8 with 2 Kings xxii. 20, and the repetition in 2 Kings xx. 6 (comp. xix. 34), which is wanting in Isa. xxxviii. 6, with 1 Kings viii, *passim*, and with the constant repetitions in the Book of Deuteronomy.

A more searching examination of the contents of the narrative considerably strengthens our position. Is it probable that Isaiah was the writer of xxxvii 36, which represents the destruction of the Assyrians as the immediate consequence of his prophecy, whereas the prophecy itself postpones complete security to the third year afterwards? Is it probable that Isaiah wrote the notice of the murder of Sennacherib, which all cuneiform scholars date about 681 B.C.? Most readers will think it is not. Is it probable (we will not presume to say, possible) that Isaiah announced a sign of such an extraordinary nature as the recession of the sun's shadow, related in xxxviii. 8? The analogy of the other signs in the Book of Isaiah (and one occurs in the very prophecy before us, xxxvii. 30), compels us to answer in the negative. Is it probable, in conclusion, that Isaiah announced so definite a prediction as that contained in xxxviii. 5? Analogy is again unfavourable to the supposition. (See note on vii. 8, and the introduction to ch. xxiii.)

However this may be, the chief interest for us belongs to the prophecy, the Isaian authorship of which has never been called in question. We may infer, from its fragmentary and unartistic character, that it was not written down by the prophet himself, but by his disciples. It might then have been inserted in the historical passage where it now occurs by a later editor, with the view of forming an epilogue to the prophetic volume. The case would then be exactly similar to that of Jer. lii.

1.

[XXXVIII. 22.] The virgin, the daughter of Zion, despiseth thee, and laugheth thee to scorn; the daughter of Jerusalem shaketh her head behind thee. Whom hast thou reproached and blasphemed? and against whom hast thou exalted thyself, and lifted up thine eyes on high? Even against the Holy One of Israel. By thy servants hast thou reproached the Lord, and hast said, 'With the multitude of my chariots am I come up to the height of the mountains, to the extremities of Lebanon; and I will cut down his tallest cedars, and his choicest cypresses; and I will enter into his most distant lodging-place, and his fruitful grove. I have digged and drunk strange waters; and will dry up with the sole of my feet all the streams of Egypt.' Hast thou not heard that long ago I made it, that in ancient days I fashioned it, and that now I have brought it to pass, laying waste defenced cities into ruinous heaps. Wherefore their inhabitants were of small power; they were dismayed and ashamed, they became as the grass of the field, and as the green herb, as the blade of the housetops, and as corn blasted before it be grown up. But I know thy sitting down, and thy going out, and thy coming in, and thy rage against me. Because thou ragest against me, and thy carelessness is come up into mine ears, therefore will I put my hook into thy nose, and my bridle into thy lips, and I will turn thee back by the way by which thou camest.

2.

[30.] And this shall be the sign unto thee. Eat ye this year that which hath fallen out; and the second year that which groweth of itself; and in the third year sow ye, and reap, and plant vineyards, and eat the fruit thereof. Then shall the remnant that is escaped of the house of Judah again take root downward and bear fruit upward; for out of Jerusalem shall go forth a remnant, and they that escape out of mount Zion. The zeal of Jehovah of Hosts shall perform this. Therefore thus saith Jehovah of Hosts concerning the king of Assyria, He shall not come into this city, nor shoot an arrow there, nor come before it with shields, nor cast a bank against it. By the way that he came, by the same shall he return, and shall not come into this city, saith Jehovah. And I will defend this city, to save it, for mine own sake, and for my servant David's sake.

Par. 1. *Behind thee*, i e on thine ignominious retreat

With the multitude of my servants. The expressions are evidently hyperbolical, with which the employment of the prophetic past tense corresponds. Sennacherib is, in effect, represented as saying that the natural barriers of Palestine and Egypt shall be ineffectual to check his progress. He boasts that he will find a pass over the highest peaks of Lebanon, and then, without condescending to mention the intervening country of the Jews, goes on to describe bombastically the real object of his expedition. The Egyptians have relied too long on the arid desert and the many-branched Nile The Assyrians will extract water from the one, and dry up the other with their countless multitudes 'Il n'y a pas de Pyrénées'

The most distant lodging-place. This is the reading of the parallel passage in 2 Kings xix 23, which seems choicer than that of the text of Isaiah, 'His highest peak.' The meaning, however, is much the same, whichever reading we adopt.

I fashioned it. The Assyrian victories had an ideal reality in the counsels of eternity Comp xxii 11.

As corn blasted. Literally, 'a blasting before the stalk' The text of Isaiah reads 'field'

Par. 2. *The sign.* The hardly-earned existence of the Jews during the next two years is a pledge of the brighter future in store, that is, of the Messianic period. See the next verse, 'Then shall the remnant,' &c.

Eat ye this year, &c. Since it was already autumn, and the Assyrian depredations had put a stop to agriculture, all that could be hoped for was a scanty harvest from the grain casually dropped in the previous season. Not till the third year would the land be quite free from the invaders, so that regular cultivation of the soil could be resumed.

XI EGYPT.

(Isa. xix)

THE prophecy against Egypt is composed of five strophes of nearly
equal length. The first of these describes the anarchy into
which Egypt has already fallen, or is on the point of falling, and which
will issue, as the prophet foresees, in a crushing despotism. The
second and third develope more in detail the disorganized condition
of the social system. This is manifested in the stagnation of the trades
on which the lower orders depend, and in the perplexity and indecision
of the upper. Yet the prospect exhibited in the concluding strophes
is by no means one of unmingled gloom. When the trouble of the
Egyptians is at its height, they will be driven by helpless terror to
adopt the religion of Israel Thenceforward they will enjoy the favour
of Jehovah, and form part of a spiritual confederacy with Israel and
Assyria

The style of the prophecy is in some respects peculiar. The first
three strophes are more prolix in description than is usual with Isaiah,
but this may be easily accounted for by the advanced age of the prophet. The phraseology, at any rate, is not unlike that of Isaiah. In
the last two strophes the forms of expression are more peculiar, but as
the ideas are developments of those which we know to be Isaiah's, and
as the supposed references to later history (see the notes) prove to be
imaginary, there is no sufficient ground for assigning the passage to a
different author. The date has been much disputed. We may be
certain, however, from the cursory manner in which Assyria is mentioned, that the power of that empire had declined, and from the gloom
of the preceding description that Egypt had already fallen into a state
of hopeless confusion. Many critics have supposed the expression 'a

, cruel lord' at the end of the first strophe to refer to Psammetichus, and certainly there is no feature in the description which points to a foreigner, but so far as the character of that king can be traced from history, it does not deserve to be called harsh or cruel. It is a further objection of some importance that, when Psammetichus became monarch of Egypt in 670, Isaiah (according to the current chronology) would be at least eighty-eight years old.· We therefore incline to place the prophecy about ten years earlier, in the troublous times which preceded the establishment of the Dodecarchy. (Herod. ii. 147–154.) ·

In fact, we have before us a republication of the well-known doctrine of the prophets, that a terrible judgment is in store for all heathen nations. The instrument selected by Jehovah on former occasions had been Assyria, but since the great humiliation of that power (see ch. xxxvii), the description of the judgment was necessarily couched in somewhat vaguer language. Probably Isaiah himself anticipated that the tyrant would be a native of Egypt; but this was a purely external matter, which left the spiritual value of the revelation unaffected. His warning, however, is softened by a passage on the religious future of Egypt, which rivals, if it does not surpass, the most evangelical portions of 'the great unknown' himself. Could there be a more fitting *Schwanengesang* for a dying prophet, a more generous farewell to his ancient foes, than the concluding words of this prophecy, 'Blessed be Egypt the people of Jehovah, and Assyria the work of his hands, and Israel his inheritance?'

1.

[XIX. 1.] Behold, Jehovah rideth upon a swift cloud, and shall come to Egypt; and the idols of Egypt shall shake before him, and the heart of Egypt shall melt in the midst of it. And I will prick on Egypt against Egypt, and they shall fight every one against his brother and every one against his neighbour; city against city, and kingdom against kingdom. The spirit of Egypt shall fail in the midst thereof; and I will destroy the counsel thereof; and they shall consult the vain gods, and the whisperers, and them that have familiar spirits, and the wizards; and the Egyptians will I give over into the hand of a cruel lord, and a fierce 'king shall rule over them: it is the utterance of the Lord, Jehovah of Hosts.

2.

[5] The waters have failed from the sea, and the river is wasted and dried up; the rivers have begun to stink, the streams of Egypt are become shallow and dry: the reeds and flags pine away. The meadows by the stream, by the brim of the stream, and everything that is sown by the stream, have vanished for dryness, and are no more. The fishers have long been sighing, and all they that cast angle into the stream have been lamenting, and they that spread nets on the face of the waters have been languishing. Moreover they that prepare combed flax, and they that weave white stuffs, are ashamed. The pillars of the land are broken to pieces, and all they that work for hire are sad of soul.

3.

[11.] Utterly foolish are the princes of Zoan; the wise men, even Pharaoh's counsellors, are become brutish. How say ye unto Pharaoh, I am the son of the wise, the son of ancient kings? Where are they, now, thy wise men? Come, let them tell thee, and let them know what Jehovah of Hosts hath purposed upon Egypt. The princes of Zoan are befooled, the princes of Noph are deceived, and Egypt hath been led astray by the corner-stone of the tribes thereof. Jehovah hath mingled in the midst of the land a spirit of disturbance, so that they have led Egypt astray in all his doings, as a drunken man staggereth in his vomit. Neither shall there be any deed for Egypt, which the head might do with the tail, the branch of the palm-tree with the rush.

4.

[16.] In that day shall Egypt be like unto women; it shall tremble and shall shudder, because of the swinging of the hand of Jehovah of Hosts, which he swingeth over it. And the land of Judah shall become a terror unto Egypt: whensoever one shall call it [Judah] to mind, he shall shudder, because of the purpose of Jehovah of Hosts, which he determineth against it [Egypt]. In that day shall there be five cities in the land of Egypt, speaking the language of Canaan, and swearing to Jehovah of Hosts; one shall be called. The city of ruined images. In that day shall there be an altar to Jehovah in the midst of the land of Egypt, and a pillar by the border thereof to Jehovah. And it shall be for a sign and for a witness unto Jehovah of Hosts in the land of Egypt; when they shall cry unto Jehovah because of oppressors, he shall send them a saviour and a champion, and shall deliver them.

5.

[21.] Thus Jehovah shall make himself known unto Egypt, and the Egyptians shall acknowledge Jehovah in that day, and shall do sacrifice and oblation, and they shall vow a vow unto Jehovah, and perform it. And Jehovah shall smite Egypt, smiting and healing it; and when they shall turn unto Jehovah, he shall suffer himself to be intreated of them, and shall heal them. In that day shall there be a highway out of Egypt to Assyria; the Assyrians shall come into Egypt, and the Egyptians into Assyria, and the Egyptians shall worship with the Assyrians. In that day shall Egypt be the third to Egypt and to Assyria, even a blessing in the midst of the earth; wherewith Jehovah of Hosts shall bless the earth, saying, Blessed be Egypt my people, and Assyria the work of my hands, and Israel mine inheritance.

Par. 1. *The whisperers*, i. e. the necromancers, who imitated the voice of the shades. See note on viii 19.

Par 2 *The sea*, i e the Nile   Comp. Job xiv. 11; Nahum iii 8.

They that prepare combed flax. Linen was universally worn in Egypt for the under-garment, and the priests were even forbidden to wear dresses of any other material. Linen was also used for the cloths in which mummies were wrapped.   The term 'white stuffs' in the parallel clause may possibly include cotton.

The pillars of the land, i. e. the upper classes. Comp Ezek. xxx 4; Ps xi 3; Gal ii 9.

Par 3. *Zoan*, i e. Tanis, the capital of an Egyptian nome or canton (Herod. ii 166), at one time a royal residence (Isa. xxx 4)   The 'princes' spoken of are probably the priests, who were renowned for their wisdom.

How say ye unto Pharaoh, &c.   'With what reason do you continue to boast of your hereditary wisdom?'

The son of ancient kings   The kings of Egypt belonged, either by birth or by adoption, to the priestly order.

Noph, generally identified with Memphis, which in the reign of Psammetichus became the capital of the monarchy.

The corner-stone, i. e the members of the order of priests collectively   See note on xxxi 9

Neither shall there be any deed, &c.   That is, the disunion of princes and people shall prevent any national enterprises

Par. 4. *The land of Judah shall become a terror.* That is, because the author of the calamities of the Egyptians is the God of Judah

Five cities, i e a very small number of cities (as in xxx 17, xvii 6) in which Jewish colonists might be found.

Speaking the language of Canaan   Isaiah appears to have anticipated the adoption of Hebrew as the sacred language of the Egyptian proselytes.

The city of ruined images. Heb. '*ir haheres*, 'city of breaking down.' An allusion to one of the Hebrew names of Heliopolis, 'city of the sun' ('*ir hacheres*), which, by a slight modification of one of the letters ('*ir haheres*), would express the zeal of its inhabitants, when converted, for the true God.' Comp Jer. xliii. 13, ' He shall break the statues of the house of the Sun,' referring to the same name, Heliopolis   A similar transformation of the Egyptian equivalent, On, is made by Ezekiel (xxx 17), 'The young men of Aven (or ' nothingness') shall fall by the sword.' This appears to be the simplest way of explaining a very peculiar phrase and thus confirming the authorship of

Isaiah; it is found as early as the Targum of Jonathan, which renders, 'One shall be called Beth-shemesh (place of the sun) which shall be destroyed,' and is adopted by the Jewish historian Herzfeld, the Roman Catholic professor Reinke, and the Protestant Delitzsch (comp his admirable note) S D Luzzatto renders somewhat differently, 'Città risorta dalle ruine,' but this is too far-fetched. Another well-attested reading is '*îr bacheres*, 'city of the sun' (or, as Ewald, 'fortunate city'), which was probably current in Egypt at the time of the foundation of the temple of Leontopolis (B.C. 160) by Onias the Jewish refugee. The latter city was, at any rate, in the canton of Heliopolis The reading of the Lxx was '*îr baṡedek*, 'city of righteousness' (comp. 1 26), which looks like a retort on the Palestinian Jews for expounding the old reading in a manner uncomplimentary to Onias, though Geiger regards it as the original one, *cheres* and *cherem* being deliberate falsifications.

An altar. Comp Josh xxii. 27; Exod. xx. 24. Probably this is the passage appealed to by Onias in justification of his Egyptian temple (Joseph Archæol. xiii 3, 1–3), and Hitzig supposes that it was really interpolated with that object. But 'an altar' is merely a symbolic expression for the religion of any particular community.

By the border, as a memorial of the Jewish origin of the adopted religion of the Egyptians.

For a sign and for a witness. For a sign that the Egyptians are worshippers of Jehovah, and for a witness that he is pledged to save them in trouble.

Par. 5 *Smiting and healing it* For the idea of the conversion of the heathen as resulting from a terrible judgment, comp. Zeph iii. 8, 9; Jer. xii. 15–17; and the vaguer but unmistakeable allusions in Isa xviii 3, 7, and perhaps originally in xvi 12

A blessing in the midst of the earth. The only distinction reserved for Israel is that of being the instrument by which the Divine blessing is communicated to others. Comp. Exod iv. 22, 'Israel is my son, even my firstborn;' and Isa. ii. 3, 'Out of Zion shall go forth doctrine.'

Blessed be Egypt my people. The Lxx renders characteristically, 'Blessed be my people in Egypt, and the work of my hands among the Assyrians,' thus converting the passage into an eulogy of the Jews of the Dispersion, who were much looked down upon by their kinsmen of Palestine.

APPENDIX I.

(Isa. xxxiv, xxxv.)

THE prophet foresees that a terrible retribution is in store for the entire heathen world, especially for the malicious foes of Israel in Edom. The latter shall be slaughtered, as it were, in one vast sacrifice to Jehovah; their territory shall be desolated, and shall become the haunt of wild beasts and evil fairies. Very different shall be the fortune of the Jews. They shall return home from exile under the Divine escort; the desert shall be transformed as they pass along it; they shall enter Jerusalem with songs of triumph.

The resemblance of this prophecy to ch. xl–lxvi dispenses us from the obligation of discussing the theory of the authorship of Isaiah. It would, in fact, be difficult to extract decisive arguments either for or against it from a work of so small an extent as this. We venture therefore to question whether the classical essay of Dr. Caspari (see the 'Lutheran Review' for 1843) on the genuineness of Isa. xxxiv, in spite of its conscientious thoroughness, has not been composed in vain. If the occurrence of parallels between Jeremiah and Isa. xl–lxvi is not a decisive argument in favour of the priority of the latter, it is not worth while to reopen the subject on behalf of Isa. xxxiv. No doubt, if this prophecy were an isolated one in the so-called Book of Isaiah, critics might, with some show of reason, argue that it was written by that prophet. But as the peculiarities of idea and of style, which are not wanting even here, are repeated on a much enlarged scale in the last twenty-seven chapters, the refutation of the Isaian theory in the latter is equally valid for the former prophecy.

It would be unwise to speak too positively as to the precise date of the composition. We may, however, be allowed to point out a few circumstances of some importance, which incline us to consider this the earliest of the prophecies written during the exile. That it was written earlier than ch. xl–lxvi seems to us to be proved by the fact that xxxv. 10 recurs as a quotation in li. 11. That it was written before the hopes of the exiles had centred round any particular deliverer, seems to follow from xxxiv. 16, and from the absence of any definite allusion to the fall of Babylon. That it was written comparatively early in the exile may be argued from the bitterness of the anathema against the Edomites, which seems to imply that the outrages offered by them to their Jewish kinsmen were still fresh in remembrance.

1.

[**XXXIV. 1.**] Come near, ye nations, to hear; and hearken, ye peoples; let the earth hear, and all that is therein: the world, and all things that come forth of it. For Jehovah hath indignation against all the nations, and wrath against all their host: he hath put a curse upon them, he hath devoted them to slaughter. Their slain also shall be cast out, and the stink of their carcases shall come up, and the mountains shall melt with their blood. And all the host of heaven shall rot, and the heavens shall roll together as a scroll; and all their host shall fade, as a leaf fadeth away from the vine, and as that which fadeth away from the fig-tree. For already my sword is drenched in heaven; behold, it shall come down upon Edom, and upon the people of my curse, to judgment. Jehovah hath a sword that is full of blood, and made juicy with fat, with the blood of lambs and he-goats, with the fat of the kidneys of rams; yea, Jehovah hath a sacrifice in Bozrah, and a great slaughter in the land of Edom. And the buffaloes shall sink down with them, and the bullocks with the oxen; and their land shall be drenched with blood, and their dust made juicy with fatness.

2.

[**8.**] For Jehovah hath a day of vengeance, and a year of

I

requital for the controversy of Zion.   And the streams of Edom
shall be turned into pitch, and the dust thereof into brimstone, and
the land thereof shall become burning pitch.   It shall not be
quenched night nor day; the smoke thereof shall go up for ever
and ever: from generation to generation it shall lie waste; none
shall pass through it for ever and ever.   But the pelican and the
hedgehog shall take it in possession; the bittern and the raven shall
dwell in it; and one shall stretch out upon it the line of desolation, and the plummet of emptiness.   As for the nobles thereof,
none shall be there to proclaim the kingdom, and all the princes
thereof shall come to nothing.   And her palaces shall be over-
grown with thorns; nettles and thistles shall be in the fortresses
thereof; and she shall become an habitation of wild dogs, and a
home for owls.   Jackals and wolves shall meet there, and the
satyr shall light on his fellow; surely Lilith shall repose there,
and find for herself a place of rest.   There shall the arrowsnake
make her nest, and lay, and hatch, and gather under her shadow;
surely there shall the vultures assemble, every one with her mate.
Seek ye out of the book of Jehovah, and read; no one of these
shall fail, none shall want her mate: for my mouth it hath commanded, and his spirit it hath assembled them.   And he hath cast
the lot for them, and his hand hath divided it unto them by line:
they shall possess it for ever, from generation to generation shall
they dwell therein.

3.

[XXXV. 1] The wilderness and the parched place shall be
glad, and the desert shall rejoice and blossom as the rose.   It
shall blossom abundantly, and rejoice with dancing and singing;
the glory of Lebanon shall be given unto it, the excellency of
Carmel and Sharon; they shall see the glory of Jehovah, and the

excellency of our God. Strengthen ye the slack hands, and confirm the tottering knees. Say to them that are of a fearful heart,
Be strong, fear not; behold, your God will come with vengeance,
with a godlike recompence; he will come himself to save you.
Then the eyes of the blind shall be opened, and the ears of the
deaf unstopped; then shall the lame man leap as an hart, and the
tongue of the dumb shout; for in the wilderness shall waters break
out, and torrents in the desert. And the sandy glistening shall
become a pool, and the thirsty land springs of water; in the
habitation of jackals, where they couched, shall be a home for
reeds and rushes. And a highway shall be there, and a way, and
it shall be called, The holy way; the unclean shall not pass over
it, for he [God] himself shall be on their side: whoso walketh in the
way, though a fool, shall not err therein. No lion shall be there,
nor any ravenous beast shall go up thereon; none shall be found
there; but the redeemed shall walk at liberty. And the ransomed
of Jehovah shall return, and come to Zion with shouting, and with
everlasting joy upon their head: they shall obtain joy and gladness, and grief and sighing shall flee away.

Par. 1. *All the host of heaven*, &c. The prophets of the Babylonian exile
delight to connect the deliverance of the Jewish nation with the destruction of
the present world and the creation of a new one. Comp. xiii. 9, xxiv. 1, li 6,
lxv. 17.

My sword is drenched, i e the acts of Divine vengeance have long been
decreed and, as it were, rehearsed in heaven.

Upon Edom. The conduct of the Edomites towards their Jewish kinsmen at
the Babylonian conquest seems to have excited in the latter the bitterest feelings of resentment. See Obad 11–14; Lam. iv 21; Ezek. xxv. 12–14, Ps
cxxxvii.

Bozrah. An Idumæan city, Gen. xxxvi. 33 See Smith's 'Dictionary of the
Bible,' s v.

I 2

Lambs and he-goats. That is, the people of Edom, as distinguished from the 'bullocks' in the next verse, i. e. the chiefs.

Par. 2. *The land is become burning pitch.* Edom is to share the fate of Sodom and Gomorrah. Comp Jer xlix. 18.

But pelican and hedgehog, &c. A favourite commonplace of the prophets in their descriptions of ruins. See xiii. 20-22, xiv. 23, and Zeph. ii. 14, the latter of which passages Ewald regards as the model on which the others were framed, Delitzsch as an imitation of them.

The line of desolation. The work of destruction shall be carried out to the smallest details.

As for her nobles. From this passage, and from Gen. xxxvi. 31, it is inferred that the king of the Edomites was elected from among the chiefs of the tribes.

Jackals and wolves. Heb *nyim . . .'iyim* The root of both words appears to represent the cry of the animals. See 'Notes and Criticisms,' p. 23.

The satyrs. That is, mythological beings, shaped like goats (whence their name in Hebrew), and believed to inhabit deserts. They appear to have been propitiated with sacrifices, Lev xvii 7, 2 Chron. xi. 15. Perhaps we may compare the usage on the Day of Atonement of dedicating a goat 'to Azazel' (mistranslated in Auth Ver. 'scapegoat'), and sending it with the sins of the people into the wilderness, Lev. xvi 8–22 Afterwards, at any rate, when the reverence for Azazel had been expelled by monotheism, the title 'king of the devils' was borne by Ashmadai (the Asmodeus of Tobit), a word evidently of Persian origin = Ashmadeva. (Levy's 'Chaldee Lexicon,' s.v.) The Arabs have a similar superstition about the Ghuls, which Sprenger deduces from the exciting air and monotonous landscape of the desert. See Sprenger's 'Leben und Lehre des Mohammad,' vol. i. p. 220.

Lilith, i. e 'the night-fairy,' like Strix and Lamia. Ben Sira (quoted by Buxtorf, 'Lex. Rabbin.' s v.) informs us that Lilith was the name of Adam's first wife Being quarrelsome, she pronounced the Divine name as a charm, and flew away, and became a devil Her passion was to murder young children, which could only be averted by exorcism. Goethe is therefore not quite accurate when he puts into the mouth of Mephistopheles the words

> 'Beware of her fair hair, for she excels
> All women in the magic of her locks,
> And when she winds them round a young man's neck,
> She will not ever set him free again.'
>   The Walpurgis-night scene in 'Faust' (Shelley's Translation).

The book of Jehovah, i e the present prophecy. This seems to imply that the fulfilment was not immediately expected.

Par. 3. *Strengthen ye* The persons addressed are the prophets of the exile. Comp. xl. 1.

In the wilderness, &c. Imitated by a later prophet in xliii. 19, xlviii. 21, xlix. 10. The allusion is to the events of the Exodus.

The sandy glistening, i e. the mirage. Comp xlix. 10.

Where they couched There is probably some corruption in the text of this clause. For 'home' Auth. Ver. renders 'grass,' but the parallel of xxxiv. 13 (last clause) is opposed to this. Comp. Job viii. 11

The unclean, i. e. the heathen. Comp. Joel iii 17: 'Then shall Jerusalem be holy, and there shall no strangers pass through her any more.'

Upon their head. An allusion to the custom of crowning the head with garlands. Comp xxv. 7. This whole verse is quoted by a later prophet in li. 11.

APPENDIX II.

(Isa. xxiv–xxvii.)

A GREAT calamity, in which all classes shall be equal sufferers, is about to befal the entire Eastern world. But it is more than an ordinary misfortune; it is the penalty of the general violation of the law of God written in the human heart. The capital city (apparently Babylon) shall be destroyed, and the population of the empire reduced to a mere handful of mourners. The Jewish exiles, however, shall seize the opportunity of returning to their native land. They shall gather by the shores of the Mediterranean, exulting over the fall of Babylon, and calling upon the heathen of the most distant countries to recognize the act of Jehovah. But, after this bright anticipation, the prophet is overcome by sympathy with the suffering which, he well knows, will ensue. The once flourishing empire will be a prey to anarchy, and the hopes of the returning Jewish exiles will be doomed, at first, to bitter disappointment. Then, gliding suddenly into another tone, the prophet continues: a great judgment shall be held on all the evil powers of heaven and earth, and the theocracy shall be visibly restored on the sacred mount.

The second part of the prophecy begins with a hymn to Jehovah, as the destroyer of the tyrannical empire, and an anticipation of the comprehension of all nations amongst the worshippers assembled at Jerusalem. Suffering and death itself shall be annihilated, and the obstinate animosity of Moab receive its final overthrow.

The third part opens with a fresh hymn to be sung by the restored exiles in the land of Judah. The ruined walls of Jerusalem, such is its purport, need not be rebuilt; for their object is more than fulfilled by spiritual bulwarks. Trust in God is the guarantee of peace and security. He who has destroyed 'the lofty city' already will henceforth grant an even course of prosperity to 'the righteous nation.' A tender, meditative strain follows. The Divine judgments of vengeance and mercy had indeed been long expected throughout the night of trouble. If these impious Babylonians (thus the exiles questioned themselves) should continue to escape the chastening of Jehovah, what hope would there be of their ever acknowledging him as the true God? This is succeeded by a series of ejaculations. The point of view in the first is the situation of the Jews before the judgment; in the two following, that produced by its accomplishment, 'Previous judgments have been in vain; therefore let the tyrants suffer a more severe one!' 'Surely thou wilt henceforth grant us lasting peace!' 'Thanks to thee alone, O Jehovah! for deliverance from the oppressors.' From the standing-point which he has thus succeeded in reaching, the prophet describes the discouragements of those who should return home from exile. He anticipates that their numbers would be small, and incommensurate with the intensity of their previous expectation, which is represented under the image of the pangs of child-birth. But, on a sudden, the prophet's faith in God's love triumphs over his despondency. An influence as potent as the dew shall draw forth the shades of the departed Israelites to fill the void in the population. 'Be patient for a while, and the last act of the Divine judgment shall be consummated.' The conclusion is formed by a description of the restoration of the exiles, quoted apparently from some earlier prophecy.

The date and origin of this prophecy have been more disputed than those of any other in the Book of Isaiah. That Isaiah himself, however, is not the author, may be inferred from the strong peculiarity of the style and the ideas. By style we do not so much mean phraseology, the argument from which is two-edged and indecisive, as the construction of the sentences, the exuberance of assonance and paronomasia (which appear comparatively seldom in Isaiah), and the unusual mode of forming a climax, by repeating and carrying on a phrase from the foregoing clause. Among the peculiar ideas may be noticed the mention of guardian-angels of kingdoms (xxiv. 21), and, above all, of the resurrection of individuals (xxvi. 19), which is wanting in the true Isaiah, and the annihilation of death (xxv. 8), which in a passage currently ascribed to that prophet (lxv. 20), is even contradicted.

More than this negative result cannot be laid down with certainty. The difficulty is chiefly owing to the generality of the description in ch. xxv, and the occasional shifting of the standing-point of the writer both in ch. xxiv and xxvi. Hence Knobel supposes the author to have been one of the Jews left in Palestine after the capture of Jerusalem by Nebuchadnezzar; Hitzig, an Ephraimite, who wrote shortly before the fall of Nineveh; Ewald, a Jew, shortly before the expedition of Cambyses against Egypt. We have not space to discuss each of these hypotheses in detail. The great catastrophe described in the early strophes can hardly, as it seems to us, be any other than the fall of Babylon, predicted in the other non-Isaian prophecies of this book. The past tenses which so frequently occur in ch. xxiv are most readily explained as idealistic or prophetic. They shew, not that the passage is a description of the past, as most modern commentators have imagined, but that the fall of Babylon was expected with eager impatience. From the anarchy anticipated in xxiv. 17, 18, we infer that the victorious march of Cyrus had not begun, otherwise the firm character of that monarch would have relieved the writer from his apprehensions. From the expression 'this mountain,' in xxv. 6, many (e. g. Knobel) have inferred that the author lived in or near Jerusalem. But xxvi. 9 seems to indicate that he had long shared the fate of the majority of the exiles, i. e. that he was resident in Babylonia. If we look at xxv. 6 more closely, we shall observe that it is but loosely connected with the foregoing passage, and probably Ewald is right in ascribing it, with vv. 7, 8, 10–12, to an earlier prophet. Similarly the mention of Assyria and Egypt in xxvii. 13, indicates that the passage is a quotation, probably from Isaiah.

PART I.

1.

[**XXIV. 1.**] Behold, Jehovah maketh the earth desert and desolate, and turneth it upside down, and scattereth abroad the inhabitants thereof. And it shall be, as with the people, so with the priest; as with the servant, so with his master; as with the maid, so with her mistress; as with the buyer, so with the seller; as with the lender, so with the borrower; as with the taker of usury, so with the giver of usury to him. The earth shall be utterly desert, and clean despoiled, for Jehovah hath spoken this word.

2.

[**4.**] The earth faileth and fadeth; the world fainteth and fadeth; the haughty people of the earth do faint. For the earth is become unholy under the inhabitants thereof, because they transgressed the precepts, violated the law, brake the everlasting covenant; therefore hath a curse devoured the earth, and they that dwell therein rue their trespass, therefore the inhabitants of the earth are burned up, and few men left.

3.

[**7.**] The new wine faileth, the vine fainteth, all the merry-hearted do sigh; the mirth of tabrets ceaseth, the noise of them that rejoice endeth, the mirth of the harp ceaseth. They shall no more drink wine with a song; strong drink shall be bitter to them that drink it. It is broken down, a city of solitude; every house is shut up, that no man may come in. In the fields is a crying for the wine; all joy has set; the mirth of the land is banished. Of the city is left desolation, and the gate is smitten to ruins.

4.

[13.] Yea, so shall it be in the midst of the earth among the peoples, as at the shaking of an olive-tree, and as at the gleaning when the vintage is done. The remnant shall lift up their voice, they shall shout; for the majesty of Jehovah they shall cry aloud from the sea, (saying,) 'Therefore in the coasts glorify Jehovah, even the name of Jehovah the God of Israel in the coasts of the sea.' From the skirt of the earth we have heard songs, 'Splendid is the lot of the righteous;' but I said, Pining is my lot, pining is my lot, alas for me! The injurious injure, and injuring they injure injuriously. A fear and a fall and a fowler are upon thee, O inhabitant of the earth; for he who fleeth from the rumour of fear shall suffer a fall, and he that ariseth from the fall shall be taken by the fowler, for the windows of heaven are open, and the foundations of the earth do shake. The earth is utterly crushed, the earth is clean dissolved, the earth shaketh exceedingly; the earth reeleth like a drunkard, and swayeth to and fro like a hammock; and the transgression thereof is heavy upon it, and when it hath fallen, it shall not rise again.

5.

[21.] And in that day shall Jehovah visit the host of heaven on high, and the kings of the earth upon the earth. And they shall be gathered together as prisoners into the pit, and shut up in the prison, and after many days shall they be visited. And the moon shall blush, and the sun be ashamed, because Jehovah of Hosts shall reign in mount Zion and in Jerusalem, and before his elders shall be glory.

Par. 1. *Behold, Jehovah maketh.* Most interpreters regard this passage as a description of the literal present, on the ground of the particularity of the details; but see the remarks at the end of the Introduction. The analogy of many other places where the Heb. *hinnéh*, 'behold,' is followed by a participle (e. g. iii. 1, xvii. 1, xix. 1) confirms us in the view that the phrase 'Behold, he maketh,' is equivalent to a future.

The earth. That is, the Babylonian empire, which embraced most of the countries with which the writer was acquainted. Comp. xiii. 5, xxxiv. 1.

Desert and desolate. Observe the fondness of the prophet for assonances, e g 'desert, desolate, despoiled,' 'faileth, fadeth, fainteth,' 'a fear, a fall, and a fowler.'

Par. 2. *The everlasting covenant.* That is, the primitive covenant of God with Noah, the representative of the human race. Comp. Gen. ix. 16, 'And the bow shall be in the cloud, and I will look upon it, that I may remember *the everlasting covenant* between God and every living creature of all flesh that is upon the earth.' The covenant being broken on the side of man, the Divine promise not to bring a second deluge on the earth is recalled, as the prophet indicates in ver. 18.

A curse. For the personification of the curse of Jehovah, comp. Dan. ix. 11; Zech. v. 3; Jer. xxiii. 10.

Hath devoured. The tense here, as throughout the description, is the prophetic past.

Par. 3. *Every house is shut up,* i. e. by the accumulation of ruins.

Par. 4. *As at the shaking of an olive-tree.* An image of a very small remnant, borrowed from Isaiah (xvii. 6).

The remnant shall lift up their voice. That is, the Jewish exiles restored to Palestine shall rejoice at the fall of their oppressors, and call upon the heathen to recognize in it the act of Jehovah. This is supposed to be answered by an anthem from the most distant heathen countries, 'Splendid is the lot of the righteous!' The prophet, however, refuses to accept these congratulations. He foresees that the consequences of the political revolution in Babylon will involve much suffering to all the inhabitants of the empire, not excepting his own people.

From the sea, i e. the Mediterranean, which is described as re-echoing with the songs of the Jews.

In the coasts, i.e. the maritime countries of the west. Read *bā'iyyîm* for *bā'urîm* (see 'Notes and Criticisms,' p. 27). For the repetition of the phrase in an amplified form, comp xxvi 6, 7

We have heard, i. e. the Jewish exiles, restored to their country, with whom the writer, in prophetic imagination, identifies himself. Immediately afterwards, he shifts his point of view, but not to any great distance. The enthusiasm of the exiles might soon be expected to cool on a clearer perception of the difficulties which surrounded them. Such was, in fact, historically the case, and hence the difference in tone between the eloquent prophet who heralded the restoration of the Jews and the prosaic Haggai and Zechariah.

The injurious injure. The prophet appears to anticipate a time of anarchy consequent on the fall of Babylon an indication that he was not contemporary with the victories of Cyrus.

O inhabitant of the earth. That is, the helpless inhabitants of the countries within the former Babylonian empire. No sooner have they escaped from one danger than they shall fall into another.

The windows of heaven. An image borrowed from the description of the deluge in Gen. vii 11.

Like a hammock, i. e. like the hanging bed erected in the vintage season for the guardian of the vineyard. Comp i 8, Job xxvii 18. 'But the true point of the comparison will not appear until the crop is over, and the lodge forsaken by the keeper. Then the poles fall down, or lean every way, and those green boughs with which it is shaded will have been scattered by the wind, leaving only a ragged, sprawling wreck.' Thomson, 'The Land and the Book,' p 362.

Par. 5. *The host of heaven,* i e. the angels, who, as in Dan x 13, 20, 21, are regarded as the patrons of earthly kingdoms. These are supposed to share the fate of the kings whom they protect, just as, perhaps, in Rev. i–iii, the 'angels' are combined with the churches they severally guard, and as in Rev. xix. 20, 'the beast' is cast into 'the lake of fire' together with his worshippers. As soon, however, as the Messianic kingdom has been established, the imprisoned angels and kings are to be released. They will then become tributaries to Jehovah, comp. xxiii 17, 18.

Before his elders shall be glory, i. e. the representatives of the people shall be admitted to a sight of the Divine glory, as in the times of Moses (Exod. xxiv. 9).

PART II.

1.

[**XXV. 1.**] O Jehovah! thou art my God; I will exalt thee, I will praise thy name, for thou hast done wonderful things; thy counsels of old are fulfilled in faithfulness. For thou hast made of a city an heap; of a defenced town a ruin; a palace of barbarians to be no city, never to be built again. Therefore shall a fierce people glorify thee, the town of terrible nations shall fear thee; for thou hast been a stronghold to the helpless, a stronghold to the poor in his distress, a refuge from the storm, a shadow from the heat, for the blast of the terrible ones was like a storm against the wall. As the heat in a dry place, so didst thou subdue the noise of the barbarians; as the heat by the shadow of clouds, the song of the terrible ones was brought low.

2.

[**6.**] 'And in this mountain hath Jehovah of Hosts made unto all peoples a feast of fat things, a feast of wines on the lees, of fat things full of marrow, of wines on the lees well refined. And he hath swallowed up in this mountain the covering cast over all peoples, and the veil that is spread over all nations; he hath swallowed up death for ever; and the Lord Jehovah hath wiped away tears from off all faces; and the reproach of his people will he take away from off all the earth: for Jehovah hath spoken it.'

3.

[**9.**] And it shall be said in that day, Lo, there is our God, for whom we waited that he should save us; there is Jehovah for whom we waited; let us exult and rejoice in his salvation. 'For on

this mountain shall the hand of Jehovah rest, and Moab shall be
trodden down in his place, like an heap of straw in the water of
the dunghill. And though he spread forth his hands therein, as
he that swimmeth spreadeth forth his hands to swim, yet despite the tricks of his hands shall Jehovah bring down his pride.
And thy defenced and lofty walls (O Moab!) shall he bring down,
lay low and bring to the ground, even to the dust.'

Par. 1. *A fierce people*, i. e. the conquerors of the Babylonians

Par. 2. *In this mountain*, i. e. mount Zion. See remarks at conclusion of
Introduction.

Hath made, i e. shall certainly make. The prophetic past

He hath swallowed up, i. e. hath annihilated, as in iii. 12.

A feast of fat things. All nations are to be admitted to the spiritual privileges
of Jerusalem. Comp. Matt. viii 11, Luke xiv. 15.

The covering An allusion to the customary sign of mourning David 'had
his head covered' as he quitted Jerusalem, 2 Sam. xv. 30, comp. Est. vi. 12.

He hath swallowed up death. Two meanings of this are possible. If this
passage was written by the author of xxvi. 19, it will imply that the Jews who
should be alive at the Messianic era, and those whom 'the dew of Jehovah'
should draw up from the underworld, should escape death. But if a quotation
from an earlier prophet (see end of Introduction), it may mean no more than
Hos. xiii. 14, which promises immortality to the regenerated *people* of Ephraim.
Certainly the greatest of the Babylonian prophets (the author of xl-lxvi) did
not anticipate the immortality of the *individual*. See lxv. 20, and comp. Zech
viii. 4.

Par. 3. *For on this mountain shall the hand of Jehovah rest.* Comp. Ezra viii
22, 31.

Moab shall be trodden down. The Moabites appear, like the Edomites, to
have shown a malignant pleasure at the fall of Jerusalem. Comp Ezek xxv
8–11.

The tricks of his hands, i. e. the artifices employed by the Moabites to escape
destruction.

PART III.

1.

[**XXVI. 1.**] In that day shall this song be sung in the land of Judah:

> ' We have a city of strength; salvation doth Jehovah appoint
>   for walls and bulwarks;
>   Open ye the gates, that a righteous nation which keep their
>   faith may enter in.'

By a sure purpose wilt thou fashion perfect peace, because in thee is their trust. Trust ye in Jehovah for ever, for Jah Jehovah is the rock of ages. For he hath brought down them that dwelt on high; the lofty city, he laid it low; he laid it low, even to the earth; he brought it even to the dust; the foot trode it down, even the feet of the suffering, and the steps of the helpless. The path for the upright is even; thou layest evenly the path of the righteous.

2.

[**8.**] Yea, for the path of thy judgments, O Jehovah, long have we waited upon thee; for thy name and thy memorial was the desire of our soul. With my soul have I desired thee in the night; yea, with my spirit within me did I seek thee carefully: for when thy judgments touch the earth, the inhabitants of the world learn righteousness. Let the wicked be favoured, then will he not learn righteousness; in the land of uprightness he will deal perversely, and will not behold the majesty of Jehovah.

3.

[**11.**] O Jehovah! thy hand was lifted up, but they saw it not.

Let them see with shame thy zeal for the people; yea, let the fire of thine enemies devour them. O Jehovah! thou wilt ordain peace for us, for thou also hast wrought for us all our work. O Jehovah our God! other lords than thee have had dominion over us, but only thee will we celebrate, even thy name. The dead will not revive, the shades will not rise; therefore didst thou visit and destroy them, and make all their memory to perish. Thou didst increase the nation, O Jehovah, thou didst increase the nation; thou didst glorify thyself; thou didst extend all the borders of the land.

4.

[16.] O Jehovah! in trouble they missed thee; they poured out a faint prayer, when thy chastening touched them. Like as a woman with child, that draweth near her delivery, is in pain, and crieth out in her pangs; so did we shrink at thy presence, O Jehovah. We were with child, we were in pain, we bore as it were a wind; we brought not the land unto full salvation, neither were inhabitants of the world begotten.

5.

[19.] O might thy dead (O Jehovah!) revive! might my dead bodies arise!—Awake and shout, ye dwellers in the dust, for thy dew is a dew of light, and the earth shall beget the shades. Go, my people, into thy chambers, and shut thy door behind thee; hide thyself for a little moment, until the indignation passeth over. For behold, Jehovah cometh out of his place to punish the inhabitants of the earth for their iniquity; and the earth shall disclose her bloodshed, and shall no more cover her slain.

6.

[XXVII. 1.] In that day Jehovah, with his sore, and great, and strong sword, shall punish the Leviathan the fleet serpent, and the Leviathan the coiled serpent; and he shall slay the dragon that is in the sea. In that day sing ye thus of the lovely vineyard:

'I Jehovah am the keeper thereof; every moment do I
 water it;
Lest harm should visit it, I keep it night and day;
I have no wrath: O might I but meet briars and thorns,
 I would march through them with war, I would kindle
 them altogether.
Or else let each one take hold of my defence; let him
 make peace with me,
With me let him make peace.'

Hereafter Jacob shall take root; Israel shall blossom and bud; and they shall fill the face of the world with fruit.

7.

[7.] Hath he smitten him as he smote those that smote him? or was he slain as his slayers were slain? By affrighting her, by sending her away, didst thou plead with her: he drove her away with his rough blast in the day of the east wind. Therefore by this is the iniquity of Jacob purged, (and this is all the fruit of putting away his sin,) that he maketh all the altar-stones as chalk-stones that are beaten in sunder, so that the Asherim and the pillars of the sun arise no more. Yea, the defenced city is solitary, a region unpeopled, and forsaken as a wilderness; there the calf feedeth, and there he lieth down, and consumeth the branches thereof. When the twigs thereof are dry, they are broken off; women come and set them on fire: yea, it is a people of no understanding; therefore he that made them hath no mercy on them, and he that formed them sheweth them no favour.

8.

[12.] 'And in that day shall Jehovah beat out ears from the flood of the River to the torrent of Egypt, and ye shall be gathered one by one, ye sons of Israel. And in that day a great trumpet shall be blown, and they shall come which were lost in the land of Assyria, and the outcasts in the land of Egypt, and shall worship Jehovah in the holy mount, even in Jerusalem.'

Par 1 *For walls and bulwarks* 'Jerusalem, which is now lying in ruins, shall be rebuilt, but without its fortifications.' Comp lx 18; Zech ii 4.

By a sure purpose. The Geneva Bible is very nearly correct: 'By an assured purpose wilt thou preserve perfite peace, because they trusted in thee' The Heb *yéser* is often, but improperly, rendered 'mind,' whereas it simply means 'a thing framed,' wheth'er materially, as in xxix 16, or mentally, as in Gen viii 21. Hence the only other admissible rendering is, 'Him that is immoveable in purpose, thou wilt keep in perfect peace,' taking *yéser* as the accusative, placed first for the sake of emphasis, like the phrase at the beginning of xxii. 2. But the use of *yissor* as the imperfect of *yasar* in ch xl–xlvi, and the fondness of the prophet for paronomasia, induce us to prefer the above rendering Comp xxv 1 (end), and 12 (beg.). Ewald (second edition) renders, 'Firm is the hope: peace, peace wilt thou form'

Jah Jehovah A combination which occurs only here and in xii. 2. Comp. xxv. 1 (Heb.).

The path for the upright. 'In strong contrast to the lot of the tyrant, the course of the righteous nation shall be prosperous.'

Par. 2 *Yea, for the path,* &c 'Indeed, how earnest was our longing, during the night of trouble, for the judgments which should usher in the Messianic blessedness!' For the connection of the following words, see Introduction.

Thy name and thy memorial. An allusion to Exod. iii 15.

The land of uprightness, i e. the land inhabited by the upright, probably alluding to Judah.

Par. 3. *The fire of thine enemies,* i e. the fire appointed for them.

Other lords than thee Jehovah was the rightful lord of Israel. Comp. lxiii 19

Will we celebrate, i e with thanksgivings for our deliverance

The dead will not revive 'There is nothing more to be feared from the oppressors, for they are dead'

K

Therefore didst thou visit and destroy them. Not, 'because the dead revive not, therefore didst thou destroy them,' but, 'because they saw not thy hand, because other lords had dominion over us.'

Par. 4 *They poured out a faint prayer* Ewald (second edition) renders: 'In affliction "thy discipline" was whispered by them' For the objections to this and other interpretations, see 'Notes and Criticisms,' pp. 27, 28.

We bore as it were a wind The prophet here places himself mentally in the position of the restored exiles, and sympathizes with their disappointment at their scanty population and precarious tenure of their country

Par. 5. *O might thy dead (O Jehovah!) revive!* These words are spoken from the standing-point of the previous verse. Their import is 'O that my fellow-exiles, who died before the fall of the oppressors, might rise from their graves, and swell the numbers of the restored nation!' This is the first indisputable anticipation of the dogma of the resurrection of *individuals*, Hos vi. 2 and Ezek. xxxvii referring only to the regeneration of the *people*. For a long time the dogma of the Resurrection was supposed to be borrowed from Zoroastrianism, and in spite of the positive assertions of Dr. Pusey ('Daniel the Prophet,' pp 512 517), this can hardly be said to have been disproved. For granting the late origin of the Bundehesh, we may still hold that 'the author of that book has in all essential points only handed on the ancient (Zoroastrian) doctrine,' a view, which, so far from being only rationalistic, is distinctly maintained by the Roman Catholic critic, Windischmann   (See his 'Zoroastrische Studien,' pp 231-260) We confess, however, that the influence of Persian ideas at so early a period appears to us improbable   If we are not mistaken, the prophecy before us was written prior to the time of Cyrus, but even if the true date be later, the idea of the Resurrection, so far as it was Persian, was not likely to be more acceptable to the prophets than that of Dualism, which one of the greatest of them (Isa. xlv. 7) most emphatically rejected   Are not the premonitions of the doctrine in Hosea and Ezekiel sufficient to account for its ultimate development ?

Awake and shout The aspiration of the previous clause has developed into a joyful hope

A dew of light. Literally, 'a dew of lights,' i e. of perfect light. The dew of Jehovah is so full of light that it draws forth the shades from the darkness of the underworld   Light and life are correlative ideas, as in Ps xxxvi. 9; Job iii 16, 20   Another rendering is 'a dew of herbs,' i e a refreshing dew, like that which falls upon the herbs. But the connection appears to require some more distinct ground for rejoicing, such as that presented above.

Par. 6. *The Leviathan.* Not only the actual enemy, Babylon, but also all conceivable hostile powers shall be subdued. The dragon is the constant symbol of Egypt; see li. 9, Ezek. xxix. 3, xxxii. 2. The two Leviathans are evidently kindred or neighbouring nations, probably Assyria and Babylonia, both mentioned in vv. 12 and 13.

The lovely vineyard. For *kerem chemer*, 'a vineyard of fiery wine,' read *kerem chemed*, 'a vineyard of desire,' with the Lxx, and most modern interpreters.

O might I but meet briars. Jehovah longs to be able to demonstrate his zeal on behalf of his people. Comp x 17.

Par 7. *Therefore by this,* &c. However painful the exile might be, it was not so severe a punishment as that suffered by Assyria. Therefore the only act required on Israel's part to render the expiation complete, and all the needful ratification ('fruit' = effect) of his conversion, is the destruction of the idolatrous altars Meantime 'the defenced city,' Babylon, is desolate and in ruins

Par. 8. *The River.* That is, the Euphrates.

The torrent of Egypt, i. e. the Wady el-Arish, on the frontier of Palestine and Egypt Comp. 1 Kings viii. 65.

Which were lost in the land of Assyria. The mention of Assyria and Egypt as the seats of the Israelitish exiles points to a time previous to the Babylonian conquest. Comp xi. 11. The passage, as Ewald has suggested, with great appearance of reason, may be quoted from some lost prophecy of Isaiah.

APPENDIX III.

(Isa. xxi. 1–10.)

A RUMOUR of the expedition of Cyrus has reached the Jewish exiles in Babylon. The prophet is instructed by a Divine revelation that nothing less is contemplated than the complete overthrow of the empire. The immediate effect of this news upon his mind is at first sight peculiar, and yet is in the highest degree natural. His sympathy with the fortunes of his foreign home almost seems to blind him to the higher interests of his own people. So much may be gathered from the first strophe of the prophecy.

An interval then elapses, during which the prophet fixes his eye intently on the progress of Cyrus, and the strange variety of tributaries which compose his army. At length the advanced guard of the Persians appears, and a second revelation rewards the prophet for his constancy. He announces, using the past tense of prophetic certainty, that 'Babylon is fallen,' that is, shall certainly fall within a brief space.

For energy and pictorial effect this prophecy can hardly be paralleled. We may imagine the deep impression it would produce, when circulated, like the kindred songs of Arndt in 1813–1815, from one to another among the Jewish patriots. Nothing short of such a popularity would have preserved so brief a composition from oblivion, and its brevity was probably the reason of the place found for it by the later editor among the minor prophecies of Isaiah. The title of 'the wilderness by the sea' attached to it in the received text is an enigmatical reference to the desolation in store for Babylon; compare with it the title of Dumah, 'silence,' prefixed, apparently by the same editor, to the prophecy against Edom, xxi. 11. The Euphrates, like the Nile (xix. 5), is called 'the sea,' probably with an allusion to its annual inundations.

1.

[**XXI. 1.**] As whirlwinds in the south pass through, so it cometh from the wilderness, from the terrible land. A grievous vision is declared unto me · 'The robber continueth to rob, and the spoiler to spoil. Go up, O Elam; besiege, O Media; all the sighing will I make to cease.' Therefore are my loins filled with pain; pangs have taken hold upon me, as the pangs of a woman that travaileth; I am so bowed down, that I cannot hear, I am so dismayed, that I cannot see. My heart panteth; horror hath affrighted me; the twilight that I delight in is changed into a time for trembling. They set the table, they spread the carpets, they eat, they drink; (a cry is heard,) 'Stand up, ye princes, anoint the shield.'

2.

[6.] For thus the Lord said unto me. ' Go, set a watchman, let him declare what he seeth; and when he seeth a troop of horsemen by pairs, a troop on asses, a troop on camels, he shall hearken diligently with much heed.' And the watchman cried with the voice of a lion, 'My lord, I stand continually upon the watchtower in the day-time, and I am set in my ward every night.' And behold, (even as he spake,) there came a troop of horsemen by pairs; and he took up his speech, and said, 'Babylon is fallen, is fallen, and all the graven images of her gods he hath broken unto the ground.' O my people threshed and trodden! that which I have heard of Jehovah of Hosts, the God of Israel, have I declared unto you.

Par 1. *From the wilderness*, i. e Media or Elymais, a region unknown to the prophet, and therefore styled by him 'the wilderness.'

All the sighing, i e the oppression of the Babylonian rule.

They spread the carpets. This rendering is due to Hitzig, and commends itself by its consistency with the parallel member of the clause The Vulgate, followed by Auth Vers, has 'contemplare in speculâ,' deriving *safith* from *safah*, to view. But *safah* may also mean 'to cover;' comp. with Furst *sif* and *sefā*, 'a mat,' in Talmudic Hebrew.

Stand up, ye princes. The banquet is in full course, when it is interrupted by a call to arms

Anoint the shield. The leathern covering of the shield was smeared over with oil, to prevent it from being injured by rain, and above all to let the weapons of the enemy glide off

Par. 2 *Set a watchman.* The personality of a prophet is, as it were, divided. Sometimes the character of the recipient of revelation predominates in him, sometimes that of the spokesman and expositor of the word whispered (Heb. *ne'ūm*) or the vision seen The watchman in this passage bears the former of these two characters Comp Hab ii. 1, which seems to be the source from which the Babylonian prophet drew

A troop on asses, a troop on camels. Some of the tribes in the Persian army rode on asses or camels, Herod. vi. 86; comp i. 80, where Cyrus gains the victory over Crœsus by his camels, and iv. 129, where the asses are of equal service to Darius Hystaspis against the Scythians.

He shall hearken, i e for a second oracle or revelation

With the voice of a lion, i e with a deep groan of impatience. Comp. v. 30.

O my people threshed and trodden. Literally, 'O my grain, and son of my threshing-floor.'

APPENDIX IV.

(Isa xiii. 2–xiv 23)

ANOTHER account from one of the exiled prophets of the doom impending over Babylon. The Medes are described in it as already crossing the mountains of the frontier. Soon they will enter on their Divinely sanctioned work of destruction, and how terribly will they perform it! The vast Babylonian empire, and more especially its guilty capital, shall be well-nigh depopulated. The foreign merchants shall barely escape by a precipitate flight, or, if they are taken prisoners, shall be savagely murdered, while the ruined palaces of Babylon shall become so awful a desolation, that even the wandering Arab shall refuse to lodge there. Yet this is the very moment selected by the Divine compassion for the deliverance of Israel. They shall return home with a train of captives and proselytes, and utter a song of triumph on their fallen tyrant. The date of the prophecy is determined by its contents, which relate to the march of Cyrus against Babylon. Comp. Part I with Jer. l, li, which seem to have been written about the same time, and Part II with Ezek xxxii, of which, as Ewald has observed, it is an imitation.

PART I.

1.

[**XIII. 2.**] Lift ye up an ensign upon a bare mountain, call aloud unto them, wave the hand, that they may go into the gates of the princes. 'I have given a charge to my consecrated ones, I have also summoned my mighty ones for mine anger, even mine own that triumph proudly.' Hark! a murmuring in the mountains, like as of a great people; hark! the rushing of the king-doms of nations gathered together: Jehovah of Hosts is mustering the host of war. They come from a far country, from the end of heaven, even Jehovah, and the weapons of his indignation to destroy the whole earth. Wail ye, for the day of Jehovah is at hand; it shall come as a mighty destruction from the Almighty. Therefore shall all hands be slack, and every man's heart shall melt; they shall be affrighted, while pangs and torments take them, writhing as a woman that travaileth, staring one at another, with faces like unto flames.

2.

[9.] Behold, the day of Jehovah cometh, cruel with fury and burning anger, to lay the earth desolate, and to destroy the sinners thereof out of it. For the stars of heaven, and the Orions thereof, shall not give their light; the sun shall be darkened in his going forth, and the moon shall not cause her light to shine. Then will I visit their evil upon the world, and their iniquity upon the wicked; and I will cause the arrogancy of the proud to cease, and lay low the haughtiness of the terrible; and I will make men more precious than fine gold, and people than the golden wedge of Ophir. Therefore will I cause the heavens to shake, and the earth shall move quaking from her place, at the fury of Jehovah of Hosts, and in the day of his burning anger. Then like a roe that is chased, and like sheep which have none to gather them, they shall every man turn to his own people, and flee every one into his own land; every one that is surprised shall be thrust through, and every one that is taken shall fall by the sword; their sucklings also shall be dashed to pieces before their eyes; their houses shall be spoiled, and their wives ravished.

3.

[**17.**] Behold, I stir up the Medes against them, which regard not silver, and have no delight in gold. Their bows shall dash youths to pieces, and they shall have no pity on the fruit of the womb; their eye shall not look kindly on children. And Babylon, the glory of kingdoms, the ornament of the Chaldees' excellency, shall be as when God overthrew Sodom and Gomorrah. It shall never be inhabited, neither shall it be dwelt in for many generations; neither shall the Arabians pitch tent there, neither shall shepherds make their fold there; but there jackals shall lie down, and owls shall fill their houses; ostriches shall dwell there, and satyrs shall dance there; wolves shall howl in the great houses thereof, and dogs in the palaces of delight: her time is well-nigh fulfilled, and her days shall not be prolonged.

Par 1. *Upon a bare mountain*, i. e. that nothing may prevent the banner from being seen at a distance

My consecrated ones. The war, to which the Medes are summoned, is a crusade against the enemies of Jehovah Comp. Ps cx 3, Jer xxii 7, Zeph 1 7.

Mine own that triumph proudly. A phrase adopted from Zeph. iii. 11.

In the mountains, i e the range of Zagros, on the Median frontier, from which an invasion might naturally have been expected According to Herod. i 189, Cyrus actually invaded Babylonia from the East, after crossing the Gyndes.

As a mighty destruction from the Almighty The original is in Joel i 15.

With faces like unto flames, i e changing in quick succession from red to pale. (Delitzsch)

Par 2. *The Orions*, i e. Orion and the constellations equal to it in splendour. Comp Joel ii 10.

They shall every man turn, i. e. the foreigners attracted to Babylon by its commerce Comp xlvii. 15.

Par. 3. The Medes. The name of 'Persians' was not yet in general circulation, we need not therefore be surprised at not finding it in our prophecy. It occurs, indeed, in Ezek. xxvii, xxxviii, but in company with other names which were certainly unfamiliar to the great majority of Hebrews.

Which regard not silver, i. e who are not to be tempted by the offer of a ransom.

It shall never be inhabited. This description has received an ideal, and not a circumstantial fulfilment, as indeed its rhetorical tone should have led us to expect. So far from being uninhabited, 'a town of considerable population (Hillah), villages, date-groves, and gardens are found still on the very site of ancient Babylon.' And so far from being deserted by the Arabs, the Birs Nimroud 'is occupied by an Arab tribe, who were actually encamped on the foot (i. e. of the Birs Nimroud) on the N.W, or Hillah side of the ruins, when I (General Chesney) was there.' See extracts from a private communication of General Chesney in B. W. Newton's 'Babylon, its Revival and Final Desolation,' pp. 38-42.

Satyrs. See note on paragraph 2 of the first of these appendices.

PART II.

1.

[**XIV. 1.**] For Jehovah will have mercy on Jacob, and will yet choose Israel, and give them rest in their own land, and the stranger shall join himself to them, and associate himself to the house of Jacob; and the peoples shall take them, and bring them to their place, and the house of Israel shall take them in possession in the land of Jehovah for servants and for handmaids. and they shall take them captives, whose captives they were, and they shall rule over their tyrants. And in the day that Jehovah shall give thee rest from thy pain and thy disquietness, and from the hard bondage which men laid upon thee, thou shalt take up this taunting speech against the king of Babylon, and say :—

[4.]   2.

How still hath the tyrant become ; how still his insolent
        dealing !
·Jehovah hath broken the staff of the wicked, the sceptre
        of the rulers,
Which smote the peoples in fury with a continual stroke,
    Which trode down the nations in anger with an untempe-
        rate step !
The whole earth is at rest, and is quiet : they break forth
        into shouting.
    The cypresses also rejoice at thee, and the cedars of
        Lebanon, (saying,)
'Since thou art laid down, no feller will come up against
        us.'

[9.]   3.

The underworld is disquieted for thee to meet thee at thy
        coming :
    It stirreth up the shades for thee, even all the leaders of
        the earth ;
        It raiseth up from their thrones all the kings of the
        nations.
They all shall answer and say unto thee,
    ' Thou also art become impotent as we ; thou art become
        like unto us !'
Thy pride is brought down to the underworld, and the
        melody of thy lutes :
    Corruption is spread beneath thee, and the worms are thy
        covering.

[12.] 4.

How art thou fallen from heaven, O Lucifer, son of the
morning!
How art thou cut down to the ground, which didst conquer the nations!
Yet *thou* didst say in thine heart, 'I will ascend into
heaven,
I will exalt my throne above the stars of God,
And I will sit upon the mountain of the gods, in the
utmost parts of the north;
I will ascend above the heights of the clouds, and make
me like the Most High.'
Nay; thou art brought down to the underworld, to the
innermost parts of the pit.

[16.] 5.

They that see thee shall narrowly look upon thee, and con-
sider thee, (saying,)
'Is this the man that made the earth to tremble, that did
shake kingdoms;
That made the earth as a wilderness, and brake down
the cities thereof;
That did not send his prisoners home at liberty?'
All the kings of the earth, even all of them, lie with honour,
every one in his house;
But thou art cast far from thy grave, as an abhorred weed;
Wrapped in them that are slain, that are thrust through
with the sword,
That go down to the stones of the pit, as a carcase trod-
den under foot.

[20.]   6.

Thou shalt not be joined with them in burial,

  Because thou hast destroyed thy land, and slain thy
    people .

No mention be made for ever of the seed of evildoers !

Prepare a place of slaughter for his sons, for the iniquity of
    their fathers ;

  That they do not arise, nor take the land in possession,
    nor fill the face of the world with ruins !

Par 1 *Shall take them in possession* The heathen shall seek admittance
within the Jewish community, whose religion has recently received so striking
an attestation, even at the price of renouncing their personal liberty. Comp.
xlv. 14.

Par 2 *His insolent dealing* For *madhēbhah* read *marhebhah* with most critics
since J. D. Michaelis (about 1770).

Step For *'urdāf* read *mirdath* with Doederlein (1789).

Par. 3 *The underworld*, here personified, is filled with an unusual agitation.
The phantom-kings (εἴδωλα καμόντων) have been hitherto seated on their
thrones in passive silence. The arrival of so eminent a guest breaks the calm
Comp 1 Sam xxviii 14, 15, where Samuel is said to 'come up' from the underworld wearing his accustomed mantle (as the kings here are still enthroned,
even among the shades), and to be 'disquieted' by being reminded of human
affairs There is also a striking parallel in Job iii 13–18, which may have
floated before the mind of the prophet.

Thy lutes For the importance attached by the Babylonians to music, see
Dan iii 5

Par. 4 *Lucifer* Literally, 'the shining one,' i e. the morning-star.

The mountain of the gods Literally, 'the mountain of the assembly' An
allusion to the myth of the mountain-abode of the gods common to various
Asiatic nations (including, apparently, the Babylonians), and exemplified in
Meru, the sacred mountain of the Vedas, and the Iranian Hara Berezaiti, or
Albordj, where Mithra and Yima were believed to dwell Possibly, too,
Ararat, where the ark of Noah rested, was originally the sacred mountain of
the Hebrews. At any rate, a peculiar sanctity is attached to the north in the
Old Testament records Thus the burnt-offering was to be sacrificed on the

north side of the altar (Lev. i. 11), and the four cherubim in the vision of Ezekiel are described as coming from the north (Ezek. i. 4). The temple itself possessed an additional distinction in the eyes of a Psalmist in virtue of its situation 'in the utmost parts of the north' (or north-east) of the city (Ps. xlviii. 3).

The innermost parts of the pit. A phrase corresponding to that in verse 13, and chosen to mark the contrast between the presumption of the tyrant and his ruin.

Par. 5. *In his house*, i. e. in a magnificent mausoleum.

Wrapped in them that are slain. Bunsen: 'Dein Todtenkleid (sind) Erschlagene.'

That go down to the stones of the pit. The other warriors receive the honours of burial, but the king of Babylon is cast out for a prey to the wild beasts.

Par. 6. *Thou shalt not be joined with them*, &c. A special dishonour for kings, 2 Chron. xxi. 20, xxiv. 25.

Ruins For *'arim*, cities, read *'iyyim*, heaps, with Hitzig. Comp. note on xxiv. 15.

APPENDIX V.

(Isa. xl-lxvi.)

BOOK I.

CYRUS THE LIBERATOR.

TOWARDS the end of the Babylonian exile, when the victories gained by Cyrus over the Medes and Lydians had begun to excite the expectations of the Jewish patriots, another eloquent herald of the advent of the liberator composed and circulated a prophecy. We may perhaps venture to fix his date approximatively B.C. 546, seven or eight years before the edict of Cyrus. His work is not a mere collection of fugitive pieces, a prophetic anthology, but an artistic whole, divided into three books of equal length, two of which are terminated by the refrain, 'There is no peace to the wicked,' and the third by a detailed description of the judgment thus vaguely indicated. The logical divisions, indeed, are not so clearly marked as the artistic. Often a subject is

treated cursorily and imperfectly, and then suddenly dropped, to receive a more complete development on some future opportunity. But
although the progress of ideas is somewhat irregular, its reality will be
evident from the salient points of each book, viz. (1) Cyrus the liberator, i. e. Jehovah has decreed the redemption of his people; (2) vicarious atonement, i. e. the suffering of the pious shall be rewarded by the
regeneration of their country; (3) the new Jerusalem, i. e. the religion
of Israel in the future shall consist, not in external ceremonies, but in
sanctification. For further details the reader is referred to the running
analysis prefixed to each book.

The first book is opened by a succession of heavenly voices which
address 'the goodly fellowship of the prophets' in Babylon,—'Comfort ye my people,' 'Prepare the way of Jehovah,' 'Cry that all flesh is
grass.' The call is obeyed, and the advent of the Divine Liberator
(not as yet of Cyrus) is proclaimed. Jehovah himself is on his way,
the valiant champion, the tender guide of his people. He is incom-
parable for wisdom and irresistible in might, and therefore is far
from deserving the strange distrust with which his people regard him
(chap. i). A more definite announcement follows. The chosen agent
in Israel's redemption will be that wonderful Eastern king, whose
victorious career the heathen are so powerless to explain (chap. ii).
The idolaters having thus been silenced, the genius of Israel is next
apostrophised as the ideal 'servant of Jehovah,' and assured of his
high spiritual destiny (chap. iii. pars. 1–4). True, that there are
serious obstacles to the attainment of this. Israel, taken as a whole,
is unconscious of its responsibility, and this is the real source of its past
calamities, but now the crisis has arrived, and Jehovah himself will
interpose. On the one hand, he will revive the spiritual energies of his
people, and on the other, he will overthrow the tyranny of Babylon,
not for Israel's sake, but out of free grace (chap. iii. par. 5—chap. v.
par. 3). One more complaint is uttered of the national unworthiness,
followed by a promise of complete forgiveness, and a justification of the
Divine procedure (chap. iv. par. 4), and then the first obstacle to redemption is dismissed, and a calmer tone succeeds.

The fifth chapter is in the main hortatory. It begins with a description of the spiritual blessings reserved for the regenerate nation, the numbers of which shall be swelled by a large accession of Gentile proselytes. The prophet then proceeds to justify his enthusiasm by an appeal to the fulfilment of prophecy and the signal failure of idolatry. He contrasts the ludicrous unreality of the heathen gods with the moral perfections and providential activity of the God of Israel. These are manifested in that great achievement, which in the language of prophetic inspiration, and in the counsels of eternity, is already past. Jehovah has removed, that is, he is about to remove, the two great obstacles to Israel's realization of its destiny, the one, by pardoning its long accumulation of sins, the other, by raising up Cyrus as the instrument of its restoration.

In the sixth chapter, Jehovah addresses Cyrus by name, gives him the title of ' Jehovah's anointed one' (Heb. *Māshiach* = Messiah) and assigns three reasons for the success vouchsafed to him, viz. (1) that he might acknowledge Jehovah as the true God, (2) that Israel might be liberated, and (3) that the world might be converted from false religions. The Messiahship thus accorded to a Gentile may seem to many Jews humiliating or even inconceivable, but the murmurers are admonished by the prophet not to criticise the plan of the Creator. Not only shall Cyrus restore the Jewish exiles freely and honourably, but three representative nations, the Egyptians, the Ethiopians, and the Sabeans, shall be impelled by a desire for the true religion to offer themselves as vassals to those who possess it. And these are but the forerunners of a much more extensive conversion. The Divine promise is clear and unmistakeable, that a day is coming when all those Gentiles, who have escaped the impending judgment, shall recognize Jehovah as the only true God.

The tone of the seventh chapter is less enthusiastic. The prophet first describes in highly picturesque language the ruin of the Chaldean idolatry. He points out the superiority of the God of Israel to the impotent and burdensome gods of Babylon. He then exhorts the polytheistic party among the exiles, who are indifferent to the prospect of redemption, seriously to reflect on the course of history and of prophecy. In the eighth chapter, the progress of ideas is interrupted by a sarcastic song on the fall of Babylon, not however from a distinctively religious point of view. This is composed of four strophes, each of which taunts the captive enemy with the loss of some envied distinction, such as luxury, foreign empire, and skill in magic and astrology.

In the ninth chapter the prophet returns to the unbelieving Jewish renegades. Their 'hardness of heart' has had a peculiar effect on the course of prophetic revelation. The 'former things,' i. e. the exile and its duration, and even the fall of Babylon, had been revealed to much earlier prophets, such as Jeremiah and the author of Isa. xxiv–xxvii, but the restoration of the Jews by means of Cyrus is so extraordinary an event, and so undeserved a mercy, that it is announced only at the eleventh hour. The book concludes with a tender appeal to the self-love of the readers, to the effect that the existence and prosperity of the nation are intimately connected with their fidelity to Jehovah. But it seems as if the prophet were afraid that his admonition was too gently expressed. He would make one last effort to rouse his countrymen from their torpor, and darts forth at a venture these sharp and menacing words, No peace to the wicked!

CHAPTER I.

1.

[**XL. 1.**] Comfort ye, comfort ye my people, saith your God. Speak ye kindly unto Jerusalem, and cry unto her, that her warfare is accomplished, that her punishment is finished, that she hath received of the hand of Jehovah double for all her sins. Hark, one crieth, saying, Prepare ye in the wilderness a way for Jehovah, lay evenly in the desert an highway for our God. Let every valley be exalted, and every mountain and hill be made low, and let the steep be made even, and the rough places plain, and the glory of Jehovah shall be revealed, and all flesh shall see it together: for the mouth of Jehovah hath spoken it. Hark, one saith, Cry. And he said, What shall I cry?—All flesh is grass, and all the goodliness thereof as the flower of the field: the grass withereth, the flower fadeth, if the breath of Jehovah but blow upon it; surely the people is grass. The grass withereth, the flower fadeth, but the word of our God shall stand for ever.

2.

[9.] Get thee up into an high mountain, O Zion, thou heraldess of joy; lift up thy voice with strength, O Jerusalem, thou heraldess of joy; lift it up, be not afraid; say unto the cities of Judah, Behold your God! Behold, the Lord Jehovah will come like a valiant one, while his arm ruleth for him; behold, his reward is with him, and his recompense before him. He shall feed his flock like a shepherd, he shall gather the lambs with his arm, and carry them in his bosom, and shall gently lead those that are with young.

3.

[12.] Who measured the waters with the hollow of his hand, and proportioned the heavens with a span, and comprehended the dust of the earth in a tierce, and weighed the mountains in scales, and the hills in a balance? Who proportioned the Spirit of Jehovah, and being a man shewed him his counsel? With whom took he counsel, that he might instruct him, and guide him in the path of right, and teach him knowledge, and shew to him the way of perfect understanding? Behold, nations are as a drop hanging on a bucket, and are counted as small dust on a balance; behold, he lifteth up the sea coasts as gossamer. Lebanon is not sufficient to burn, nor the beasts thereof sufficient for burnt offerings. All nations are as nothing before him; he reputeth them as things of nought and vanity. To whom then will ye liken God? and what likeness will ye compare unto him?

4.

[19.] As for the image, a craftsman hath cast it, and a smith spreadeth it over with gold, and fasteneth it with silver chains! He that is too poor for a great oblation chooseth a wood that will not decay; he seeketh unto him a cunning workman, to set up an image that will not shake! Will ye not perceive? will ye not hear at last? hath it not been told you from the beginning? have ye not understood it since the foundations of the earth? It is he that sitteth upon the vault of the earth, so that the inhabitants thereof are as locusts, that stretcheth out the heavens as gauze, and spreadeth them out as a tent to dwell in; that bringeth potentates to nothing, and maketh the judges of the earth as a chaos. They are scarce planted or sown, and scarce has their stock taken root in the earth, when he bloweth upon them, so that they wither, and a tempest taketh them away as stubble. To whom then will ye liken me, that I may be equal to him? saith the Holy One. Lift up your eyes on high, and behold. Who hath made yonder heavens? It is he that bringeth out their host by number, that calleth them all by names, by whose infinite might and abundant power not one is wanting.

5.

[27] Why sayest thou, O Jacob, and speakest, O Israel, My way is hidden from Jehovah, and my right is passed over by my God? Hast thou not perceived? hast thou not heard? Jehovah is an everlasting God, the maker of the ends of the earth; he fainteth

not, neither is weary; there is no searching of his understanding. He giveth power to the faint, and unto the feeble sendeth abundant strength. Youths may faint and be weary, and the strongest men may stumble; but they that wait upon Jehovah shall renew their strength; they shall lift up their wings as eagles; they shall run and not be weary; and they shall walk, and not faint.

Par. 1 *Kindly* Literally, 'to the heart' Comp. Gen. xxxiv. 3, l. 21.

Her warfare The Babylonian exile is likened to the comfortless condition of a soldier on a campaign. Comp Job vii 1, 'Hath not man a warfare upon earth?'

Double for all her sins The key to this passage is furnished by Jer xvi 14–18, where the unparalleled grandeur of the second restoration of the Jews is justified by the extreme severity of their previous chastisement. Comp Isa. lxi. 7, 'For your shame ye shall have double'

Hark, one crieth. A celestial voice is heard by the prophet and his companions, i e. they are conscious of a Divine revelation.

In the desert. An allusion to the deliverance of the Jews from their first captivity in Egypt, which was typical of the second.

And he said, i e. the prophet Observe the studious self-concealment of the author.

All flesh is grass. The prophet's first emotion on receiving the revelation of the fall of Babylon is one of awe; his second, one of gratitude Comp. xxi. 1–10.

Par 2 *O Zion* The Zion of this prophecy is an ideal personage,—the spirit or genius of Jerusalem, which still hovered, as it were, over the ruins Comp xlix 14–19, lii 1, 2, 7–9, lxii 6.

His arm, i e. the manifestation of God's power, as in li 9, lxiii 12. Similarly the word of God is personified in lv. 11.

His reward, i e. the fulfilment of his promise to the faithful.

Par. 3. *A tierce;* probably the third part of an ephah, or a little more than a peck. The word occurs besides only in Ps lxxx. 6.

His counsel, i. e. that of restoring Israel; comp. xli. 28.

The sea coasts, i e. the countries bordering on the Mediterranean.

Par. 4. *The image,* i. e 'Will ye liken such an image as this to me?' A derisive description of this kind is natural in a prophet who had mixed much with the heathen. Comp. Jer. x. 3, 4

As a chaos, i. e. like the condition of the universe before the 'creation' of light. The word *Tohu*, 'chaos,' occurs in Gen. 1. 2.

The vault of the earth. The heaven, according to the Hebrew cosmogony, was a circular arch resting on the waters which surrounded the flat round surface of the earth. Comp. Prov. viii. 27.

The Holy One. Isaiah's phrase, 'the Holy One of Israel,' is shortened by our prophet into a quasi-proper name.

Par. **5.** *My right;* with an allusion to the oppression exercised by the Babylonians.

CHAPTER II.

1.

[XLI. 1] Keep silence towards me, O coasts of the sea, and let the peoples renew their strength: let them draw near, then let them speak; let us approach the judgment-seat together. Who hath stirred up from the east the man that is accompanied by victory? Who giveth up nations before him, and causeth him to trample on kings, and maketh their sword as dust, and their bow as driven stubble? Meantime he pursueth them, and passeth safely, by a way that before he had not trodden. Who hath wrought and performed this? He that called forth the generations from the beginning; even I, Jehovah, am the first, and with the last I am the same.

2.

[5] The sea coasts have seen it, and are afraid; the ends of the earth tremble; they already approach and come; they help every one his neighbour, and every one saith to his brother, Be of good courage. The caster encourageth the goldsmith, and he that smootheth with the hammer him that striketh the anvil; he saith of the sodering, It is good, so he fasteneth it with nails, that it may not shake.

3.

[8] But thou, Israel, my servant, and Jacob whom I have chosen, seed of Abraham my friend; thou, whom I have fetched from the ends of the earth, and called from distant parts thereof, and unto whom I said, Thou art my servant, I have chosen thee, and not cast thee away:—fear thou not, for I am with thee; be not dismayed, for I am thy God; I will strengthen thee; yea, I will help thee; yea, I will uphold thee with the right hand of my righteousness. Behold, all they that were incensed against thee shall be ashamed and confounded, and they that strive with thee shall be as nothing, and shall perish. Thou shalt seek them, but shalt not find them, even them that contended with thee; they that warred against thee shall be as nothing, and as a thing of nought. For I Jehovah am thy God, which hold thy right hand, which say unto thee, Fear not; I will help thee.

4.

[14.] Fear not, thou worm Jacob, and ye few men of Israel; I will help thee, (the utterance is Jehovah's,) and the Holy One of Israel is thy redeemer. Behold, I will make thee a threshing-instrument, even a new and sharp one, having many teeth: thou shalt thresh the mountains, and beat them small, and shalt make the hills as chaff; thou shalt fan them, so that the wind shall carry them away, and the tempest shall scatter them; but thou shalt exult in Jehovah, and glory in the Holy One of Israel.

5.

[17.] Ah, the afflicted and the poor, which seek water, but there is none, and their tongue is parched with thirst!—I Jehovah will hear them, I the God of Israel will not forsake them. I will open rivers on barren hills, and fountains in the midst of the valleys; I will make the wilderness a pool of water, and the dry land springs of water. I will plant in the wilderness the cedar, the shittah-tree, and the myrtle, and the oil tree; I will set in the desert the cypress, and the plane and the larch together; that men may see and perceive, and consider and understand at once, that the hand of Jehovah hath performed this, and the Holy One of Israel hath made it.

6.

[21.] Produce your cause, saith Jehovah; bring forth your strong reasons, saith the King of Jacob. Let them bring forth and shew unto us what shall happen: yea, shew ye the former things, what they be, that we may consider them, and perceive the latter end of them: or declare us things for to come. Shew the things that are to come hereafter, that we may perceive that ye are gods; yea, do good, or do evil, that we may be amazed and see it together. Behold, ye are of nothing, and your work is of nought: an abomination is he that chooseth you.

7.

[25] I stirred up one from the north, and he came; yea, one from the east, who shall call upon my name; and he shall tread upon governors as upon mortar, and as the potter that treadeth clay. Who shewed this from the beginning, that we might know it, and before-time, that we might say, It is right? Yea, there was none that shewed; yea, there was none that declared; yea, there was none that heard your words. I am the first to give unto Zion an herald, even unto Jerusalem one that saith, Behold, behold them. For though I look, there is none; even from these there cometh no counsellor, that I might ask them, and they might give

an answer. Behold, they are all vanity; their works are nothing; their molten images are wind and confusion.

Par. 1. *The judgment-seat*, i. e. the tribunal of reason.

That is accompanied by victory. Literally, ' that righteousness meeteth at his foot.' Observe that throughout this prophecy the word ' righteousness' is equivalent to ' victory,' ' prosperity,' ' salvation' (see xlv. 8, li. 5, &c.), not without an allusion, however, to the fact that these blessings were in some sense or other merited by their recipients. Thus the tyranny and idolatry of the Babylonian empire rendered the cause of Cyrus a just one, and the ' righteousness' of Jehovah, that is, his fidelity to his revealed principles of action, was the guarantee to the prophet of its success So far there is nothing doctrinally peculiar in the use of the word. The Psalmists frequently claim the protection of God as a just recognition of their own righteousness. But the extension of the term in this prophecy to the interposition of Jehovah in behalf of the Jewish nation, the majority of whom are declared to be personally unworthy of it, is highly remarkable, and marks an advanced period in the development of Jewish religion. See note on par. 2 of next chapter.

Who hath wrought this? ' Who can be most easily conceived of as the author of the victories of Cyrus, Jehovah or the gods of the heathen? Certainly not the latter, for Cyrus is the bitter enemy of their worshippers.'

Par. 2. *The sea coasts.* Probably the subjects and allies of Crœsus.

They approach and come, i. e. they combine their forces to meet the invader.

The caster encourageth, &c. The gods, whom the heathen expect to rescue them, have first of all to be cast and gilded.

Par. 3. *My servant.* See note on the phrase ' servant of Jehovah,' in Par. 1 of next chapter.

From the ends of the earth, i. e. either from Mesopotamia or from Egypt (comp. Hos. xi. 1). If the former, we must suppose the writer to have shifted his point of view for the moment to Palestine.

Par. 4. *Ye few men.* Heb. *mĕthé*, an archaic word, of obscure origin, meaning ' men.' The plural is used designedly to imply the scattered and disorganised condition of the Jewish exiles. Lxx. ὀλιγοστὸς Ἰσραήλ.

A threshing-instrument. Imitated from Mic. iv. 13.

Par. 5. *I will plant*, &c. Some have inferred from the variety of trees mentioned that the prophecy could not have been written in Babylon But the acacia (' the shittah-tree') was common in Babylonia, and the other trees might have been found in the neighbouring mountains.

Par. 6. *Produce your cause.* The prophet returns to his previous subject,—

the futility of idolatry. The gods of the heathen are challenged to specify any of their predictions, which might now be in course of fulfilment, or else, to foretell something at once, whether good or evil, as a proof of their divinity.

Let them . . . shew unto us, i. e. unto Jehovah and his worshippers.

Par. 7. *From the north . . . from the rising of the sun,* i. e. from Media and from Persia, which were united under Cyrus.

Who shall call upon my name, i e who shall be converted to the religion of Jehovah For the affinities of the Persian religion to that of the Jews, consisting in the worship of a single supreme God, and a strong aversion to idolatry, see Rawlinson's ' Five Great Monarchies,' vol. iv. ch. vi.

Governors Heb. *seghanim,* a word probably of Persian origin, found only in writings of the Babylonian period. Delitzsch renders well ' satraps.'

Behold, behold them, i e. the Jews shall soon return from exile.

Counsellor, here used in the sense of prophet; comp xliv 26.

CHAPTER III.

1.

[**XLII. 1.**] Behold my servant, whom I uphold, mine elect, in whom my soul delighteth: I have put my spirit upon him, he shall bring religion to the nations. He shall not cry, nor call, nor cause his voice to be heard in the street; a bruised reed he shall not break, and a smoking wick he shall not quench; he shall bring forth religion truthfully. He shall not fail, nor be discouraged, till he have set religion in the earth, and the sea coasts wait for his doctrine.

2.

[**5**] Thus saith God, even Jehovah, that made the heavens, and stretched them forth, he that spread forth the earth and that which cometh out of it; he that giveth breath unto the people upon it, and spirit to them that walk therein; I Jehovah called thee in righteousness, that I might take hold of thee by the hand, that I might form thee and appoint thee for the covenant of the

people, for the light of the nations; to open the blind eyes, to bring out the captives from the prison, and them that sit in darkness from the house of restraint. I am Jehovah; that is my name: and my glory will I not give to another, neither my praise to graven images. Behold, the former things are come to pass, and new things do I declare; before they spring forth I tell you of them.

[10.]　　　　　　　　　　3.

Sing unto Jehovah a new song, and his praise from the end
　　of the earth,
　Ye that go down to the sea, and all that is therein; the
　　　sea coasts, and the inhabitants thereof.
Let the wilderness and the cities thereof lift up their voice,
　　the villages that Kedar doth inhabit;
　Let the inhabitants of Sela shout; let them cry from the
　　　top of the mountains;
Let them give glory unto Jehovah, and shew his praise in
　　the sea coasts!
　Jehovah shall go forth as a mighty man, he shall stir up
　　　his jealousy like a man of war;
He shall cry, yea, shout for the battle; he shall approve his
　　might against his enemies.

4.

[14.] I have long time holden my peace; I have been still, and refrained myself; now will I pant like a travailing woman, I will gasp and groan at once. I will make waste mountains and hills, and dry up their herbs; and I will make the rivers mainlands, and dry up the lakes. And I will bring the blind by a way that they knew not; I will lead them in paths that they have not known; I will make darkness light before them, and rough places plain. These things will I perform, and not forsake them. But they shall draw backward, and be greatly ashamed, that trust in graven images, that say to molten images, Ye are our gods.

5.

[18] Hear, ye deaf; and look, ye blind, that ye may see! Who is blind, but my servant? or deaf, as my messenger that I send? Who is blind as he that is devoted to God, and blind as the servant of Jehovah? Thou hast seen many things, but thou observest not; the ears are opened, but none heareth! Jehovah was pleased for his righteousness' sake to give them a doctrine great and glorious. Yet they are a people robbed and spoiled; they are all of them snared in holes, and hid in houses of restraint; they are become a prey, and there is no deliverer, a spoil, and there is none that saith, Restore. Who among you will give ear to this? who will hearken and be obedient for the time to come? Who gave up Jacob unto spoiling, and Israel unto robbers? Did not Jehovah, he against whom we sinned, in whose ways men would not walk, and unto whose doctrine they were not obedient? Therefore did he pour upon them the fury of his anger, and the fierceness of war. and it set them on fire round about, yet they perceived not; and it consumed them, yet they laid it not to heart.

Par. 1 *My servant* This phrase expresses, in general, an absorbing attachment to Jehovah, as distinguished from all false gods. So Daniel is called by Darius 'servant of the living God' (Dan. vi 20), and so Abdallah, 'servant of Allah,' has become a favourite Mohammedan surname The difficulty of explaining it in ch. xl–lxvi arises from a certain degree of confusion in the various passages in which it occurs Sometimes the prophet surveys the people of Israel from an ideal, sometimes from a historical point of view. Hence in several important sections the 'Servant of Jehovah' (like the Zion of xl. 9, &c.) is a purely poetical figure, personifying the ideal character of the pious Israelite, and decorated by the prophet with all the noblest achievements of faith, whether actually realized in the past, or merely hoped for from the future. In other words, it is a glorification of the prophetic office, and an aspiration after the time when the office of a few should become that of the entire nation, and the words of Joel be fulfilled, 'Your sons and your daughters shall prophesy.' In this secondary sense alone can the passages xlii. 1-7, xlix. 1-9, l. 4-10, lii. 13-liii. 12, be termed unconscious predictions of our Lord. But there are several other passages, in which the title 'Servant of Jehovah' is simply collective, and represents the actual contemporaries of the prophet in Babylon, who had to a large extent forgotten their exalted ideal, and degenerated into formal worshippers of Jehovah, or even into undisguised polytheists. (Comp Ezek. xiv, xx, xxxiii) These passages are xli. 8, 9, xlii. 19, xliii. 10, xliv. 1, 2, 21, xlv. 4, xlviii. 20.

Religion Literally, 'judgment,' i. e. the revealed religion on its practical side as the rule of action. Similarly the Arabic *dín*, 'judgment,' is used by Mohammed in the sense of 'religion.'

His doctrine. Heb *thōrāthō.* The word Thorah (Auth. Vers 'law') should, throughout the prophetical books written previously to Ezra, be rendered by some general term, such as 'doctrine,' 'precept.' See Isa ii 3, viii. 16; Jer. xviii. 18, Ezek. vii 26; Hagg. ii. 12; Zech. vii. 12 Even in Malachi, who wrote after the recognition of the Pentateuch as the 'Law of Moses,' there is but one passage (iv. 4) where the reference to a written law can be established

Par. 2. *I Jehovah called thee in righteousness.* Divesting this passage of its poetical dress we may interpret it thus. The ideal standard enshrined in the heart of the pious exiles was placed there by Jehovah himself, as an evidence of his 'righteousness,' i. e. of his faithful adherence to his covenant with Israel. The performance of this covenant on Jehovah's side had been interrupted by the national defection of the Jews, and could only be resumed when the more pious members of the nation had been awakened to a due sense of their responsibilities This had now taken place; there was already a numerous band of prophets and prophetically-minded persons; and these were the mediators between Jehovah and the great body of their spiritually-blind countrymen. This is what the prophet means by saying that the 'Servant of Jehovah' was destined to be a 'covenant of the people' (comp xlix 8), and 'to open the blind eyes, to bring out the captives from the prison.' Comp the development of the same ideas in Par. 5.

The former things . . . new things, i. e. the termination of the exile, which had been foretold by Jeremiah, on the one hand, and the restoration of the Jews by Cyrus, on the other.

Par. 3 *Sing unto Jehovah* Here the prophetic writer shifts his point of view to the time immediately following the liberation of the Jews At the end of the song he returns to the present, unless, with Delitzsch, we regard the battle in the last verse as a final and decisive victory over the heathen

Kedar. See note on xxi 16

Par. 4 *I will gasp and groan at once* The assonance is strongly emphatic. 'Jehovah has long been travailing with redemption; he shall now by a sudden effort be delivered of it.'

I will make waste mountains. 'The land, where the Jews have so long languished in exile, shall be laid waste.'

Par 5 *Hear, ye deaf* The mention of the idolaters and their fate reminds the prophet of the failings of his own countrymen. Comp Par. 2.

He that is devoted to God. Literally, 'he that has been brought into a state of submission' Heb. *meshullam*, the passive corresponding to the Arabic *Moslim*.

CHAPTER IV.

1.

[**XLIII. 1**] But now, thus saith Jehovah that made thee, O Jacob, and he that formed thee, O Israel: Fear not, for I have redeemed thee, I have called thee by name; thou art mine. When thou passest through the waters, I will be with thee; and through the rivers, they shall not overflow thee: when thou walkest through the fire, thou shalt not be scorched, neither shall the flame kindle upon thee. For I, Jehovah thy God, the Holy One of Israel, thy Saviour, have given Egypt for thy ransom, Ethiopia and Seba for thee. Since thou art precious in my sight, and honourable, and I love thee, therefore will I give men for thee, and peoples for thy life. Fear not, for I am with thee; I will bring thy seed from the east, and gather thee from the west; I will say to the north, Give up, and to the south, Keep not back: bring my sons from far, and my daughters from the end of the earth, even every one that is called by my name, that I have made for my glory, that I have formed, and also fully prepared.

2.

[8.] Bring forth the blind people that have eyes, and the deaf that have ears. Let all the nations gather together, and let the peoples assemble: who among them can declare such things? Or let them shew unto us former things! Let them bring forth their witnesses, that they may be justified; and let those hear, and say, It is truth. Ye are my witnesses, saith Jehovah, and my servant whom I have chosen, that ye may perceive and believe me, and understand that I am he,—before me there was no God formed, neither shall there be after me; I am Jehovah, and beside me there is no saviour; I alone shewed, and saved, and declared, there was no strange god working among you; ye are my witnesses, saith Jehovah, that I am God. Yea, from this day forth I am he, and there is none that can deliver out of my hand: I will work, and who shall let it? Thus saith Jehovah your redeemer, the Holy One of Israel, For your sake have I sent to Babylon, and will drive them all down as fugitives, even the Chaldeans into the ships of their pride; I, Jehovah, your Holy One, the Maker of Israel, your King.

3.

[16.] Thus saith Jehovah, which maketh a way through the sea, and a path through mighty waters, which bringeth forth the chariot and horse, the army and the power,—they lie down together, and shall not rise, they are extinct, and quenched as a wick: Remember ye not the former things, neither consider the things of old. Behold, I prepare a new thing; it springeth forth already, shall ye not perceive it? Yea, I will make a way in the wilderness, and rivers in the desert. The beasts of the field shall honour me, the jackals and the ostriches: because I set waters in the wilderness, and rivers in the desert, to give drink to my people, my chosen. The people which I have formed for myself, they shall shew forth my praise.

4.

[22.] But thou hast not called upon me, O Jacob; much less art thou weary in my service, O Israel! Thou hast not brought me the small cattle of thy burnt offerings, neither hast thou honoured me with thy sacrifices; howbeit I burdened thee not with offerings, nor wearied thee with incense. Thou hast bought me no sweet cane with money, neither hast thou filled me with the fat of thy sacrifices; thou hast rather burdened me with thy sins, and wearied me with thine iniquities. I, even I, am he that blotteth out thy transgressions for mine own sake, and will not remember thy sins. Put me in remembrance: let us plead together: declare thou, that thou mayest be justified. Thy first father sinned, and thine interpreters rebelled against me, therefore did I profane consecrated princes, and gave Jacob to outlawry, and Israel to revilings.

Par 1 *I have redeemed thee*, i e Jehovah has decreed Israel's redemption.

I have called thee by name, i e chosen thee as my familiar acquaintance.

Have given Egypt for thy ransom 'Egypt and the neighbouring states, which escaped subjection to Babylon, shall be granted to the Persians in compensation for their generosity towards the Jews.' The prophecy was realized in the conquest of Egypt by Cambyses. 'Seba' is the northern half of Ethiopia, including Meroe and its inhabitants Comp. note on xlv. 14

I will bring thy seed, &c. The central body of Jewish exiles in Babylon shall be reinforced by those of Israel dispersed in previous 'captivities.'

That I have made Auth. Vers. 'that I have created,' but the word 'create' in English is associated with ideas foreign to the Old Testament. The doctrine of creation from nothing cannot be traced before the Greek version of Aquila (about 180 A.D.), who renders the Hebrew *bārā* in Gen. 1 1, by ἔκτισεν instead of ἐποίησεν. In fact *bārā* differs from other verbs meaning 'to form, or make' only in its exclusive application to Jehovah. In the last twenty-seven chapters of Isaiah it is used metaphorically of the extraordinary operations of Divine Providence.

Par. **2.** *Bring forth* Two parties are summoned before the tribunal of reason, the Israelites, who are to be cured of their spiritual blindness, on the one hand, and the heathen, as witnesses of the false gods, on the other. The question is then put to the latter, Which of their gods is the peer of Jehovah in prophecy? 'Such things,' i.e. such as the restoration of Israel 'Former things,' i e prophecies which have been ratified by the event.

I am Jehovah. The proper name Jehovah (Yahveh = the Existent, or, perhaps, the Life-giver) supplies the place of an appellative As if the Divine speaker would say, I am the only true God, the Giver and Preserver of Life.

Shewed and saved and declared. The second of these verbs, which harmonizes but ill with the other two, might, by altering a single consonant ('Shin' into 'Daleth'), be corrected into 'made known' (Note in Bunsen's 'Bibelwerk.') If we retain 'saved,' we must explain it as an allusion to 'saviour' in the preceding verse. 'Shewed' = promised; 'declared' = prophesied.

No strange god working among you. Literally, 'no stranger (Deut xxxii 16) among you,' i. e. your only protector was Jehovah

From this day forth The long period of Jehovah's inaction is at an end

Have I sent Cyrus has already received a commission to destroy Babylon.

The ships of their pride Literally, 'the ships of their shouting,' where 'shouting' is perhaps used in the double sense of triumph and despair Comp. the equivocal use of 'cheer' in xvi. 9, 10.

Par. **3.** *Through the sea* The overthrow of Babylon is compared to that of the Egyptians in the Red Sea

The former things, i e Jehovah's former interpositions on behalf of Israel, as in xlvi. 9

Par. 4 *Thou hast not called upon me.* The service which Jehovah demanded of his people during the exile was that of prayer and moral obedience. The ceremonial duties of the Israelites were suspended by their forced residence in a foreign land (comp. Ps. li 18, 19)

Thy first father hath sinned Either Abraham or Jacob; probably the latter, since Abraham was reverenced as the ideal of a religious Israelite. Comp. James i. 23

Thine interpreters, i.e. the prophets, who were the recognized channels of communication between Jehovah and his people.

Consecrated princes, i. e. the four last kings of Judah.

CHAPTER V.

1.

[XLIV. 1.] Yet now hear, O Jacob, my servant; and Israel, whom I have chosen. Thus saith Jehovah that made thee, and formed thee from the womb, which will help thee; Fear not, my servant Jacob; and thou, Jeshurun, whom I have chosen. For I will pour water upon him that is thirsty, and floods upon the dry ground; I will pour my spirit upon thy seed, and my blessing upon thine offspring; and they shall spring up as among the grass, as willows by the water-courses. One shall say, I am Jehovah's; and another shall proclaim the name of Jacob; and another shall subscribe with his hand unto Jehovah, and give flattering titles by the name of Israel.

2.

[6] Thus saith Jehovah, the king of Israel, and his redeemer Jehovah of Hosts; I am the first and I am the last; and beside me there is no God. And who calleth continually as I, since I established the most ancient people? let him declare it and lay it before me: or let them declare things for to come, and those that shall happen shortly. Tremble not, neither be afraid; have not I told thee heretofore, and have declared it? ye are my witnesses. Is there a God beside me? yea, there is no God: I know not any. They that make images are all of them vanity, and their delectable things shall not profit; and their witnesses see not, neither perceive, to the end that they may be ashamed.

3.

[10] Who hath formed a god, or molten an image that is profitable for nothing? Behold, all the fellows thereof shall be ashamed; and the artificers themselves are men: let them all gather together, let them stand up; yet they shall tremble and be ashamed together. The smith sharpeneth an axe, he worketh in a fire of coals, and formeth it with hammers; he worketh it with the strength of his arms; he is also hungry, and his strength faileth; he drinketh no water, and is faint. The carpenter stretcheth out the line, he marketh it out with the graver; he prepareth it with planes, and marketh it out with the compass; and maketh it after the figure of a man, like a stately person, to dwell in a house. He heweth him down cedars, and taketh the holm-oak and the oak, and reareth for himself the best trees of the forest; he planteth a pine, and the rain doth nourish it. Then it serveth for men to burn; he taketh thereof, and warmeth himself; yea, he kindleth it and baketh bread; yea, he worketh it into a god, and worshippeth it: he maketh it an image, and falleth down thereto. Half thereof he hath burned in the fire; by the fuel thereof he eateth flesh; he roasteth roast, and is satisfied; yea, he warmeth himself, and saith, Aha, I am warm, I have felt the fire; and the residue thereof he maketh a 'god, even his image; he falleth down unto it, and worshippeth it; he prayeth unto it, and saith, Deliver me, for thou art my god! They do not perceive, nor understand; for Jehovah hath besmeared their eyes, that they cannot see; and their hearts, that they cannot understand. And he layeth it not to heart, neither hath he knowledge nor understanding to say, I have burned half thereof in the fire; and have also baked bread upon the coals thereof; I roasted flesh, and ate; and shall I make the remnant thereof an abomination? shall I fall

M

down to the stock of a tree? Whoso feedeth on ashes, a deluded heart hath turned him aside, that he cannot deliver his soul, nor say, Is there not a lie in my right hand?

4.

[21.] Remember these things, O Jacob; and Israel, for thou art my servant: I have formed thee; thou art my servant; O Israel, thou art not forgotten of me. I have blotted out as thick clouds thy transgressions, and as vapours thy sins: return unto me, for I have redeemed thee. Sing, O ye heavens; for Jehovah hath done it; shout, ye depths of the earth: break forth, ye mountains, into singing, O forest, and every tree therein; for Jehovah hath redeemed Jacob, and glorifieth himself in Israel.

5.

[24] Thus saith Jehovah, thy redeemer, and he that formed thee from the womb; I am Jehovah, that maketh all things; that stretched forth the heavens alone; that spread abroad the earth; who was with me? that frustrateth the tokens of the liars, and maketh diviners mad; that turneth wise men backward, and maketh their knowledge foolish; that confirmeth the word of his servant, and performeth the counsel of his messengers; that saith of Jerusalem, Let her be inhabited; and of the cities of Judah, Let them be built, and I will raise up the decayed places thereof; that saith to the flood, Be dry, and I will dry up thy streams; that saith of Cyrus, He is my shepherd, and shall perform all my pleasure; even saying of Jerusalem, Let her be built, and let the foundation of the temple be laid.

Par. 1. *O Jacob my servant.* The title 'Servant of Jehovah' is here extended to the pious minority of the nation, whose early hopes had been damped by the apparent hesitation of Cyrus to invade Babylonia.

Jeshurun, a poetic synonym for Israel, formed on the analogy of proper names from *Yashar*, righteous. It occurs elsewhere only in the song and blessing of Moses, Deut xxxii. 15, xxxiii. 5, 26. Comp. also Num. xxiii. 10, where 'righteous' is parallel and synonymous with Israel.

One shall say, &c. Gentile proselytes shall vie with one another in proclaiming their attachment to Jehovah and his people. 'Proclaim the name of Jacob,' i e. with gratitude and admiration, as in xii. 4 'Subscribe ... unto Jehovah,' i e. testifying that the writer is a worshipper of Jehovah. 'Give flattering titles,' &c i. e. shall adopt Israel as a *cognomen*, or title of distinction, for himself and his friends.

Par. 2. *Calleth*, or crieth, i. e. prophesieth, as in xl. 2. The same word is used by Mohammed, e. g. Koran, xcvi. 1, 'Cry thou in the name of thy Lord.'

The most ancient people, i. e. the earliest families of mankind. Hitzig well renders, 'der Urzeit Volk.' Comp. Job xxii. 15, 16 (Heb.).

To the end that they may be ashamed. The consequence of an action is frequently described as having formed part of the intention of the agent Comp. vi. 9, xxviii 13, xxx. 1.

Par. 3 *Who hath formed a god?* Who is so foolish or so bold as to make an idol?

All the fellows thereof, i.e. all the worshippers of the idol. Comp Hos. iv. 17, 'Ephraim is in fellowship with idols,' and 1 Cor. x. 20 (Knobel).

The smith sharpeneth an axe. The verb is wanting in the Hebrew, but the omission is evidently a clerical error. See 'Notes and Criticisms,' p. 38.

Reareth for himself. The word occurs in the same sense in Ps. lxxx 16, on which see Hupfeld's note.

Hath besmeared their eyes, i. e. made them spiritually blind. Comp. vi. 10.

Half thereof. One half of the wood is used as fuel, i. e. for cooking food, the other is made into an idol. 'By the fuel thereof,' lit. 'by the half thereof.'

Feedeth on ashes, i. e. cherisheth hopes as vain and unsubstantial as ashes.

Par. 5. *The liars*, i. e. the Babylonian soothsayers. Comp. xlvii 13.

His servant ... his messengers, i e. the author and his prophetic contemporaries. This interpretation is established by the use of the word 'counsel' in the second member of the verse, which, as in xli. 28, evidently signifies 'prediction.'

The flood, i. e. the river Euphrates.

Cyrus. According to a theory of Havernick, Cyrus, 'the Sun,' was a common titular name of the Persian kings, and might therefore have come to the ears of Isaiah in a natural way, either through Persian travellers, or the Medes in the army of Sennacherib.　Unfortunately the meaning thus ascribed to the name of Cyrus has long been disproved by Lassen, and is only worth mentioning on account of its revival in England by Professor Plumptre ('Biblical Studies,' p. 195).　The analogy of Pharaoh, quoted as meaning 'the sun' by the latter critic is equally insecure.

CHAPTER VI.

1.

[**XLV. 1**] Thus saith Jehovah to his anointed, to Cyrus, whom I hold by the right hand, that I may subdue nations before him, and loose the loins of kings, that I may open before him the two-leaved doors, and that the gates may not be shut: I will go before thee, and make the rough places even; I will break in pieces the doors of brass, and cut in sunder the bars of iron; and I give thee the treasures of darkness, and hidden riches of secret places, that thou mayest know that it is I, Jehovah, which call thee by thy name, even the God of Israel.　For Jacob my servant's sake, and Israel mine elect, I called thee hither by thy name; I surnamed thee, though thou didst not know me.　I am Jehovah, and there is none else; beside me there is no God: I girded thee, though thou didst not know me, that men might know from the rising of the sun, and from the setting thereof, that there is none except me,— I am Jehovah, and there is none else, that form the light and make the darkness, that prepare peace and make evil,—I am Jehovah, that do all these things.

Distil, ye heavens, from above, and let the skies pour down
　　righteousness;
　Let the earth open that salvation may grow up, and let it
　　cause righteousness to spring forth together·
I, Jehovah, have made it

2.

[9.] Woe unto him that striveth with his Maker, a potsherd among potsherds of earth! Shall the clay say to him that formeth it, What makest thou? or thy work, He hath no hands? Woe unto him that saith to his father, What begettest thou? or to the woman, What bringest thou forth? Thus saith Jehovah, the Holy One of Israel, and his Maker, Ask me of things to come; trust me with the care of my sons, and of the work of my hands. I myself prepared the earth, and made the men upon it; mine own hands stretched out the heavens, and I gave charge to all their host: I myself have stirred him up in righteousness, and will make all his ways even; he shall build my city, and he shall let go mine exiles, not for price nor reward, saith Jehovah of Hosts.

3.

[14.] Thus saith Jehovah, The wealth of Egypt, and the gains of Ethiopia, and the Sabeans, men of stature, shall come over unto thee, and they shall be thine; they shall go after thee, and pass on in chains; they shall fall down and pray unto thee, saying, 'Surely God is in thee; and there is none else; there is no God.' Verily, thou art a God that hidest thyself, O God of Israel, the Saviour! They are ashamed, and also confounded, all of them; they meet with confusion together that are makers of idols: but Israel is saved by Jehovah with an everlasting salvation; ye shall not be ashamed nor confounded world without end.

4.

[18.] For thus saith Jehovah, that made the heavens, (he is the God,) that formed the earth and prepared it, (it was he that established it, that made it not for a chaos, but formed it to be inhabited:) I am Jehovah, and there is none else. I have not spoken in secret in some place of the land of darkness: I said not unto the seed of Jacob, Seek ye me in vain; for I am Jehovah, that promise with righteousness, that declare with up-rightness. Assemble yourselves and come, draw near together, ye that are escaped of the nations. (They have no knowledge that carry about the wood of their image, and pray unto a god that cannot save.) Declare ye and bring it forth; yea, let them take counsel together: who hath proclaimed this from ancient time, and declared it of old? Have not I Jehovah? and there is no God else beside me, a righteous God and a Saviour; there is none beside me.

5.

[22] Turn unto me, and be ye saved, all the ends of the earth; for I am God, and there is none else. By myself I swear it, out of my mouth proceedeth righteousness, even a word, and it shall not return, That unto me every knee shall bow, every tongue shall swear. And one said unto me, In Jehovah only is righteousness and strength; all they that were incensed against him shall come unto him and be ashamed. In Jehovah shall all the seed of Israel be justified, and shall glory.

Par. 1. *To his anointed.* Cyrus is the only heathen king who receives the title of 'The anointed of Jehovah.' But we are not to suppose that, by thus investing him with 'Messiahship,' the prophet intended to connect him with what we are in the habit of calling the Messianic idea. The function of Cyrus was merely preparatory, he was to be instrumental in the removal of obstacles to the realization of that idea. The actual establishment of God's kingdom on earth, so far as it could be devolved on human agents, was reserved by the prophet for the regenerate people of Jehovah

Loose the loins of kings, i. e. render them incapable of resistance.

The doors of brass. According to Herodotus (i. 179) Babylon had a hundred gates of brass.

I surnamed thee, i. e. gave thee the titles ' My shepherd,' ' My anointed.'

That form the light and make the darkness This is generally supposed to be a warning against Dualism The opportuneness of such a declaration is shewn by the fact that Ahriman, the Persian name of the power of evil, survived among the later Jews as ' the impious Armilos ' Just as Ahriman was to be ultimately overcome by Ormazd, the supreme god, so Armilos, the Jews believed, should be slain by his enemy the Messiah. (Levy's ' Chaldee Lexicon,' vol. i. p. 66.)

Par. 2. *Woe unto him that striveth,* &c. Some of the Jews in Babylon seem to have disbelieved in the promises of which Cyrus was the centre, or to have considered the announcement of his Messiahship as an offence against patriotism. The prophet points out first the absurdity, and next the want of natural piety, involved in such murmurs.

Ask me of things to come, i. e. if you are disquieted about the future, apply to Jehovah through the prophet, and acquiesce in his revelations.

Par. 3. *The wealth of Egypt,* &c. ' When the Jews shall have returned to Palestine, the richest and most powerful nations shall become their voluntary prisoners, in the hope of acquiring from them the true religion.' Comp. xviii 7; Ps. lxviii 31. No particular stress is to be laid on the selection of these three nations; they are representatives of the whole world. In xliii. 3, on the other hand, the prophetic announcement respecting them is to be understood literally.

A God that hidest thyself. An exclamation of surprise at the splendid and far-reaching consequences of the Babylonian exile.

Par. 4. *Thus saith Jehovah,* &c. The sense of this rather intricate passage seems to be, that God in all His acts is guided by a definite purpose. Thus the formation of the earth involved that of the human race, and the clear and unambiguous promises made known by a long succession of prophets, should inspire all true Israelites with a confidence in their fulfilment

The land of darkness, i e the underworld (Sheol), comp. Job x. 21; Ps lxxxviii. 12. The allusion is to necromancy.

Ye that are escaped, i. e. the Gentiles who may survive the great judgment to be executed on the enemies of Jehovah See lxvi. 15-19.

Par. 5. *And one said unto me.* This refers to a mysterious heavenly voice, similar to those mentioned at the beginning of the book. For the abrupt introduction of the author's personality, comp xlviii. 16.

CHAPTER VII.

1.

[**XLVI. 1.**] Bel boweth down, Nebo stoopeth; their idols are given to the beasts and to the cattle: your carriages are heavy loaden; they are a burden to the weary beast. They stooped, they bowed down together; they could not deliver the burden, but themselves went into captivity.

2.

[**3.**] Hearken unto me, O house of Jacob, and all the remnant of the house of Israel, which are borne by me from the birth, which are carried from the womb; (and even to old age I am the same, and even to hoar hairs will I carry you; I have done it, and I will bear, and I will carry, and will deliver you :) To whom will ye liken me, and make me equal, and compare me, that we may be like? They that lavish gold out of the bag, and weigh silver in the balance, hire them a goldsmith, that he may make it a god · they fall down; yea, they worship. They bear him upon the shoulder, they carry him, and set him in his place, and he standeth; from his place shall he not remove; yea, one may cry unto him, yet will he not answer, nor save him out of his trouble.

3.

[**8.**] Remember this, and shew yourselves men; lay it to heart, O ye renegades. Remember the former things of old, how that I am God, and there is none else, I am God, and there is none like me; that declare the end from the beginning, and from ancient times the things that are not yet done; that say, My counsel shall stand, and I will do all my pleasure; that calleth the vulture from the east, the man that executeth my counsel from a far country: that which I have spoken, I will bring to pass; that which I have purposed, I will also accomplish. Hearken unto me, O ye stubborn of heart, that are far from righteousness: I have brought near my righteousness; it is not far distant, and my salvation shall not tarry: and I will give in Zion salvation; to Israel I will give my glory.

Par. 1. *Bel . . Nebo* Observe the infrequency of the prophet's references to Babylon. He is apparently too much absorbed in the fortunes of his own country to make more than a few passing allusions to the hated scenes of his captivity. The few which occur are therefore specially valuable, and they imply a degree of acquaintance with Babylon, which we cannot reasonably suppose Isaiah to have possessed In this passage the prophet refers to Bel-Merodach, the Jupiter, and Nebo, the Mercury of the Babylonians The former had a temple at Babylon, the latter at Borsippa, each with a tower attached, in which the ark or tabernacle of the god was deposited. Herodotus, in his description of the temple of Bel, seems to have inserted some architectural details, which apply in reality to the temple of Nebo See Rawlinson's ' Herodotus,' vol i pp 321, 627-629, 637, 638

Your carriages, i e the idols which were carried about in solemn religious processions Comp xlv 20; Jer. x 5; Amos v. 26

They bowed. Here the prophet changes his point of view. In the first verse he represented the idols as falling before his eyes, in the second he relates their destruction as an event of the past

Par. 2. *Which are borne* Literally, ' which are loaden.' The phrase corresponds to that in verse 1, and is chosen to mark the contrast between the rival objects of worship.

Par. 3. *Shew yourselves men*, i e. renounce your childish hankering after idolatry

That are far from righteousness, i. e that refuse to believe that God is so soon about to fulfil his promises.

CHAPTER VIII.

[**XLVII. 1.**]   1.

Come down and sit in the dust, O virgin-daughter of Babylon;
Sit on the ground without a throne, O daughter of the Chal-
     deans!
  For thou shalt no more be called tender and delicate.
Take the millstones, and grind meal ·
  Raise thy veil, strip off thy train,
  Uncover the leg, pass through the rivers.
Let thy nakedness be uncovered, yea, let thy shame be seen:
  I will take vengeance, and spare no man.
As for our redeemer, Jehovah of Hosts is his name, the
     Holy One of Israel.

[**5.**]   2.

Sit thou silent, and get thee into darkness, O daughter of
     the Chaldeans!
  For thou shalt no more be called, The lady of kingdoms
I was wroth with my people, I polluted mine inheritance,
     and gave them into thine hand:
  Thou didst shew them no mercy;
  Upon the ancient thou hast very heavily laid thy yoke.
And thou saidst, I shall be a lady for ever:
  So that thou didst not lay these things to thy heart,
  Neither didst remember the latter end of it.

[**8.**]   3

Therefore hear now this, thou that art given to pleasures,
    that dwellest carelessly,

That sayest in thine heart, I am, and there is none else;
> I shall not sit as a widow, neither shall I know the loss of children.

These two things shall come to thee in a moment in one day, the loss of children and widowhood;
> They shall come upon thee in their perfection,

Notwithstanding the multitude of thy sorceries, and the great abundance of thine enchantments.

And because thou hast trusted in thy wickedness, and hast said, None seeth me,
> And because thy wisdom and thy knowledge perverted thee,
> So that thou saidst in thine heart, I am, and there is none else:

Therefore shall an evil come upon thee, which thou shalt not have skill to charm,

And mischief shall fall upon thee, which thou shalt not be able to appease,

And desolation shall come upon thee suddenly, which thou shalt not know.

[12.]   4.

Continue now in thine enchantments, and in the multitude of thy sorceries,
> Wherein thou hast laboured from thy youth;

Haply thou mayest profit thereby, haply thou mayest quell the trouble!

Thou art wearied with the multitude of thy counsellors;
> Let now the astrologers, the star-gazers, stand and save thee,
> Prognosticating monthly the things that shall come upon thee.

Behold, they are as stubble; the fire hath burned them;
   They cannot deliver their own soul from the power of the
      flame:
It is not a coal to warm at, nor a fire to sit before!
Thus grievous is their lot, for whom thou hast laboured:
And they which have trafficked with thee from thy youth have
      wandered every one straight forward;
   There is none that saveth thee!

Par. 1. *Pass through the rivers.* The 'daughter' or population of Babylon is to wade through the rivers on her way to the scene of her captivity.

Par 2. *Get thee into darkness*, i e hide thyself from the scornful looks of the bystanders.

I was wroth with my people, &c. The Babylonians (like the Assyrians, x 6, 7) had exceeded the limits of their commission from Jehovah Comp. the pathetic language of Zechariah (1. 15).

Upon the ancient Comp Lam. iv 16, v 12

Par. 3. *As a widow*, i.e. deserted by the merchants, who were attracted to Babylon by its extensive commerce.

In their perfection, i. e in the full extent of their bitterness

To charm . . . to appease. No magic spells will be potent enough to avert the threatened calamity Comp verse 12, 'Haply thou mayest quell (literally, 'strike fear into') the trouble.'

Par 4 *The astrologers* Literally, 'the dividers of the heavens.' Most of the astronomical tablets discovered at Babylon 'are of an astrological character, recording the supposed influence of the heavenly bodies, singly, in conjunction, or in opposition, upon all sublunary affairs' Rawlinson's 'Five Great Monarchies,' vol iii. p 425.

The star-gazers. The Zodiacal system is probably in a great measure due to the Babylonians.

They which have trafficked with thee, i. e not the astrologers, but the foreign merchants. Comp. xiii 14

CHAPTER IX.

1.

[XLVIII. 1.] Hear ye this, O house of Jacob, which are called by the name of Israel, and are come forth out of the waters of Judah; which swear by the name of Jehovah, and make mention of the God of Israel, but not in truth, nor in righteousness. For they call themselves of the holy city, and stay themselves upon the God of Israel, whose name is Jehovah of Hosts! I declared the former things of old; they went forth out of my mouth, and I shewed them; I performed them suddenly, and they came to pass. Because I knew that thou wast stubborn, and thy neck was an iron band, and thy forehead of brass, therefore I declared it to thee of old; before it came to pass, I shewed it thee; lest thou shouldest say, Mine idol hath done it, and my graven image, and my molten image, hath appointed it.

2.

[6.] Thou hast heard it; see it fulfilled; and yourselves, will ye not acknowledge it? From this time do I shew thee new things, even hidden things, and those which thou knewest not. Now are they made, and not of old, and before this day thou heardest them not, lest thou shouldest say, Behold, I knew them. Thou heardest them not, neither didst thou know them, neither was thine ear opened of old: for I knew that thou wast very treacherous, and wast called a renegade from the womb. For my name's sake I defer mine anger, and for my praise I refrain towards thee, that I cut thee not off. Behold, I have refined thee, but not as silver; I have proved thee in the furnace of affliction.

For mine own sake, even for mine own sake, will I do it: for how should my name be polluted? and I will not give my glory unto another.

3.

[12.] Hearken unto me, O Jacob; and thou, Israel, my called: I am he: I am the first, I also am the last. Mine hand also laid the foundation of the earth, and my right hand spread out the heavens: when I call unto them, they stand up together. All ye, assemble yourselves, and hear; which among them declared these things? He that Jehovah loveth shall perform his pleasure on Babylon, and his arm shall be on the Chaldeans. I, even I, have spoken; yea, I have called him; I have brought him, and his way shall be prosperous. Come ye near unto me, hear ye this; (from the first I have never spoken in secret, from the time that the earth was, there have I been; and now hath the Lord Jehovah sent me with his Spirit:) thus saith Jehovah, thy redeemer, the Holy One of Israel, I am Jehovah thy God, which teacheth thee to profit, which leadeth thee by the way that thou shouldest go. O that thou didst hearken to my commandments! then should thy peace be as a river, and thy righteousness as the waves of the sea; thy seed also should be as the sand, and the offspring of thy body as the grains thereof; thy name should not be cut off nor destroyed from before me.

4.

[20] 'Go ye forth of Babylon, flee ye from Chaldea;' declare ye this, and tell it with a merry shout; utter it even to the end of the earth, say ye, 'Jehovah hath redeemed his servant Jacob. And they thirsted not in the deserts through which he led them: he caused water to flow out of the rock for them; he clave the

rock, and water gushed out.' There is no peace, saith my God, for the wicked.

Par. 1. *The waters of Judah* The founder of the nation is compared to a fountain, as in Ps lxviii. 26.

I declared the former things of old, &c. The gloom of the future had to a certain extent been illuminated, as a restraint upon idolatry, but the restoration of the Jews through Cyrus was so extraordinary, that it was revealed only on the eve of its accomplishment, 'lest thou shouldest say, Behold, I knew it,' i. e. to avoid impairing its religious effect. The writer seems to imply that an older prophet, as for instance Isaiah, would have contravened the Divine will, had he uttered such a prediction.

Par 2 *Behold, I have refined thee,* i. e thy troubles were not designed for thine extinction, but for thy purification. 'Not as silver,' i. e. not literally refined, but metaphorically.

I will not give my glory unto another. A continuance of the exile would have seemed a confession of weakness on the part of Jehovah. 'Another,' i. e. the god of the Babylonians

Par. 3. *Who among them,* i e among the gods of the heathen The persons addressed are the Jews

That the earth was. Literally, 'that it was,' referring to the events described in verse 13. Comp. viii. 21 (Heb.).

There have I been, i e from the beginning of the world I have raised up a succession of prophets, each bearing his own unambiguous message; 'and now,' as the prophetic writer subjoins, Jehovah has crowned his previous work with this grandest of revelations. A similar transition from Jehovah to the prophetic writer occurs in xlv. 24

With the grains thereof Or, 'with the brood thereof.' The obscurity is produced by a play upon words, which can scarcely be reproduced.

Par. 4. *For the wicked,* i. e. for the idolatrous party among the Jewish exiles. See chaps lxv, lxvi.

BOOK II.

VICARIOUS ATONEMENT.

THE second book consists of mingled warnings and promises, all
derived from the certainty of the termination of the exile. In the first
chapter, the general subject is stated anew. The ideal of Israel, expressed in a condensed form by means of personification, can only be
fully realized by a world-wide proclamation of the true religion. Israel
indeed may cherish suspicions of her Lord, but the intercourse between
God and His people is only interrupted, not destroyed. The next
chapter describes the troublous experience of the 'Servant of Jehovah.'
The latter is introduced in person, declaring his 'apostolical' gifts, his
perfect devotedness to his mission, and the acquiescence in torture and
shame produced by an unceasing consciousness of the presence of God.
Then, turning to the Jewish exiles, the prophet encourages the faithful
to copy the sublime confidence of God's 'servant,' and threatens their
enemies with a mysterious punishment. Three times are these or
similar exhortations reiterated, and then the prophet bursts on a
sudden into a rapturous invocation, first, of the wonder-working arm
of God, and then of Zion or Jerusalem, soon to be again thickly
peopled, and in character, as well as in name, 'the holy city,' (chap. iv.)
He seems already to descry the bounding feet of the heralds of good
tidings, and adjures the 'armour-bearers of Jehovah' to remember the
awful sanctity of their charge.

The fifth chapter opens with a declaration on the part of Jehovah,
to the effect that the splendour of the 'servant's' victory should bear
a marked proportion to his previous sufferings. All that the pious
Israelites had endured for the sake of their religion is attributed in the
fullest measure to their ideal representative. The sufferings of the
latter are described as being perfectly unmerited. They are imposed
by Jehovah, and cheerfully endured by the 'servant,' in expiation of the
sins of His people. A wonderful result follows. The genius of Israel

rises from the ashes of martyrdom to an undecaying supremacy, and the actual nation is so transformed in character as to correspond to its Divine ideal.

The sixth chapter developes at greater length the bright prospects of Israel. The sufferings of the exile are transitory, and, like the flood of Noah, they shall not be repeated, for the security and prosperity of Zion are guaranteed by the righteousness of its inhabitants. Then follows a succession of warnings and complaints, mingled with encouragements. The highest spiritual and temporal blessings are offered freely for acceptance, and a renewal of the promises of the covenant given long before to David. The single condition demanded is the renunciation of all selfish and sinful projects, founded in disbelief of the Divine faithfulness. The wondrous character of Jehovah's promises is a sufficient pledge of their fulfilment, for celestial principles of action must be widely different from those of earth (chap. vii). One duty is specially singled out as a test of obedience,—the observance of the Sabbath. Even 'strangers and foreigners,' provided they keep holy the day of Jehovah, will be gladly admitted within the house of universal prayer (chap. viii).

The prophet then abruptly changes his tone (chap. ix). He complains that the guides and teachers of the nation are utterly depraved, and so absorbed in the pursuit of luxury, that they even fail to observe how the few righteous men left are dying out. 'May these enjoy (so the prophet exclaims) their well-earned repose! But as for you, whose apostacy from Jehovah is put to shame by their fidelity, I bid you appear before the Divine tribunal! Your hereditary sins shall meet with a terrible retribution, which none of the idols in your Pantheon will be able to avert.' But now a celestial voice is heard, announcing the liberation of the exiles, and its ultimate source in the Divine character. Jehovah has looked down with compassion on his erring people, and will now restore and console them. But not to all the Jewish exiles is this bright prospect unfolded. The warning at the close of the first book is repeated in yet sterner accents, There is no peace for the wicked.

N

CHAPTER I.

1.

[XLIX. 1.] Listen unto me, ye sea-coasts; and hearken, ye peoples that are far off: Jehovah hath called me from the womb; since my mother conceived me hath he made mention of my name. And he made my mouth as a sharp sword, hiding me in the shadow of his hand, and made me a polished shaft, covering me in his quiver; and said unto me, Thou art my servant, O Israel, by whom I will glorify myself. Then I said, I have laboured in vain, I have spent my strength for nought and in vain, yet surely my right is with Jehovah, and my recompense with my God. But now saith Jehovah, that formed me from the womb to be his servant, that I might bring Jacob again to him, and that Israel might be gathered unto him, (for I am honoured in the eyes of Jehovah, and my God is become my strength,) It is too light a thing that thou shouldest be my servant to raise up the tribes of Jacob, and to restore the preserved of Israel; therefore I appoint thee for a light of the nations, that my salvation may reach unto the end of the earth.

2.

[7] Thus saith Jehovah, the redeemer of Israel, and his Holy One, unto him whose life is despised, that is abhorred of the people, and a servant of tyrants, (yet kings shall see and arise, even princes, and shall worship, because of Jehovah that is faithful, and of the Holy One of Israel, in that he chose thee;) thus saith Jehovah, In the season of acceptance have I heard thee, and in the day of salvation have I helped thee; and I will form and appoint thee for a covenant of the people, to establish the land, to

assign the desolate heritages, saying to the prisoners, Go forth,
and to them that are in darkness, Shew yourselves. They shall
feed in the ways, and find their pasture on the barren hills; they
shall not hunger nor thirst; the glistening of the sand shall not
deceive them, neither shall the sun smite them; for he that hath
mercy on them shall lead them, and guide them unto the springs
of water And I will make all my mountains a road, and my
highways shall be exalted. Behold, these shall come from far;
and lo, these from the north and from the west, and these from
the land of the Sinim.

Shout, O heavens, and dance for joy, O earth, and break
forth into shouting, O mountains!
For Jehovah hath comforted his people, and hath mercy
upon his afflicted.

3.

[14.] But Zion said, Jehovah hath forsaken me, and the Lord
hath forgotten me! Can a woman forget her sucking child, that
she should not yearn upon the son of her womb? Yea, though
they should forget, yet will I not forget thee! Behold, I have
graven thee upon the palms of my hands; thy walls are continually before me. Soon shall thy children hasten hither; thy
destroyers and they that made thee waste shall go forth of thee.
Lift up thine eyes round about, and behold: they all gather themselves together, and come to thee. As I live, saith Jehovah, thou
shalt surely clothe thee with them all, as with an ornament, and
bind them on thee, as a bride doeth. For thy wastes, and thy
desolate places, and thy land laid in ruins—yea, thou wilt then be
too strait for the inhabitants, and they that destroyed thee shall
depart far away. The children of thy bereavement shall yet say

in thine ears, The place is too strait for me; make room for me that I may sit down. Then shalt thou say in thine heart, Who hath begotten me these, seeing I was childless and unfruitful, an exile and taken away? and who hath brought up these? Behold, I was left alone; these, where had they been?

4.

[22.] Thus saith the Lord Jehovah, Behold, I will lift up mine hand to the nations, and set up mine ensign to the peoples, and they shall bring thy sons in their bosom, and thy daughters shall be carried on the shoulder. And kings shall become thy foster-fathers, and their queens thy nursing-mothers; they shall bow down unto thee with their face toward the earth, and kiss the dust of thy feet; and then shalt thou know that I am Jehovah, in whom they that hope are never ashamed. Can the prey be taken from the mighty, or the captives of the violent escape? For thus saith Jehovah, Yea, though the captives of the mighty should be taken away, and the prey of the violent should escape, yet with him that contendeth with *thee* I will contend, and I will save thy children. And I will feed them that oppress thee with their own flesh, and they shall be drunken with their own blood, as with sweet wine: and all flesh shall know that I Jehovah am thy saviour, and that thy redeemer is the hero of Israel.

5.

.1.] Thus saith Jehovah, Where is the bill of your mother's divorcement, wherewith I put her away? or which of my creditors is it to whom I sold you? Behold, for your iniquities were ye sold, and for your transgressions was your mother put away. Wherefore, when I came, was there no man? when I called, was there none to answer? Is my hand indeed too short to redeem? or have I no power to deliver? Behold, at my rebuke I dry up the sea, I make the rivers a wilderness, that their fish stinketh for want of water, and dieth for thirst; I clothe the heavens with blackness, and I make sackcloth their covering.

Par. 1. *Listen unto me*, &c. The abrupt introduction of the 'Servant of Jehovah' need not surprise us it is, as Hengstenberg remarks, 'A necessary result of the dramatic character of prophetic speech.' ('Christology,' vol. ii. p. 227.) In fact, without these dramatic alternations, the frequent repetitions in this prophecy might have been intolerable. The soliloquy before us, for instance, is, except in one point, a development of ch. xlii verses 1–7, although it must be admitted that this single exception (see the next note) is one of the highest importance.

O Israel Observe the speaker's assumption of the name of Israel He is the agent in the regeneration of Israel, and yet in some sense he claims to be Israel himself This seems to prove conclusively that the 'Servant of Jehovah' is neither the prophet nor the Messiah, but, primarily at least, the personified ideal of the Israelitish nation.

Par. 2. *Unto him whose life is despised*, i. e. who is not considered worthy to live. Ewald renders, 'Unto the object of deepest contempt,' comp Ezek. xxxvi. 5, xxv. 6, 15; Ps xvii. 9.

The people; or, more generally, 'people' The phrase denotes primarily the heathen, without altogether excluding the large body of unbelieving Jews. Comp Ps. xxii. 6

I will form and appoint thee Comp the parallel passage in xlii. 6, 7.

The glistening of the sand, i e. the mirage. Comp xxxv. 7

The land of the Sinim, probably China, an outlying portion of which seems to have been known to the Indians, and through them to the Babylonian merchants. We know at any rate that the west of China was under the dominion of the *Thsin* princes for several centuries before the Christian era. As early as the eighth century B C they are said to have borne the title of 'heavenly kings,' and to have occupied one of the capitals of the empire. From 249 to 206 they were emperors of China This view of the 'Sinim' is now generally accepted; it agrees admirably with the Babylonian origin of our prophecy See the note of Gesenius on this passage, and Geiger's 'Ursprung der Sprache,' p. 456.

Par. 3. *But Zion said*. Here the prophet shifts his point of view to the sorrowful times of the exile. Zion, he says, has never ceased to exist in the mind of Jehovah, which is a pledge of her future restoration. Comp note on xl. 9

Yea, thou wilt then be too strait. A sudden alteration in the construction, re-minding us of St. Paul in the Epistles.

The children of thy bereavement, i e. as Auth. Vers. renders, 'The children which thou shalt have after thou hast lost the other.'

Par. **4.** *The captives of the violent.* For *saddíq,* 'righteous,' read *áris,* 'violent,' with Lowth and Ewald, supported by the Syriac and the Vulgate.

Yea, though the captives, &c Faith in Jehovah, the prophet had said, shall never be disappointed. But it would be so, if, after having been delivered for awhile, the Jews were to be once more enslaved Therefore, 'though even the captives of the mighty,' &c.

The hero of Israel Borrowed from Gen. xlix. 24, Isa. i. 24.

Par. **5.** *Where is the bill,* &c. Since no bill of divorce had been written, no second husband could have any right over Jehovah's bride, and since no price had been received by Jehovah in payment for his children (comp lii. 3), it de-pended only on himself to reinstate them in his family.

Wherefore, when I came, was there no man? Why did not Israel welcome my advances ?

CHAPTER II.

1.

,[L 4.] The Lord Jehovah hath given me the tongue of a dis-ciple, that I should know how to succour with the word him that is weary: he wakeneth morning by morning, he wakeneth mine ear to hearken like a disciple. The Lord Jehovah hath opened mine ear, and I am not rebellious, neither have I turned back. I have given my back to the smiters, and my cheeks to them that plucked out the hair· I have not hidden my face from shame and spitting Yet the Lord Jehovah will help me ; therefore am I not confounded : therefore have I set my face like flint, and I know that I shall not be ashamed. He is near that justifieth me ; who will contend with me ? let us stand together. Who is mine ad-

versary? let him come near unto me Behold, the Lord Jehovah
will help me; who is he that shall condemn me? lo, they all shall
fall to pieces as a garment, the moth shall eat them up.

2.

[10] Who is among you that feareth Jehovah, that hearke
to the voice of his servant, that walketh in darkness, and hat
light? Let him trust in the name of Jehovah, and stay upon his
God. Behold, all ye that kindle a fire, that make your arrows to
burn; get you hence into the flame of your fire, and into the
firebrands that ye have lighted. This shall befal you from mine
own hand; ye shall lie down in pain.

Par. 1. *The tongue of a disciple*, i. e. such as the disciples of Jehovah possess.
Comp. viii. 16, liv 13 Similarly 'the word' means the Divine word.

I have given my back, &c. An anticipation of ch. liii. Comp. also Ps xxii,
which is evidently a description of an ideal personality (similar to that of the
'Servant of Jehovah') in which all the best qualities of the Jewish exiles are
intensified

That justifieth me, i. e. that declareth my innocence.

Par. 2. *Who is among you*, &c. The prophet addresses his readers, 'Who
among you understands the true sense of these words of the servant?'
(Ewald.)

That make to burn. For *me'azzere*, 'girding,' read *me'ire*, with Hitzig.

In pain, or, in a place of pain. An anticipation of lxvi 24

CHAPTER III.

1.

[LI. 1.] Hearken unto me, ye that follow after righteousness,
ye that seek Jehovah: look unto the rock whence ye are hewn,
and to the hole of the pit whence ye are digged. Look unto
Abraham your father, and unto Sarah that bare you: though he

was alone when I called him, yet I blessed him and increased him. For Jehovah will comfort Zion, he will comfort all her waste places; and make her wilderness as Eden, and her desert as the garden of Jehovah; joy and gladness shall be found therein, thanksgiving and the voice of melody.

2.

[4] Hearken unto me, my people, and give ear unto me, O my nation: for doctrine shall proceed from me, and my religion will I establish for a light of the peoples. My righteousness is near; my salvation is gone forth, and mine arms shall judge the peoples: for me the coasts shall wait, and upon mine arm shall they trust. Lift up your eyes to the heavens, and look upon the earth beneath; for the heavens shall vanish away like smoke, and the earth shall fall to pieces as a garment, and they that dwell therein shall die miserably: but my salvation shall be for ever, and my righteousness shall not be abolished.

3

[7] Hearken unto me, ye that know righteousness, the people in whose heart is my doctrine; fear ye not the reproach of men, neither be afraid at their revilings. For the moth shall eat them up like a garment, and the worm shall eat them like wool: but my righteousness shall be for ever, and my salvation from generation to generation.

Par 2 *My righteousness*, i e the exhibition of my righteousness in the deliverance of Israel and the destruction of their enemies

Miserably Gesenius and most modern critics render 'like a gnat,' but it seems better with Delitzsch (see his note) to take the word *kén* as an adverb ('thus') qualified by the gesture of the speaker Comp 2 Sam xxiii 5; Num xiii. 33; Job ix 35; and the 'hujus non facio' of the Latin comic writers.

CHAPTER IV.

1.

[**LI. 9.**] Awake, awake, put on strength, O arm of Jehovah; awake, as in the ancient days, in the generations of old. Art thou not it that hewed the sea-monster in pieces, that pierced the dragon? Art thou not it that dried up the sea, the waters of the great flood, that made the depths of the sea a way for the ransomed to pass over? 'And the redeemed of Jehovah shall return, and come unto Zion with shouting, and with everlasting joy upon their head: they shall obtain joy and gladness; and grief and sighing shall flee away.'

2.

[**12.**] I, even I, am he that comforteth you: who, then, art thou, that thou fearest the frail creature that shall die, and the son of man which shall be made as grass; and forgettest Jehovah thy maker, that stretched forth the heavens, and laid the foundations of the earth; and tremblest all the day long for the fury of the oppressor, because he taketh aim to destroy? and where is the fury of the oppressor? He that bendeth with the yoke shall soon be released; he shall not perish unto the grave, neither shall his bread fail; for I am Jehovah thy God, which stirreth up the sea, that its waves roar, whose name is Jehovah of Hosts. And I did put my words in thy mouth, and covered thee in the shadow of mine hand, that I might plant the heavens, and lay the foundations of the earth, and say unto Zion, Thou art my people.

3.

[**17.**] Arouse thee, arouse thee, stand up, O Jerusalem, which

hast drunk at the hand of Jehovah the cup of his fury, which
hast drunken the chalice of the cup of reeling, and supped it out!
There was none to lead her of all the sons whom she had born,
neither any to take her by the hand of all the sons whom she
had brought up. Twofold is that which befell thee: who shall
be sorry for thee? desolation and destruction, and famine and the
sword: how shall I comfort thee? Thy sons lay fainting at the
corners of all the streets, like the antelope in a net, being full of
the fury of Jehovah, the rebuke of thy God. Therefore hear now
this, thou afflicted, and drunken, but not with wine. Thus saith
thy Lord Jehovah, and thy God that pleadeth the cause of his
people, Behold, I have taken out of thine hand the cup of reeling;
yea, the chalice of the cup of my fury, thou shalt never drink it
more. and I have put it into the hand of them that plagued
thee, which said to thy soul, Bow down, that we may go over;
and thou didst make thy back as the ground, and as the street
for them that go over.

4.

[LII. 1] Arouse thee, arouse thee, put on thy strength, O
Zion; put on thy glorious garments, O Jerusalem, the holy
city: for henceforth there shall no more come into thee the
uncircumcised and the unclean. Shake thyself from the dust;
arise, and sit down, O Jerusalem · loose thyself from the bands
of thy neck, O captive daughter of Zion. For thus saith Jehovah,
Ye were sold for nought, and ye shall not be redeemed with
money. For thus saith Jehovah, My people went down aforetime
to Egypt to sojourn there, and Assyria oppressed him without
cause. And now, what shall I do here? saith Jehovah; for my
people is taken away for nought; they that rule over him howl,

(this is the utterance of Jehovah,) and all the day long is my name reviled. Therefore my people shall know my name: therefore they shall know in that day that I am he that promised, saying, Here am I.

5.

[7.] How graceful upon the mountains are the steps of the herald that publisheth peace, that is an herald of good tidings, that publisheth salvation, that saith unto Zion, Thy God reigneth. Hark, thy watchmen lift up the voice; they sing together: for they see eye to eye the return of Jehovah to Zion. Break forth into shouting together, ye waste places of Jerusalem: for Jehovah hath comforted his people, he hath redeemed Jerusalem. Jehovah hath made bare his holy arm in the eyes of all the nations; and all the ends of the earth have seen the salvation of our God. 'Depart ye, depart ye, go ye out from thence, touch no unclean thing; go ye out of the midst of her; keep yourselves pure, ye that bear the armour of Jehovah. For ye shall not go out in haste, nor go by flight: for before you goeth Jehovah, and the God of Israel is your rereward.'

Par. 1. *The sea-monster*, i e Egypt. An allusion to a mythological legend, which represented God as having subdued a rebellious sea-monster (Rahab), and fastened it as a constellation on the sky—an everlasting warning to man against impiety. See Job ix. 13 (with Ewald's note), xxvi 12, where the Lxx has κήτη, 'sea-monsters,' and compare the similar legend of 'the giant' Orion Isaiah (xxx 7) employs the same word Rahab here rendered 'sea-monster,' as a synonym for Egypt, but assigns to it the pure Hebrew meaning of 'arrogance.' 'Dragon' is also a poetic expression for Egypt; comp xxvii. 1.

And the redeemed, &c. A quotation from xxxv. 10 Comp lxv. 25.

Par. 2. *Who, then, art thou*, &c. That is, What right have those who are comforted by Jehovah to give way to despondency?

He that bendeth with the yoke A figurative description of the sufferings of the patriotic Jews during the exile.

I did put my words in thy mouth. The prophetic eloquence, and security under the Divine protection, ascribed in xlix. 1, 2 to the ideal 'Servant,' are here predicated of the pious minority among the prophet's contemporaries. We must admit, therefore, that the distinction between the ideal and the actual 'Servant' is from time to time imperfectly adhered to. This was only to be expected, considering that the effect principally aimed at by the prophet was not poetical, but practical.

That I might plant heaven. See lxv. 17, lxvi. 22. 'Plant,' i. e. set up as a tent.

Par. 3. *The cup of reeling.* 'Reeling,' i e terror, perplexity, and despair, is the consequence of God's providential judgments. Comp xix 14; Jer. xxv. 15, 16. 'The chalice of the cup of reeling.' Comp. the similar expression, 'The way of thy paths,' iii. 12.

Par. 4. *There shall no more come into thee,* &c. Comp the parallel passage in Joel iii. 17.

Ye were sold for nought. See analysis prefixed to this book.

To sojourn, i e as guests, not slaves

Here, i. e in Babylonia. The necessity for the intervention of Jehovah is as great in Babylon as it was formerly in Egypt and Assyria. 'Howl,' i. e. triumph.

That I am he that promised, i e that the prophetic promises proceeded from a faithful and almighty God.

Par. 5. *How graceful upon the mountains.* The heralds of the Divine deliverer are seen bounding, like graceful gazelles, over the mountains

Thy God reigneth, i. e. Jehovah has resumed his functions as the true king of Israel

Thy watchmen. The ideal Jerusalem (see note on xl 9) is represented as stationing watchmen on the (ideal) walls, to announce the first tidings of the return of the exiles

Depart ye. A heavenly voice is heard, summoning 'the armour-bearers of Jehovah' (so Luzzatto renders), i e. his faithful worshippers, to depart from Babylon. Unlike the Exodus of old, their march is to be distinguished by calmness and solemnity, and by a rigid abstinence from the spoils of the idolaters

CHAPTER V.

1.

[LII 13.] Behold, my servant shall be prosperous; he shall be exalted and extolled, and be very high. According as many were astonished at thee, (his visage was so marred unlike to a man, and his form unlike to the sons of men,) so shall he cause many nations to admire; kings shall shut their mouths at him; for that which had not been told them shall they see, and that which they had not heard shall they consider.

2.

[LIII. 1.] Who hath believed our revelation? and to whom was the arm of Jehovah disclosed? He grew up before him as a tender plant, and as a root out of a dry ground; he had no form nor majesty, that we should regard him, and no beauty, that we should desire him. He was despised, and forsaken of men, a man of pains, and acquainted with sickness; and we hid as it were our faces from him; he was despised, and we esteemed him not.

3.

[4.] Surely he did bear our sicknesses, and carry our pains, whilst we esteemed him stricken, smitten of God, and afflicted. But he was pierced for our transgressions, bruised for our iniquities; the chastisement of our peace was upon him, and through his stripes we are healed. All we like sheep did go astray; we turned every one to his own way; and Jehovah laid upon him the iniquity of us all.

4.

[7.] He was tormented, but he suffered freely, and opened not his mouth, as the sheep that is led to the slaughter, and as the ewe that before her shearers is dumb; and he opened not his mouth. From oppression and from punishment was he taken,—and, as for his generation, who considered that he was cut off out of the land of the living, for the transgression of my people he was stricken? And his grave was appointed with the wicked, and his tomb with the oppressor, although he had done no violence, neither was any deceit in his mouth.

5.

[10.] Yet it pleased Jehovah to bruise him, and to smite him with sickness: for if he should make his soul a trespass-offering, he should see a seed, he should prolong his days, and the pleasure of Jehovah should prosper in his hand; he should see the gains of his soul, and should be satisfied; by his knowledge should my righteous servant make many righteous, and he should take up the burden of their iniquities. Therefore will I divide him a portion among many, and with a great company shall he divide the spoil, because he poured out his soul unto death, and was numbered with the transgressors, though he had borne the sin of many, and made intercession for the transgressors.

Par 1 *Behold, my servant.* According to Ewald, this chapter (like lvi 9-lvii. 11) is a quotation from an earlier prophecy composed in the reign of Manasseh, and referred originally to the martyrdom of an individual. He bases this theory on the historical tone of the description, on the peculiar abruptness of the style, and the singularity of particular words or significations. He might have added the abrupt introduction of the idea of vicarious atonement, which disappears again at the end of this chapter The objections to his hypothesis are, (1) the evident connection of some of the ideas in this chapter with those in xlii 1, 4, 6, xlix 6, 7, l 4–11, (2) the exaggerated weight it requires us to attach to a few slight differences in shades of meaning. The peculiarity in the style of the chapter may be sufficiently accounted for by the excitement of the prophet, labouring after an adequate expression of new and grand ideas. (We may notice, in passing, a recent misconception of Ewald's meaning in 'The Witness of the Old Testament to Christ,' by Professor Leathes, p. 262. Ewald merely intends to say that certain Hebrew words are used by the writer of this chapter in a sense peculiar to himself.)

Behold, my servant shall be prosperous. A soliloquy of Jehovah, which may, perhaps, be thus interpreted: 'The ideal, which even one of the greatest of the prophets (liii. 1) confesses himself incapable of realizing, shall one day be universally recognized as the religious standard.'

His visage was so marred. The genius of Israel was 'marred' or disfigured in the persons of its representatives, the faithful worshippers of Jehovah among the exiles.

Cause to admire. Literally, 'make to spring,' an expression of joy or astonishment The verb is found in Arabic and Assyrian 'Shall shut their mouths,' i.e. shall be lost in contemplation.

Par. 2. *Who hath believed*, &c. The speaker is carried on the wings of prophetic imagination to the period when the foregoing oracle should be in course of fulfilment. He represents the actual nation of Israel, who had outlived the exile, as musing penitently on their guilt in disregarding their lofty ideal. But does the prophet, we may be asked, include himself in the confession? Remembering the humility of the righteous Job, when contemplating the infinite ideal of Jehovah (xlii. 5, 6), we need not hesitate to answer in the affirmative; besides, the histories of Elijah and Jonah shew that even a prophet, the representative of the Divine ideal, could in moments of weakness become a backslider from it.

A man of pains, &c., i.e the ideal of Israel, during the troubles of the exile, had to wage a constant struggle for its existence.

Par. 3. *He did bear our sicknesses*, &c. So far as the more pious of the exiles represented the ideal of the 'Servant of Jehovah,' they suffered undeservedly. To the greater part of the Jewish community they must have appeared in the light of unpractical enthusiasts, because they refused to adopt the ways and feelings of their heathen neighbours. To the latter, on the other hand, their ardent religious patriotism must have seemed a treasonable exhibition of disaffection to Babylon. Hence they were persecuted by both parties (see lxvi 5, xlix. 7, 1 5-7) But the sufferings thus endured by the faithful were not only undeserved, but accepted by Jehovah as a vicarious atonement for the nation. They were imperfect in themselves, it is true, but were transfigured in the light of the ideal which produced them. In other words, they proved that the chosen people was still capable of regeneration, and as a reward for them the offences of the mass of the nation were forgiven, and a glorious spiritual future guaranteed. Strictly speaking however, it was not the suffering of the faithful, but the ideal which this did but imperfectly express, that formed the atonement for the nation, or, to use a New Testament metaphor, the faithful who suffered were mystical members of the supreme 'Servant of Jehovah.'

Par 4. *As the sheep* Comp Jer. xi 19, where however the sheep is an image of Jeremiah's ignorance of the conspiracy formed against his life

He was taken, i e. snatched away by a violent death   Comp lii 5.

He was stricken. Heb *negá lámo* The original phrase, taken singly, is equivocal; it may signify either 'a stroke (came) to him,' or, '. . . to them' There is no doubt that *lámo* occasionally means 'to him,' e.g Gen. ix. 26, Ps xxviii 8, lxiii 10, Isa xliv 15; but Gesenius asserts that 'it is so used only with reference to collectives.' On this shewing the 'Servant of Jehovah' must be a collective, and not a person, whether historical or ideal Gesenius, however, is for once inaccurate *É* and *Ém* in Phœnician are both forms of the suffix of the third person singular, and there can be no reasonable doubt that the latter form was adopted with much besides in the poetic usage of Hebrew The final *m* was probably a remnant of the primitive Semitic Nunnation or Mimmation; in other words, the pronoun of the third person singular, like the noun, was terminated by *n* or *m*. When the Jews had forgotten the origin of the *m* in *lám*, they added a final *o*, thus making the forms of the suffixes in both singular and plural identical See Schröder's 'Phœnician Grammar,' p 153, and Bickell in 'Theologisches Literaturblatt,' 1869, p 366

And his tomb with the oppressor Auth Vers 'And with the rich in his death,' which mars the symmetry of the verse the second member should correspond to the first, as the fourth does to the third Besides, this rendering is not literal; it should be 'in his deaths' For though some critics have explained this as a 'plural of exaggeration,' equivalent to 'in his violent death,' analogies are altogether wanting. (Ezek xxviii 8 is hardly to the point, for (1) *móthé* should be corrected to *mĕmóthé*, see verse 10, and (2) *chalal*, 'the slain,' is used generically, and answers to the plural *árélím*, 'the circumcised,' in verse 10) We must therefore have recourse to conjecture For *áshér*, 'the rich,' we read with Ewald, *'áshók*, 'the oppressive.' The other word *bĕmótháv*, 'in his deaths,' seems to us hopelessly corrupt, and the words 'his tomb,' given above, are only intended as a substitute for the true reading, not as a translation Many critics indeed are of a different opinion, and, by simply changing a vowel-point, read *bámótháv* (with three MSS.), which they render either 'his tombs,' with an allusion to the collective character ascribed by them to the 'Servant,' or, as Ewald, 'his tomb,' omitting entirely to account for the plural suffix. (A plural of extension, such as 'habitations' in liv. 2, is scarcely suitable) The word in question, however, never occurs elsewhere in Biblical or Rabbinic Hebrew in that sense, though frequent enough in the sense of 'high place' or 'altar ' an objection which is scarcely answered by quoting the imperfect analogy of a different word in Job xxi. 32.

His generation, i. e his contemporaries, as in Jer. ii. 31.

Par. 5. *If he should make*, i e the sufferings described above were imposed by Jehovah and endured by the 'Servant' with a high spiritual object in view. The received text has, 'If thou shouldest make,' but so harsh an alternation can hardly be paralleled elsewhere

A trespass-offering, i e a sacrifice by way of satisfaction, as opposed to a sin-offering, or sacrifice by way of expiation See Lev v 15–19

He should see his seed, &c. These expressions appear sufficient of themselves to prove that the 'Servant of Jehovah' is not a historical, but an ideal person. In the course of the paragraph, however, the personification gradually fades away into the Jewish church of the Messianic period. (Comp. note on li. 16)

By his knowledge, &c. That is, the members of the regenerate Jewish church should stand in the twofold relation of prophets and of priests to the Gentile world Comp. xlii 1, 4, 6, &c.

Therefore will I divide. The chapter concludes, as it commenced, with a Divine oracle. The personification is now completely dissolved, and the spiritual recompense of God's 'Servant' is divided among a 'great company.'

The sin of many The 'many' and the 'transgressors' are evidently the Jewish exiles, on the analogy of similar expressions in an earlier paragraph.

CHAPTER VI.

1.

[LIV. 1] Sing, O barren, thou that didst not bear; break forth into singing, and cry aloud, thou that didst not travail with child: for more are the children of the desolate than the children of the married wife, saith Jehovah. Enlarge the place of thy tent, and let them stretch forth without restraint the curtains of thine habitation; lengthen thy cords, and strengthen thy stakes. For thou shalt break forth on the right hand and on the left; and thy seed shall inherit the nations, and make the desolate cities to be inhabited. Fear not, for thou shalt not be ashamed; neither be thou confounded, for thou shalt not blush : yea, thou shalt forget the shame of thy youth, and shalt not remember the reproach of thy widowhood any more. For thy Maker is thine husband, Jehovah of Hosts is his name; and thy Redeemer is the Holy One of Israel, the God of the whole earth is he called. For as a woman forsaken and grieved in spirit Jehovah called thee, and that a wife of youth should be refused, how can it be? saith thy God. For a small moment did I forsake thee, but with great mercies will I gather thee: in my vehement indignation I hid my face from thee for a moment, but with everlasting kindness will I have mercy upon thee, saith Jehovah thy Redeemer.

2.

[9.] For this is as the waters of Noah unto me: as I sware that the waters of Noah should no more go over the earth, so do I swear that I will not be wroth with thee, nor rebuke thee. For though the mountains should move, and the hills should tremble, yet not removed from thee shall be my kindness, neither tremble shall the covenant of my peace, saith Jehovah that hath mercy upon thee. O thou afflicted, tossed with tempest, and not comforted, behold, I will lay thy stones with fair colours, and lay thy foundations with sapphires; and I will make thy battlements of rubies, and thy gates of carbuncles, and all thy borders of precious stones; and all thy children shall be the disciples of Jehovah, and great shall be the bliss of thy children. Through righteousness shalt thou be established: think not on oppression, for thou hast nought to fear, neither on thy terror, for it shall not come nigh thee. If thine enemies should stir up strife, it is not of my counsel; whosoever hath stirred up strife against thee shall fall away unto thee. Behold, I myself made the smith, which bloweth upon the fire of coals, and bringeth forth a weapon fitted for the purpose thereof; I myself made the destroyer to do mischief. No weapon that is formed against thee shall prosper; and every tongue that shall rise against thee in the judgment thou shalt prove guilty. This is the heritage of the servants of Jehovah, and their justification that is of me: the utterance is of Jehovah

Par. 1 *The children of the desolate,* &c. That is, the population of Jerusalem, which now lies in ruins, shall be more numerous than in the most flourishing times of old. Comp. l. 1, lxii. 4.

Thy stakes, i e. thy tent-pins Comp xxxiii. 20

The shame of thy youth . . . the reproach of thy widowhood, i. e. the Egyptian and the Babylonian servitudes.

For Jehovah called thee, &c That is, 'If God freely chose Israel as his own people in spite of its miserable condition during the forty years' wanderings, and if an early love is ever the hardest to be destroyed, then the sufferings of the Babylonian exile can only be a temporary chastisement' (So Ewald.) The assonance of the original is inimitable in English. Ruckert, a master in reproducing Oriental forms of poetry, renders, 'Denn als Weib verdrängtes und bedrängten Geistes.'

Par. 2. *With fair colours* Literally, 'with antimony.' Comp. 2 Kings ix. 30, where Jezebel is said to have 'set her eyes in antimony,' i e. to have painted or coloured them with it.

Shall fall away unto thee, i. e. go over to thy side. Vulgate, 'adjungetur tibi.'

The servants of Jehovah Henceforth we meet only with the phrase 'the servants (not the servant) of Jehovah.' Comp. lxiii. 17, lxv. 8, 9, 13, 14, 15, lxvi 14

CHAPTER VII.

1.

[LV. 1.] Ho, every one that thirsteth, come ye to the waters, and he that hath no money, come ye, buy and eat; yea, come, buy wine and milk without money and without price. Wherefore do ye spend money for that which is not bread, and your gains for that which cannot satisfy? Hearken diligently unto me, and eat ye that which is good, and let your soul delight itself in fatness. Incline your ear, and come unto me; hear, and you shall live; and I will make an everlasting covenant with you, even the sure mercies of David. Behold, I appointed him for a witness to the peoples, a leader and commander of the peoples. Behold, thou shalt call a people whom thou knowest not, and a people that knew not thee shall run unto thee, because of Jehovah thy God, and for the Holy One of Israel, for he hath glorified thee. Seek ye Jehovah while he may be found; call ye upon him while he is near. Let the wicked forsake his way, and the unrighteous man his thoughts; and let him return unto Jehovah, and he will have mercy upon him; and to our God, for he will abundantly pardon

2.

[8.] For my thoughts are not your thoughts, neither are your ways my ways, saith Jehovah. Yea, as the heaven is higher than the earth, so are my ways higher than your ways, and my thoughts than your thoughts. For as the rain cometh down, and the snow, from heaven, and returneth not thither, till it hath watered the earth, and made it bring forth and bud, and given seed to the sower, and bread to the eater; so shall my word be that goeth forth out of my mouth: it shall not return unto me void, till it hath accomplished that which I please, and prospered in the thing whereto I sent it. For ye shall go out with joy, and be led forth with peace; the mountains and the hills shall break forth before you into shouting, and all the trees of the field shall clap the hand. Instead of the thorn shall come up the cypress, and instead of the nettle shall come up the myrtle-tree; and it shall be unto Jehovah for a name, for an everlasting sign, that shall not be cut off.

Par. 1. *The sure mercies of David.* The point of this and the next two verses is, that the wide dominion granted by Jehovah to David, and guaranteed in 2 Sam. vii. 12–16 to David's descendants, shall be restored to the regenerate nation of Israel. Comp a parallel in one of the Psalms written after the return from exile, lxxxix. 39.

For a witness, i e of the true religion Ewald and others render, 'for a law-giver,' giving the original word a sense not found elsewhere, though barely defensible by the Hifil conjugation of its verb.

Par. 2. *So shall my word be.* The word or promise of God is personified as a messenger, who returns when he has performed his commission.

CHAPTER VIII.

[**LVI. 1.**] Thus saith Jehovah, Keep ye justice, and do right-eousness; for my salvation is soon to come, and my righteousness to be revealed. Happy is the man that doeth this, and the son of man that layeth hold on it; that keepeth the Sabbath, that he may not pollute it, and keepeth his hand, that he may do no evil! And let not the alien, that hath joined himself to Jehovah, speak, saying, Assuredly will Jehovah separate me from his people; neither let the eunuch say, Behold, I am a dry tree. For thus saith Jehovah of the eunuchs that keep my Sabbaths, and choose the things that please me, and lay hold on my covenant: I will give unto them in mine house and within my walls a memorial and a name better than sons and daughters ; I will give them an everlasting name, that shall not be cut off. And as for the aliens that join themselves unto Jehovah, to minister unto him, and to love the name of Jehovah, that they may be his servants, even every one that keepeth the Sabbath, that he may not pollute it, and layeth hold on my covenant, I will bring them to my holy mountain, and make them joyful in my house of prayer ; their burnt-offerings and sacrifices shall be acceptable on mine altar : for mine house shall be called the house of prayer for all peoples. This is the utterance of the Lord Jehovah, which gathereth together the outcasts of Israel, Yet will I gather others to them, when they are gathered.

That keepeth the Sabbath Note the contrast between the genuine Isaiah and the later prophets, beginning with Jeremiah. The former, to say the least, depreciates the observance of the Sabbath (i 13, see note), the latter inculcate it with extreme earnestness, as if the future of the nation depended upon it See lviii 13, 14 , Jer. xvii. 19-27 , Ezek xx 12-21. In fact, during the exile it was almost the only bond of religious union which remained

The alien . the eunuch The allusions in this passage are obscure Comp Deut xxiii 2-8.

A memorial and a name, i. e. the memory of their voluntary adhesion to the true religion.

I will bring them, &c That is, the Gentile proselytes shall be allowed to accompany the Jews on their departure from Babylon

Yet will I gather, &c ' When Israel is restored, other Gentiles besides those mentioned shall be converts to the faith.'

CHAPTER IX.

1.

[LVI. 9.] All ye beasts in the field, yea, all ye beasts in the forest, come to devour! His watchmen are blind; they are all without power to discern; they are all as dumb dogs, which cannot bark, murmuring in their dreams, lying down, loving to slumber. Yet the dogs are greedy, and can never have enough, and those are shepherds which cannot understand; from the first even to the last they all turn their own way, each one after his gain. Come, say they, let me fetch wine, and let us fill ourselves with strong drink, and tomorrow shall be as this day, and that beyond measure abundant.

2.

[LVII 1.] The righteous perisheth, and no man layeth it to heart, and godly men are taken away, none considering that the righteous is taken away from the evil which compasseth him. May he depart in peace; may they rest upon their beds, whosoever walked in his own straight path! But as for you, draw near hither, children of the sorcerers, the seed of the adulterer and the whore! Against whom do ye sport yourselves? against whom make ye a wide mouth, and draw out the tongue? are ye not children of transgression, a seed of falsehood; which inflame yourselves with lust hard by the oaks, even under every green tree, which slay the children in the beds of the torrents under the clifts of the rocks? The smooth stones of the torrent-bed are thy portion; they, they are thy lot; unto them also didst thou pour out drink-offerings, thou didst offer meat-offerings. Should I pacify myself for these things?

3.

[7.] Upon a lofty and high mountain didst thou set thy bed: thither also wentest thou up to offer sacrifice. Behind the door also and the post didst thou set thy memorial; yea, afar off from me didst thou uncover thy bed, and go up and enlarge it; thou didst require a covenant from them, thou didst love their bed; thou didst view the hand. And thou didst travel to the king with oil, and didst make thy perfumes to abound, and didst send thy messengers afar off, and wentest even down to the underworld; thou wast wearied with thy much journeying; yet saidst thou not, There is no hope; thou didst gain fresh life in thine arm, therefore thou wast not weakened. And of whom wast thou afraid, and whom didst thou dread, that thou didst deal falsely, and didst not remember me, nor lay it to thy heart? Surely I have long time holden my peace, therefore thou fearest me not. I make known to thee thy justification; but as for thy works, they shall not profit thee. When thou criest, let the idols which thou hast heaped up deliver thee! but the wind shall carry them all away; even a breath shall take them: but he that trusteth in me shall inherit the land, and shall possess my holy mountain.

4.

[14.] And one said, Cast ye up, cast ye up, prepare the way, take up the stumbling-block out of the way of my people. For thus saith the high and lofty One, that abideth the same for ever, whose name is Holy; I abide in the high and holy place, with him also that is of a bruised and lowly spirit, that I may revive the spirit of the lowly, and revive the heart of them that are bruised. For I will not contend for ever, neither will I be always wroth; for the spirit would faint before me, and the souls which I have made. For his unlawful desires was I wroth, and smote him, I hid me, and was wroth; for he walked frowardly in the way of his own heart. I have seen his ways, and will heal him; I will lead him also, and will repay comforts to him and his mourners. Thus saith Jehovah that maketh the fruit of the lips, Peace, peace to him that is far off, and to him that is near, and I will heal them. But the wicked are like the troubled sea, for it like them cannot stay at rest, and the waters thereof cast up mire and dirt. There is no peace, saith my God, for the wicked.

Par. 1. *All ye beasts of the field*, &c. This is merely a poetical way of describing the dangers to which the Jews were exposed by the neglect of their teachers. A complete moral and religious reform was the only means of preserving their nationality unimpaired, but the elders and the prophets were too degenerate to pay any heed to this. Comp. Ezek. viii 1, xiii 1–23, xiv 1, xx 1, Jer. xxix. 8, 9, 21–23.

According to Ewald and Bleek, this passage (lvi 9–lvii 11, beginning) is a quotation from an earlier prophet, who lived probably in the reign of Manasseh. Idolatry, as we know from this prophecy and from that of Ezekiel, was not uncommon among the Jewish exiles, and our prophet may have designed to add force to his denunciation by citing words which had received the sanction of antiquity. (Comp. ii 2, 5, xv, xvi 1–12, xxv 6–8, 10–12, xxvi 12, 13.) The principal reasons in favour of this hypothesis are, (1) the abruptness with which the section is introduced—though we venture to think that such abrupt transitions are quite in the manner of this prophet, and fail to observe any indication of a change in style in lvii 11, (2) the description of Jewish idolatry which follows, some of the features of which are rather Palestinian than Babylonian. In answer to the latter objection it may be urged that a Semitic race, when transplanted to a distant country, preserves a lively recollection of its earlier home. The Arabic poets in Spain delighted in allusions to Arabian localities, and descriptions of the events of desert-life. Why should not a prophecy of the exile contain some such allusions to the scenery of Palestine, and at least one such retrospect of events, some of which had happened previously to the fall of Jerusalem, events, it should be remembered, which had left a deep impression on the religious condition of the Jews in

Babylon? It will perhaps not be out of place to compare the allusions in this section to oaks and hills and torrent-beds, with the frequent and touching references of Ezekiel to the mountains and rivers of Israel. See Ezek. xxxiv. 13, xxxvi. 1, &c.

Par. 2. *Hard by the oaks.* Comp. i. 29 and note; Ezek. vi. 13.

Which slay the children. Sacrifices of children were offered to Moloch and to Baal, 2 Kings xxiii 10; Jer. xix 5

The smooth stones . are thy portion. This was a return to the primitive Semitic religion. Sacred stones were worshipped as symbols of the Divine presence prior to the rise of idolatry. Comp. Herod iii. 8, and the black stone of the Caaba at Mecca.

Par 3 *Didst thou set thy bed* The religious defection of Israel is compared to adultery. Comp. Ezek. xvi, xxiii.

Thy memorial, i e the words, 'Jehovah is our God, Jehovah is One,' which, according to Deuteronomy (vi 9, xi 20), were written on the posts of the house and on the gates The polytheists apparently placed this 'memorial' of Jehovah '*behind* the door and the post' by way of putting it out of sight. Others understand the phrase of some obscure idolatrous emblem.

Thou didst view the hand. Probably an euphemism.

To the king, i e. to Baal, who bears the title of 'king' in Phœnician inscriptions. Baal's consort, Asherah, is called 'queen of heaven' in Jeremiah (vii. 18, xliv. 17–19, 25).

Afar off, i. e to renowned foreign shrines.

To the underworld, i e. to the infernal gods Comp note on lxv 4

Of whom wast thou afraid? That is, as long as the Jews were under the protection of Jehovah, they had no real cause for alarm. Then follows the secret motive of the idolatry practised during the exile Jehovah seemed to have renounced his relation to his people, 'to have been silent a long time' (comp. xlii. 14, lxiv. 11); the Jews therefore conceived themselves at liberty to change their religion.

Thy justification, i e. the justification of thy cause in the eyes of the world, or, in other words, the restoration of the Jews to Palestine. 'Thy works'='thine idols'

Par. 4 *And one said,* i e. a heavenly voice was heard. Comp. note on xlv. 24

A bruised spirit, i e. one depressed by affliction Comp lxi 1, lxv 14, lxvi 2.

For his unlawful desires Literally, 'for the iniquity of his covetousness,' which is explained afterwards as = 'walking frowardly in the way of his own heart,' i e the imitation of foreign culture and religions.

And will repay comforts. Comp note on xl 2

That maketh the fruit of the lips, 1. e. who designed the lips for offering the sacrifice of praise. Comp. Hos xiv. 2.

To him that is far off and to him that is near, i e to the whole body of Jewish exiles, in whatever country they might be dispersed.

BOOK III.

The New Jerusalem.

In the second book the prophet had abstracted his view alike from Cyrus and from Babylon, and concentrated it on Israel's glorious horizon, and the grave question whether his countrymen were morally prepared for the crisis. The third book is equally destitute of any express reference to Cyrus or to Babylon, but it contains several passages from which we may plausibly infer that the expectations at first entertained of Cyrus had met with a temporary disappointment. If so, we may proceed to the further conclusion that some months at least had elapsed between the composition of the first book of the prophecy and the third. In the period covered by the second book we may suppose the patriotic Jews to have been waiting for news of the advance of Cyrus upon Babylon: in the course of the third we seem to hear the accents of disappointment and complaint. Not that the prophet himself shared these discontented feelings; he even wins his way through the apparent failure of his anticipations to a still bolder faith in the immediate interposition of Jehovah.

The first chapter of this book refutes the objection that Israel has a right, based on its scrupulous observance of fast-days, to complain of Jehovah for not interfering in its behalf. The second, in more direct language, indicates the moral degradation of all classes among the Jews as the cause of Jehovah's displeasure. Then follows a confession of sin, in which the prophet, as on a similar occasion (chap. liii), includes himself. Sin alone is the reason why the people of Jehovah have so long languished in exile. But now, since the hopes formerly fixed on

Cyrus have been disappointed, Jehovah himself will interpose for the destruction of all the foes of the theocracy, and the spiritual regeneration of his own people. Here the connection of ideas is interrupted by a digression extending over the next three chapters. And first of all by an ode on the glory of the new Jerusalem, which divides itself into five strophes: (1) the dawn of Zion's prosperity; (2) the restoration and beautification of the temple; (3) the rebuilding of Jerusalem; (4) the peace and splendour of the Jewish state; (5) the inalienable character of all these mercies. In the fourth chapter the 'Servant of Jehovah' reappears for the last time, dwelling in glowing terms on his pre-eminent function of consolation, and exulting in the speedy fulfilment of the Divine promises. In the beginning of the fifth chapter Jehovah himself is the speaker; he declares that he will not desist until he has attained his object in the glorification of Zion. Indeed, he has himself appointed angelic watchmen, who allow themselves no rest until Jehovah shall interpose for the relief of his people. Here the prophet returns to his contemporaries in Babylon, and urges them not to linger in the accursed city, for their redemption is won.

At this point the digression is ended, and the reader is transported by the prophet's vivid imagination to the position occupied at the end of the second chapter. The judgment already announced has by this time actually taken place. It is described in a dialogue between the prophet and a victorious warrior on his return from the field of battle in Edom. The latter turns out to be none less than the Divine champion of the cause of Israel. He had noticed with wonder that no human agent (an allusion to the delay of Cyrus in Asia Minor) had offered himself for the sacred enterprise, and therefore he was constrained to take vengeance in person on his own and Israel's enemies. Edom indeed is among the first to feel the weight of his displeasure, yet Edom is only the representative of the entire heathen world. (Comp. lxiii. 6, 'I trode down the *peoples*,' and lix. 18, 'to the sea-coasts (i. e. to his most distant enemies) he will repay recompense.') The three chapters which succeed are evidently designed to form an artistic conclusion to the whole prophecy. The seventh chapter is an expression of thanksgiving intermingled with penitence and supplication. It begins with a retrospect of the early history of Israel, when Jehovah stood in intimate relationship to his people, and constantly delivered them. Then it passes into a tender expostulation with Him, who has done so much, but now seems to be inaccessible to entreaty. 'O that Jehovah would descend, as once before on Sinai!' Indeed, the prophet exclaims, if chastisement was designed to lead the Israelites back to their God, it has completely missed its aim with the great majority of the nation. Calamity has but led to a despair of God's forgiveness, and, as a natural consequence of this, to a general and undisguised depravity. The eighth chapter contains the answer of Jehovah to the prayers offered by the prophet in the name of the church. It begins with rebuke, but ends with gracious consolations. The Divine speaker points out the moral impossibility of granting any relief as long as the majority of the exiles commit such open violations of the true religion. But, he continues, although the unbelievers and the polytheists shall soon be punished still more fearfully, the truly pious Israelites shall be spared amidst the general destruction. He concludes with a glowing description of the blessings reserved in Palestine for the faithful. The ninth and last chapter contains a further answer to the church's prayer, with special reference to the case of the unbelieving Jews, who had treated the patriotic zeal of the prophet and his disciples with bitter contempt. It declares that even if any insincere worshippers of the true God should desire to co-operate in building a temple to Jehovah, He, the friend of the poor in spirit, will not accept their service. Then the prophet turns to his own disciples, and announces the terrible destruction of their unbelieving countrymen. But here he is transported to the time when the faithful few have returned to Palestine, and Jehovah has resumed his throne on Mount Zion. Representatives of all nations shall throng to the new Jerusalem as spectators, and even the polytheistic exiles, who had remained in Babylon, shall at last resolve to claim a share in the patrimony of Israel (chap. ix. par. 2). But a sudden catastrophe shall take place; the enemies of Jehovah shall be consumed by fire and sword. A few only shall escape from the scene of destruction, but these shall be transformed into instruments for the fulfilment of Jehovah's purposes respecting Israel. They shall carry tidings of the great God of the Jews to their distant homes, and prevail upon those Gentiles, amongst whom any Jews may still be dwelling, to conduct these swiftly and honourably to Jerusalem. Last of all, the prophet returns to the unbelievers and their awful doom. Even after death (if we are not mistaken in so interpreting the passage) they shall have some consciousness of the bitter resentment of Jehovah.

CHAPTER I.

1.

[LVIII. 1] Cry aloud, spare not; lift up thy voice like a trumpet, and shew my people their transgression, and the house of Jacob their sins. Yet they seek me daily, and desire to know my ways, as a nation that did righteousness, and forsook not the precept of their God: they demand of me judgments of righteousness, they desire that God would approach. Wherefore do we fast, say they, and thou seest not? wherefore do we chasten our soul, and thou takest no knowledge? Behold, in the day of your fast ye go after your business, and exact all your labours. Behold, ye fast for strife and debate, and to smite with the fist of wickedness: ye do not so fast this day, that ye make your voice to be heard on high. Is this the fast that I have chosen, the day when a man doth chasten his soul? Is it to bow down his head as a bulrush, and to spread sackcloth and ashes under him? wilt thou call this a fast, and an acceptable day to Jehovah? Is not this the fast that I have chosen? to loose the bands fastened by wickedness, to undo the thongs of the yoke, and to let the oppressed go free, and to burst in sunder every yoke? Is it not to deal thy bread to the hungry, and to bring home them that wander abroad in misery? when thou seest the naked, to cover him, and not to hide thyself from thine own flesh?

2.

[8.] Then shall thy light break forth as the morning, and thine healing shall spring forth speedily, and thy righteousness shall go before thee: the glory of Jehovah shall be thy rereward. Then shalt thou call, and Jehovah shall answer; thou shalt cry, and he shall say, Here I am. If thou take away from the midst of thee the yoke, the putting forth of the finger, and speaking maliciously; and if thou offer thy pleasant things to the hungry, and satisfy the afflicted soul; then shall thy light rise in obscurity, and thy darkness be as the noon-day, and Jehovah shall guide thee continually, and satisfy thy soul in sultry heat, and make strong thy bones: then shalt thou be like a fresh watered garden, and like a fountain whose waters fail not. And they that shall be of thee shall build the old waste places; thou shalt raise up the foundations of many generations, so that men shall call thee, The repairer of the breach, The restorer of paths, that the land be inhabited.

3.

[13.] If thou turn away thy foot from the Sabbath, not doing thy business on my holy day, and call the Sabbath a delight, and the holy of Jehovah honourable; and if thou honour it, not doing as thou art wont, nor going after thy business, nor speaking vain words: then shalt thou have thy delight in Jehovah, and I will cause thee to ride over the high places of the land, and feed thee with the heritage of Jacob thy father; for the mouth of Jehovah hath spoken it.

Par. 1. *They demand of me judgments of righteousness.* i. e. they claim the destruction of their enemies, as a just recognition of their own innocence

Wherefore do we fast. The tendency of the Jews during the exile seems to have been to substitute fast-days for Sabbaths, the ostensible motive of the former being the commemoration of the great national calamities. Thus there were fasts in the fourth, fifth, seventh, and tenth months, in memory of the capture of Jerusalem, the burning of the temple, the murder of Gedaliah, and the beginning of the siege of Jerusalem, respectively. See Zech. vii. 3–5, viii. 19. The only fast prescribed by the law was that of the day of atonement.

Is this ... the day when a man doth chasten his soul. The word 'to fast' (*ṣūm*) does not occur in the Pentateuch; its place is supplied by the phrase 'to afflict, or chasten, one's soul,' Lev. xvi. 29, 31. The prophet's meaning therefore seems to be, Is this a fast in the true and original sense of the word, i. e. a prolonged act of self-denial?

The thongs of the yoke. For the cruelty of Jewish masters to their slaves at a somewhat earlier period, see Jer. xxxiv. 8–22

From thine own flesh, i. e. thy poorer countrymen. Comp. 2 Sam. v. 1.

Par. 2. *Then shall thy light,* &c. That is, a thorough moral and spiritual reformation is the condition of participation in the promised redemption. The prophet alludes apparently to the complaints called forth (ver. 2) by the delay of Cyrus to invade Babylonia.

Thy righteousness, i. e. the prosperity granted by Jehovah in his 'righteous' fulfilment of his covenant.

The putting forth of the finger, i. e. the gesture of contempt towards the poor and the pious. Comp. lxvi. 5.

Par. 3. *To ride over the high places of the land,* i. e. to take triumphal possession of Palestine with its hills and fortresses

CHAPTER II.

1.

[**LIX. 1.**] Behold, the hand of Jehovah is not too short to save, neither his ear too heavy to hear; but your iniquities have separated between you and your God, and your sins have concealed his face from you, so that he heareth not. For your hands are defiled with blood, and your fingers with iniquity; your lips speak lies, and your tongue muttereth perverseness. There is none that preacheth in sincerity, nor any that pleadeth in faithfulness: they trust in vanity, and speak deceitfully; they conceive misery, and bring forth mischief. They hatch basilisks' eggs, and weave spiders' webs, he that eateth of their eggs dieth, and, if an egg be crushed, it breaketh out into a viper. Their webs serve not for clothing, neither with their works can men cover themselves: their works are works of mischief, and the act of violence is in their hands. Their feet run to evil, and they make haste to shed innocent blood: their thoughts are thoughts of mischief; desolation and destruction are in their highways. The way of peace they know not, and there is no justice in their tracks; they have made them crooked paths; whosoever goeth therein shall not know peace.

2.

[9.] Therefore hath judgment been far from us, and righteousness doth not overtake us: we wait for light, but behold obscurity; for the perfect brightness, but we walk in darkness. We grope for the wall like the blind; we grope as those that have no eyes: we stumble at noon-day as in the twilight; among the wealthy we are as dead men. We all murmur like bears, and moan feebly like doves: we wait for judgment, but there is none; for salvation, but it is far from us. For our transgressions are many before thee, and our sins testify against us; for we have the conscience of our transgressions, and as for our iniquities, we know them,—rebellion and belying Jehovah, and drawing back from following our God, speaking oppression and frowardness, conceiving and uttering from the heart words of falsehood. Justice hath been driven backward, and righteousness standeth afar off; yea, truth hath stumbled in the street, and uprightness cannot enter; therefore truth faileth, and he that shunneth evil is spoiled of strength.

3.

[15.] And Jehovah saw it, and it displeased him that there was no judgment; and he saw that there was no man, and was astonished that there was no champion; therefore his arm brought salvation unto him, and his righteousness it sustained him. And he put on righteousness as a coat of mail, and the helmet of salvation upon his head; and he put on garments of vengeance for clothing, and clad himself with zeal as a mantle. According to their deeds, accordingly he will repay, fury to his adversaries, recompence to his enemies; to the sea-coasts he will repay recompence. Then shall they fear the name of Jehovah from the west, and his glory from the rising of the sun; for it shall come like a pent-up stream, which the blast of Jehovah hath driven, but as a Redeemer shall he come unto Zion, and unto them that are converted from transgression in Jacob: the utterance is of Jehovah.

4.

[21.] And as for me, this is my covenant with them, saith Jehovah, My spirit that is upon thee, and my words which I have put in thy mouth, shall not depart out of thy mouth, nor out of the mouth of thy seed, nor out of the mouth of thy seed's seed, saith Jehovah, from henceforth and for ever.

Par 1. *There is none that preacheth in sincerity* Literally, 'there is none that crieth in righteousness.' Comp. the use of 'to cry' or 'to call' = 'to prophesy,' in xl 2, 6, xliv 7, of 'report' = 'revelation,' in liii. 1, and of 'righteous' = 'right' or 'veracious,' in xli 26 The sense appears to be, that none of the popular prophets had courage to expose the moral degradation of their hearers

None that pleadeth in faithfulness, i e. none whose evidence can be trusted

If an egg be crushed, &c. That is, if any of their plans are opposed, they will take a cunning and malicious revenge.

Their webs serve not for clothing. A qualification of the metaphor. They are weavers, not of any useful object, but of deeds of violence.

Par. 2. *Therefore hath judgment*, &c. That is, therefore has Jehovah so long refrained from interposing in your behalf.

We wait for light, &c. A description of the disappointment felt by the patriotic Jews at the apparent hesitation of Cyrus to attack the Babylonians.

Among the wealthy, i. e. among the prosperous inhabitants of Babylon. The origin of the word rendered 'wealthy' is doubtful; see 'Notes and Criticisms,' p. 39.

Is spoiled of strength. This passage has been very variously interpreted, but the most probable sense is that deduced from Ps. lxvi. 5, where the expression, 'the stout-hearted are spoiled,' is explained by the subsequent words (Auth. Vers.), 'and none of the men of might have found their hands,' i. e. they have lost the power of resistance.

Par. 3. *He saw that there was no man.* The hopes of the Jews, which had centred in Cyrus and the Persians, appeared to be ending in disappointment. See the analysis prefixed to this book.

His arm brought salvation. That is, Jehovah himself will interpose, and execute vengeance on all his enemies. This is described in the past of prophetic certainty.

It shall come, i. e. the name of Jehovah shall come. Comp. xxx. 27, where there is a similar transition from 'the name of Jehovah' to Jehovah himself.

Par. 4. *My spirit that is upon thee*, &c. See notes on li. 16, lxi. 1.

CHAPTER III.

[LX. 1]   1.

Arise, shine; for thy light is come,
    And the glory of Jehovah is risen upon thee.
For, behold, the darkness shall cover the earth, and gross
        darkness the peoples,
But upon thee shall Jehovah rise, and his glory shall be
        seen upon thee;

And the nations shall journey unto thy light,
   And kings to the brightness of thy shining.
Lift up thine eyes round about, and see : they all gather to-
   gether, and come unto thee ;
   Thy sons come from afar, and thy daughters are borne on
     the side.

[5.]   **2.**

Then shalt thou see, and be lightened; and thine heart shall
   throb, and be enlarged;
   Because the wealth of the sea shall be turned unto thee, the
     riches of the nations shall come unto thee.
A multitude of camels shall cover thee, the young camels of
   Midian and Ephah, they all shall come from Sheba,
   Bearing gold and incense, and spreading abroad the praises
     of Jehovah ;
All the flocks of Kedar shall gather together unto thee, the
   rams of Nebaioth shall minister unto thee:
   They shall come up acceptably on mine altar, and I will
     glorify the house of my glory
Who are these that fly as the clouds, and as doves to their
   cotes ?
Yea, for me the sea-coasts wait, and the ships of Tarshish first,
   To bring thy sons from far, their silver and their gold
     with them,
For the name of Jehovah thy God, and for the Holy One of
   Israel, because he hath glorified thee.

[10.]   **3.**

And aliens shall build thy walls, and their kings shall minister
   unto thee,

For in my wrath I smote thee, but in my favour will I
have mercy upon thee.

And thy gates shall be open continually, they shall not be
shut day nor night,

That men may bring unto thee the riches of the nations,
and their kings in a train of captives;

For the nation and kingdom that will not serve thee shall
perish,

Yea, those nations shall be utterly wasted.

The glory of Lebanon shall come unto thee, the cypress and
the plane and the larch together,

That I may glorify the place of my sanctuary, and make
my footstool honourable.

And the sons of them that afflicted thee shall go crouching
unto thee, and all they that reviled thee shall bow
down at the soles of thy feet,

And men shall call thee, The city of Jehovah, The Zion
of the Holy One of Israel.

[15.]   4.

Whereas thou wast forsaken and hated, and no man passed
through thee,

I will make thee an eternal excellency, a delight of many
generations;

And thou shalt suck the milk of the nations, and shalt suck
the breast of kings,

And thou shalt know that I Jehovah am thy saviour, and
that thy redeemer is the Hero of Israel.

For brass I will bring gold, and for iron I will bring silver,
and for wood brass, and for stones iron;

And I will make thine officers peace, and thy governors righteousness.

Violence shall no more be heard in thy land, desolation nor destruction within thy borders,

But thou shalt call thy walls Salvation, and thy gates Praise.

[19.]   5.

The sun shall be no more thy light by day, neither for brightness shall the moon give light unto thee,

But Jehovah shall be unto thee an everlasting light, and thy God thy glory:

Thy sun shall no more go down, neither shall thy moon withdraw itself,

For Jehovah shall be unto thee an everlasting light, and the days of thy mourning shall be ended.

And thy people shall be all righteous, they shall possess the land for ever,

The plant of my garden, the work of mine hands, that I may be glorified

The smallest shall become a thousand, and the weakest a great nation;

I Jehovah will hasten it in the season thereof.

Par. 1. *Arise, shine.* Jerusalem is personified as a woman lying prostrate on the ground in deep melancholy. The rest of the world is metaphorically described as being shrouded in thick darkness, for the great judgment-day of Jehovah is but just past. Suddenly a light is seen approaching the spot where Jerusalem is lying, it is the glory of Jehovah, who is returning with the exiles to his sanctuary

On the side. An allusion to the Oriental custom of carrying children on the hip

Par. 2. *Be lightened* Literally, ' shine for joy.' The same expression occurs in Ps. xxxiv. 5.

The young camels of Midian. The caravans of the Midianites, especially those of Ephah (Gen. xxv. 4), appear to have gone to Sheba, i. e. to Arabia Felix, or Yemen, for gold and spices. Kedar and Nebaioth are the names of nomad Arabian tribes. See Gen. xxv. 13.

Who are these that fly as the clouds? Indistinct forms are seen in the distance; they are the ships which bear the returning exiles.

Par 3. *Their kings in a train of captives.* See note on xlv. 13, where the captivity of the heathen nations is described as being voluntary.

The glory of Lebanon shall come unto thee, i. e. the new Jerusalem shall excel the fairest regions of Palestine in beauty.

CHAPTER IV.

1.

[LXI 1] The Spirit of the Lord Jehovah is upon me, because Jehovah hath anointed me to preach good tidings to the afflicted, because he hath sent me to bind up the broken-hearted, to proclaim liberty to the captives, and the opening of the prison to them that are bound; to proclaim the acceptable year of Jehovah, and the day of vengeance of our God, to comfort all who mourn; to grant unto them that mourn in Zion, yea, to give unto them a coronal for ashes, the oil of joy for mourning, the garment of praise for a heavy spirit, that men should call them oaks of prosperity, the garden planted of Jehovah that he might be glorified.

2.

[4.] Then shall they build the old wastes, and raise up the former desolations, and they shall repair the waste cities, the desolations of many generations. And strangers shall stand and feed your flocks, and aliens shall be your ploughmen and your vinedressers; but ye shall be named the priests of Jehovah, men

shall call you the ministers of our God : ye shall eat the riches
of the nations, and shall make your boast of their glory.   For
your shame ye shall have double, and for infamy they shall
triumph in their portion ; therefore in their land they shall
possess the double; everlasting joy shall be unto them.   For
I Jehovah love justice, I hate wrongful violence; and I will
give them their reward faithfully, and make with them an
everlasting covenant, so that their seed shall be renowned
among the nations, and their offspring in the midst of the
peoples : all that see them shall acknowledge them, that they
are a seed which Jehovah hath blessed.

3.

[10.]   I will greatly rejoice in Jehovah; my soul shall exult in
my God ; for he hath clothed me with the garments of salvation,
he hath wrapped me in the mantle of prosperity, as a bridegroom
that putteth on a priestly coronal, and as a bride that decketh herself with her jewels.   For as the earth bringeth forth her buds, and
as a garden causeth the things that are sown in it to bud forth, so
the Lord Jehovah will cause prosperity to bud forth, even renown ,
before all nations.

Par. 1. *The spirit of the Lord Jehovah is upon me.*   This is probably another
soliloquy of the ' Servant of Jehovah,' and not, as most modern critics suppose,
of the prophetic author.   Perhaps the only objection to our view is the exclusive use of the expression, ' the servants of Jehovah,' from chap. liv. onwards,
which might seem to indicate a resolution of the personality of the ' Servant'
into its elements, but is not such a sudden renewal of an old subject in complete accordance with the characteristics of the prophecy?   At any rate, the
objection is counterbalanced by the absence from our prophet of anything
like self-assertion.   Five times indeed we have seemed to trace allusions to
his own privileged position, but each of these is confined within a mere frag-

ment of a sentence, and thus the impersonal character of the composition is on the whole carefully maintained. The present soliloquy differs in no essential respect from the preceding ones, the reference of which to the servant has (except in chap 1) never been disputed

Hath anointed me, i e hath appointed me to a sacred office. So in 1 Kings xix 16, Elijah is directed to 'anoint' Elisha, and so in Isa. xiii. 3, the Medes are called ' Jehovah's consecrated ones.'

To proclaim liberty. An allusion to the legal phrase for the privilege of the year of jubilee, Lev xxv 8.

Oaks of prosperity Literally, ' oaks of righteousness.' But the context shews that ' righteousness' means here the external justification of a good cause, i. e success. See note on xli. 2, and for the rendering ' oaks,' note on 1. 29.

Par. 2 *The priests of Jehovah.* That is, the position of Israel in relation to the Gentiles shall be analogous to the primacy of Levi among the tribes. Comp Exod. xix. 6, ' Ye shall be unto me a kingdom of priests '

For your shame ye shall have double An enigmatical expression, which is explained by the following words, ' they shall possess the double.' Comp. note on xl. 2 (p. 147), ' double for all her sins '

Wrongful violence, i. e. the oppression exercised by the Babylonians.

Par. 3. *I will greatly rejoice* The ' Servant' places himself mentally in the period when God's promises will have been fulfilled, and expresses his delight.

A priestly coronal. Comp. Exod. xxix. 9; Song of Sol. iii. 11.

CHAPTER V.

1.

[LXII. 1] For Zion's sake I will not be silent, and for Jerusalem's sake I will not rest, until the prosperity thereof go forth as the dawn, and the salvation thereof as a burning torch. And the nations shall see thy prosperity, and all kings thy glory, and thou shalt be called by a new name which the mouth of Jehovah shall give thee; and thou shalt be a crown of glory in the hand of Jehovah, and a royal diadem in the palm of the hand of thy God.

2.

[4.] Thou shalt no more be termed The forsaken, neither shall thy land any more be termed The desolation; but thou shalt be called My delight is in her, and thy land The married, forasmuch as Jehovah delighteth in thee, and thy land shall be married. Yea, as a young man marrieth a virgin, so shall thy sons marry thee, and with the joy of the bridegroom over the bride shall thy God rejoice over thee.

3.

[6] I have set watchmen upon thy walls, O Jerusalem; they are never silent by day nor by night. O ye that are Jehovah's remembrancers, take not your rest; and give no rest to him, until he establish Jerusalem, and make it a renown in the earth.

4.

[8.] Jehovah hath sworn by his right hand, and by the arm of his strength, Surely I will no more give thy corn to be meat for thine enemies, and the aliens shall not drink thy wine, for the which thou hast laboured; but they that gather it shall eat it, and praise Jehovah, and they that bring it into the storehouse shall drink it in my holy courts.

5.

[10] Go through, go through the gates; prepare ye the way of the people; cast up, cast up the highway; gather out the stones; lift up an ensign for the peoples. Behold, Jehovah hath proclaimed unto the end of the earth, Say ye to the daughter of Zion, Behold, thy salvation cometh; behold, his reward is with him, and his recompence before him. And men shall call them,

The holy people, The redeemed of Jehovah; and thou shalt be called, The sought out, A city not forsaken.

Par. 1. For Zion's sake will I not be silent . . . until, &c. The speaker here is Jehovah, as is shewn by par. 3, and by the parallel expression, lxv. 6, 'I will not be silent, until I have recompensed;' comp. also lvii. 11, lxiv. 12.

A new name. Comp. Jer. xxxiii. 16, 'This is the name wherewith she shall be called, Jehovah is our righteousness' (i e the promise of Jehovah is the warrant of our security).

In the band of Jehovah. Jerusalem is compared to a crown, which Jehovah holds forth proudly for the admiration of the world

Par. 3. I have set watchmen upon thy walls. The key to this passage is furnished by lii. 8, where the ideal representative of Zion (comp. note on xl. 9) is described as having 'watchmen' (perhaps angelic beings, Zech. i. 12), whose duty it is to give the first tidings of the return of Jehovah with the exiles. In the present passage these 'watchmen' are said to have been stationed on the (ideal) walls by Jehovah himself. Comp. the pathetic apostrophe in Lamentations ii 18,

> 'Cry heartily unto Jehovah, O wall of the daughter of Zion!
> Let tears run down like a river day and night!
> Give thyself no rest; let not the apple of thine eye cease!'

O ye that are Jehovah's remembrancers. The prophet adjures the 'watchmen' to continue reminding Jehovah of his promises.

Par. 4. Shall drink it in my holy courts. An allusion to the feasts of the tithes, which, according to Deut. xiv. 23–27, were to be eaten 'before Jehovah'

CHAPTER VI.

[LXIII. 1.] 'Who is this that cometh from Edom, with purple garments from Bozrah? this that is glorious in his apparel, that throweth back his head in the pride of his strength?' 'I that promised in righteousness, mighty to save.' 'Wherefore is there red in thine apparel, and thy garments like his that treadeth in the wine-press?' 'I have trodden the wine-trough alone, and of the

peoples there was no man with me ; so I trode them in mine
anger, and trampled them in my fury, and their blood besprinkled
my garments, and I have stained all my raiment. For a day of
vengeance was in mine heart, and the year of my redeemed had
come ; and I looked, but there was none to help, and wondered in
myself, but there was none to uphold , therefore mine own arm
brought salvation unto me, and my fury it upheld me ; and I trode
the peoples in mine anger, and brake them to pieces in my fury,
and caused their blood to run down to the earth.'

Who is this that cometh from Edom ? The prophet here returns to the standing-
point occupied at the end of chap ii Edom is the representative of the
heathen world, as in chap xxxiv (old arrangement), the notes on which may
illustrate this chapter For the connection of ideas, and especially for the sense
of the expression, 'there was no man with me,' see analysis prefixed to this
book

I that promised in righteousness. An allusion to the promises contained in the
preceding chapters Comp lii 6

That treadeth in the wine-press. Compare, for this metaphor, Joel iii. 13 ;
Lam. i. 15 ; Rev xix. 15.

Their blood Literally, 'their juice.' Similarly wine is sometimes called 'the
blood of the grape,' Gen xlix 11 , Deut. xxxii 14.

Broke them to pieces For *'ashakkĕrém*, 'I made them drunk,' read *'ashabbĕrém*,
with the Targum, and many MSS and critical editors.

CHAPTER VII.

1.

[**LXIII. 7**] I will celebrate the loving-kindness of Jehovah, and
the praises of Jehovah, according to all that Jehovah hath bestowed on us, and the great goodness toward the house of Israel,
which he hath bestowed on them, according to his mercies, and
according to the multitude of his loving-kindnesses. He said,

Surely they are my people, children that will not lie, and became unto them a saviour. In all their affliction he was afflicted, and the angel of his presence saved them · in his love and in his pity he redeemed them, and he took them up, and carried them all the days of old. But they rebelled, and vexed his holy Spirit, so he turned himself to be their enemy; he himself fought against them.

2.

[11.] Then they remembered the days of old, and the true Moses of his people, saying, Where is he that brought them up out of the sea with the shepherds of his flock? Where is he that placed his holy Spirit among them? That caused his majestical arm to journey at the right hand of Moses, that divided the water before them, to make himself an everlasting name? That made them go through the floods, as horses through the pasture-land, without stumbling? Like the beast that goeth down into the valley, the Spirit of Jehovah led them: thus didst thou guide thy people, to make thyself a name of majesty.

3.

[15.] Look down from heaven, and behold, from the habitation of thy holiness and thy majesty. Where are thy zeal and thy mighty acts? Thine inward yearnings and compassion have restrained their issues toward me. Surely thou art our father, for Abraham knoweth us not, and Israel doth not acknowledge us; thou, Jehovah, art our father, our redeemer was thy name from of old. O Jehovah, why dost thou make us to err from thy ways, and harden our heart that we should not fear thee? Return for thy servants' sake, the tribes of thine inheritance. Thy holy people possessed it but a little while : our adversaries have trodden down thy sanctuary.   We are become like those over whom thou hast never borne rule, who have not been called by thy name.

4.

[**LXIV. 1.**] Oh that thou wouldest rend the heavens, that thou wouldest come down, that the mountains might quake before thee, (as when the fire kindleth the brushwood, as when the fire causeth the water to boil,) to make thy name known to thine adversaries, so that nations might tremble before thee, when thou didst terrible things which we hoped not for ; oh that thou wouldest come down, that the mountains might quake before thee, (for none from of old have heard it, nor perceived it by the ear, neither hath the eye seen any God beside thee, who would perform such things for him that waiteth for him)! Oh that thou wouldest meet favourably him that worketh righteousness with joy, that remembereth thee, walking in thy ways! Behold, thou wast wroth, therefore we sinned; our adversities continued long, therefore we went astray.   And we all became as one that is unclean, and our righteous deeds as a menstruous garment ; we all did fade as the leaves, and our iniquities like the wind carried us away; and there was none that called upon thy name, that stirred up himself to take hold on thee ; for thou hadst hid thy face from us, and delivered us into the hand of our sins.

5.

[**8**] Yet now, O Jehovah, thou art our father· we are the clay, and thou our potter, and we all are the work of thy hands!   O Jehovah, be not wroth very sore, neither remember iniquity for ever: behold, consider, we pray thee; we are all thy

people! Thy holy cities are a wilderness, Zion is a wilderness, Jerusalem a desolation. Our holy and our glorious house, where our fathers praised thee, is burned up with fire, and all our pleasant things are laid waste. Wilt thou refrain thyself for these things, O Jehovah? wilt thou hold thy peace, and afflict us very sore?

Par. 1 *I will celebrate*, &c. Compare the historical retrospect which follows with the analogous passages in Ps. lxxvii, written probably during the Babylonian exile.

The angel of his presence A combination of two phrases in the Pentateuch, 'the angel of Jehovah' (Gen. xvi. 7, &c.), and 'my presence' (Exod. xxxiii. 15). The former phrase is frequently used as a synonym for Jehovah, the personality of an angel being regarded as unimportant, except so far as it was an organ of the Divine will

He took them up. A favourite image with the prophets. Comp. xlvi. 3; Hos. xi. 3, Deut. i. 31. For the meaning of 'vexed his holy Spirit,' see below.

Par. 2 *The true Moses of his people*, i. e. Jehovah. Compare the parallel clause, 'Where is he that brought them up out of the sea?' The literal rendering is, 'he that draweth out, or delivereth (Heb. *mōsheh*), his people,' where we seem to trace an allusion to the Hebrew etymology of Moses, Exod. ii. 10. The passage, however, is obscure, and not improbably corrupt. Ewald renders, 'And his people remembered the ancient days of Moses,' taking the noun at the end of the sentence as expressing the subject of the verb at the beginning, which seems too harsh a construction to be tolerated.

The shepherds of his flock, i. e. Moses and Aaron Comp. Ps. lxxvii. 20; Mic. vi 4.

Where is he that put his holy Spirit among them? This is a poetic personification of the religious and practical wisdom divinely vouchsafed to Moses, his companions, and his successor. Hence the expression, 'they vexed his holy Spirit,' which occurs above, will refer to the religious and political decay of Israel in the period of the Judges Comp. Num. xi. 17; Deut. xxxiv 9; Hagg. ii. 5; Neh. ix. 20.

Like the beast that goeth down into the valley, i. e. that is driven down by the shepherd from the bare mountain-side to the green pastures of the valley.

Led them For *tĕnîchennu*, 'made them to rest,' read *tanchennu* with the ancient versions, Bishop Lowth, and Ewald.

Par. 3 *Abraham knoweth us not.* 'Proud as we are of our descent from Abraham (John viii. 33), he is unable to relieve us.'

Why dost thou make us to err from thy ways ? The necessity of evil actions is preached as emphatically by the prophets as the moral responsibility of the human agent. Compare, on the one side, Isa. i. 19, 20, v. 4–7 ; Deut. xi. 26 ; and, on the other, Exod. vii 3 ; Deut. ii. 30 ; Isa. vi. 9, 10, xxix. 10. The difficulty of reconciling these doctrines seems from our passage to have been keenly felt

We are become like those over whom, &c. This expression must be explained by the close connection which existed between the religion of the Jews and their politics Even in the last days of Jerusalem a large proportion of the inhabitants imagined the city of Jehovah to be impregnable (Jer. vii. 4, xxviii. 1–11, &c), and Jeremiah himself, though he deprecated such exaggerations, looked forward to a permanent restoration of the theocratic state (xxxiii 15–18).

Par 4. *Oh that thou wouldest rend the heavens,* &c One of the most involved periods in the Old Testament, extending properly to the words, 'walking in thy ways.' For other instances, see in the Hebrew, Gen i. 1–3, ii. 4–7, v. 1, 2 ; Josh. iii. 14–16 ; 1 Sam iii 2–4, 1 Kings viii. 41–43, &c. (evidently by a prophetic writer, and therefore an unexceptionable parallel to our passage).

Therefore we sinned The calamities of the Jews had only increased their inclination to sin ; on the ground of this the prophet supplicates for mercy

Our adversities continued long Literally, 'therein (i e. in the tokens of thine anger) a long time.' The verb seems to have fallen out, or to have intruded into some neighbouring passage. For the use of the plural *bāhem*, comp. xxx. 6, xxxviii. 16, xliv 15 ; Ezek xxxiii 18, quoted by Delitzsch.

Therefore we went astray For *věnivvashéá*, 'and we shall be saved' read *vannéthá* with Ewald, following the Lxx. ἐπλανήθημεν

And delivered us. For *vattemūgénu*, 'and thou didst melt us,' read *vattěmag-gěnénu* with Ewald, following the Lxx, the Targum, and the Syriac. Comp. Gen. xiv 20

Par. 5 *We are the clay,* &c As the potter never wantonly destroys his own work, so Jehovah cannot have given his people over to irreversible ruin.

The holy cities, i e. the cities of the Holy Land.

CHAPTER VIII.

1.

[LXV.1] I gave access to them that asked not for me; I was at hand unto them that sought me not I said, Behold me, behold me, unto a nation that called not upon my name. I spread out my hands all the day unto a rebellious people, which walked in a way that was not good, after their own thoughts, a people which provoke me continually to my face, which sacrifice in the gardens, and burn incense upon the bricks, which sit in the graves, and lodge in hidden places, which eat swine's flesh, and broth of abominable things is in their vessels, which say, Stand by thyself, come not near unto me, for I am holy. These are a smoke in my nose, a fire that burneth perpetually. Behold, it is written before me, I will not keep silence, until I have recompensed, and recompensed into your bosom, your own iniquities, and the iniquities of your fathers together, saith Jehovah, which burned incense upon the mountains, and reviled me upon the hills; yea, I will measure their reward first into their bosom.

2.

[8.] Thus saith Jehovah, As when new wine is found in the cluster, one saith, Destroy it not, for a blessing is in it, so will I do for my servants' sakes, that I may not destroy it all. And I will bring forth a seed out of Jacob, and out of Judah a possessor of my mountains, and mine elect shall possess it, and my servants shall dwell there And Sharon shall be a pasture of flocks, and the valley of Achor a place for herds to lie down in, for my people that have sought me.

Q

3.

[11.] But as for you that forsake Jehovah, that forget my holy mountain, that prepare a table for Fortune, and fill up spiced wine for Destiny; I have destined you for the sword, and ye shall all bow down to the slaughter; because when I called, ye did, not answer; when I spake, ye did not hear; but did that which was evil in mine eyes, and did choose that wherein I delighted not. Therefore thus saith the Lord Jehovah, Behold, my servants shall eat, but ye shall hunger; behold, my servants shall drink, but ye shall thirst; behold, my servants shall rejoice, but ye shall be ashamed; behold, my servants shall sing for gladness of heart, but ye shall cry for sorrow of heart, and shall howl for vexation of spirit. And ye shall leave your name for a curse unto my chosen, they shall say, 'The Lord Jehovah slay thee in like manner;' but he shall call his servants by another name; so that he who blesseth himself on earth shall bless himself by the God of faithfulness; and he that sweareth on earth shall swear by the God of faithfulness; because the former troubles are forgotten, and because they are hid from mine eyes.

4.

[17] For, behold, I make new heavens and a new earth; and the former shall not be remembered, nor come into mind. But rejoice ye and exult for ever in that which I make; for, behold, I transform Jerusalem into exultation, and her people into joy; and I will exult in Jerusalem, and rejoice in my people, and the voice of weeping shall be no more heard in her, nor the voice of crying. There shall no more be born of her an infant of a few days, nor an old man that filleth not up his days; for he, that dieth at a hundred years, shall die a child, and the sinner, that dieth at a

hundred years, shall be deemed accursed. And they shall build houses, and inhabit them; and they shall plant vineyards, and eat the fruit of them: they shall not build, and another inhabit; they shall not plant, and another eat; for as the days of a tree shall be the days of my people, and mine elect shall long enjoy the work of their hands. They shall not labour in vain, nor bring forth for calamity; for they are the seed of the blessed of Jehovah, and their offspring with them. Before they call, I will answer, and while they are yet speaking, I will hear. 'The wolf and the lamb shall feed together, and the lion shall eat straw like the ox,' and the meat of the serpent shall be dust: 'they shall not hurt nor destroy in all my holy mountain, saith Jehovah.'

Par 1 *I gave access to them*, &c The faithful had complained, through the prophet, that Jehovah had broken off his relationship to his people. Jehovah replies, that the fault lay on their side, for he had always been ready to renew his intercourse with them. For *qōrā* '(where my name was not) invoked,' it is more natural to read *qārā* with Ewald.

A people which provoke me. Some of the idolatrous rites mentioned in this passage were common in Palestine before the exile; others first arose in Babylonia, as the prophet himself intimates by the distinction which he draws between the sins of his hearers, and those of 'their fathers,' who lived in a land of 'mountains and hills' To the former class belong the sacrifices in the gardens (comp. i. 29), and perhaps the initiation in heathen mysteries, to the latter, all the remainder of the description

Upon the bricks, i. e upon altars made of bricks, which were implicitly prohibited by the law (Exod. xx. 24, 25), but were of prime necessity to any system of ritual in Babylonia. Ewald however explains the phrase of the tiling on the roofs, and in the preceding clause alters *gannoth*, 'gardens,' into *gaggoth*, 'roofs,' in accordance with the theory, which no one but himself has adopted, that this prophecy was written by a Jewish refugee in Egypt. The obvious objection is that the preposition in the former clause is not 'upon,' but 'in'

Which sit in the graves. In order, that is, to consult the spirits of the dead, or perhaps the infernal deities of the Babylonians, Anu and Martu. Comp Sir H. Rawlinson, in Rawlinson's 'Herodotus,' vol. i. p 591.

In hidden places, i. e. in subterranean caves and passages, where the mysteries might be celebrated.

That eat swine's flesh, &c. That is, that partake of the 'unclean' food of sacrificial feasts The swine was forbidden by the law, Lev. xi. 7.

I am holy Literally, 'I am holy to thee,' i. e 'thou shouldest treat me as holy.' Thus the Jewish renegades marked the completeness of their defection from Jehovah. A good Israelite, on the other hand, regarded himself as holy, i. e. as one devoted to Jehovah, and the heathen as unclean, Acts x. 28.

Upon the mountains. Comp. lvii. 7; Hos. iv. 13.

Par. 2. *Destroy it not*, i e destroy not the whole cluster because of a few bad grapes.

My mountains This reminds us of Ezekiel's affectionate allusions to the mountains and hills of Palestine, e g. xxxviii. 21, 'I will call for a sword against him throughout all my mountains.' The same expression occurs once in Isaiah (xiv 24), 'Upon my mountains will I tread him under foot.'

Sharon . . . Achor. That is, the whole of Palestine, from Carmel, where the plain of Sharon began, to Jericho, in the neighbourhood of which the valley of Achor (Josh. vii. 24–26) was situated Observe the prophet's accurate acquaintance with the geography of his ancestral country, derived no doubt partly from the traditions of the preceding generation, and partly from a deep study of the sacred writings. Comp note on p 201

Par. 3. *That prepare a table* For these feasts of the gods, the Latin *lectisternia*, see Jer vii. 18, li 44

Fortune Heb. *Gad;* comp. Gen. xxx 11. This is probably the planet Jupiter, called by the Arabs, 'the greater fortune,' and by the Babylonians, *Bel-Merodach.* In the age of Nebuchadnezzar this god 'was considered the source of all power and blessings, and had in fact concentrated in his own person the greater part of that homage and respect, which had been previously divided among the various gods of the Pantheon' (Sir H. Rawlinson, in Rawlinson's 'Herodotus,' vol. i. p 629.) A place called Baal-gad is mentioned in Josh. xi 17, xii. 7, which doubtless derived its name from a Phœnician deity corresponding to Bel-Merodach.

Destiny. Heb. *Měnî*, from *mānāh,* 'to measure, or assign' Meni, we may venture to conjecture, is the same as Nana, or the Babylonian Venus, the slight alteration being due to the fondness of the Jews for attaching Hebrew etymologies to foreign names. On the cylinder of Tiglath-Pileser, Nana is said to be styled 'the queen of victory,' and 'the fortunate' (Rawlinson's 'Herodotus,' vol. i. p. 635.) The latter title corresponds to the Arabic epithet of the planet Venus, 'the lesser fortune.' The Elymean Venus is also called Nanæa in 2 Maccab. i. 13.

The Lord Jehovah slay thee, i e. mayest thou die as fearfully as the renegades of old   The most extreme formula of imprecation.

By another name.   What this name is, we are not yet told, but its signification may be guessed from the fact that the name of Jehovah shall enter into the current formula of blessing.   Comp. note on lxii. 2.

Par. 4. *I make new heavens and a new earth*   Because the former heavens and earth had been defiled by sin, xxiv. 5.

I transform Jerusalem into exultation, i. e. joy shall be a constant habit of mind among the restored Israelites.

He that dieth at a hundred years, &c.   This excellent rendering is due to Bishop Lowth.   The meaning is, Death at the age of a hundred shall be regarded either as premature, or as an evidence of God's wrath.   The same thought is expressed by another prophet of the exile (Isa. xxv. 8) under the slightly different form of the absolute annihilation of death.

Nor bring forth for calamity.   That is, their offspring shall not be cut off by sudden death.

The wolf and the lamb.   This is a condensed quotation from xi. 6-9, with the addition of one original clause, 'the meat of the serpent shall be dust,' i. e. the enmity between the serpent and other animals shall cease.

CHAPTER IX.

1.

[**LXVI 1**] Thus saith Jehovah, The heaven is my throne, and the earth is my footstool; what manner of house will ye build for me, and what manner of place for my rest?   For all these things did mine hand make, and thus all these things arose, saith Jehovah: but on this man will I look favourably, even on him that is oppressed, and is bruised in spirit, and trembleth at my word. He that killeth an ox is as if he slew a man; he that sacrificeth a sheep, as if he brake a dog's neck; he that offereth an oblation, as if he offered swine's blood; he that burneth incense, as if he blessed an idol. According as they have chosen their own ways, and their soul delighteth in their abominations, even so I will choose their contumelies, and will bring their fears upon them; because when I called, none did answer; when I spake, they did not hear, but did that which was evil in mine eyes, and chose that in which I delighted not.

2.

[5] Hear the word of Jehovah, ye that tremble at his word; Your brethren that hate you, that cast you out for my name's sake, say, Let Jehovah glorify himself, that we may look on your joy; but they themselves shall be ashamed. A crashing of thunder from the city, a crashing from the temple, it is the voice of Jehovah that rendereth recompence to his enemies! Before she travailed, she brought forth; before her pain came, she was delivered of a man child. Who hath heard such a thing? who hath heard the like of these things? Is a land brought forth in a day? or is a nation born at once? for Zion hath travailed, and also brought forth her children! Should I bring to the birth, and not cause to bring forth? saith Jehovah; or should I, which cause to bring forth, restrain it? saith thy God.

[10.]
3.

Rejoice ye with Jerusalem, and exult on her account, all ye
    that love her;
  Dance for joy with her, all ye that mourned over her;
That ye may suck, and be satisfied, from the breast of her
    consolations,
  That ye may draw forth with delight from the udder of
    her glory.

For thus saith Jehovah, Behold, I will extend peace to her like a river, and the glory of the nations like an overflowing torrent, so that ye shall suck therefrom ; ye shall be borne on the side, and be dandled upon the knees : as one whom his mother comforteth, so will I comfort you, and ye shall be comforted in Jerusalem. And when ye see this, your heart shall dance for joy, and your bones shall flourish like young grass, and the hand of Jehovah shall be made known for his servants, but he shall pour out his anger on his enemies.

4.

[15.] For, behold, Jehovah will come in fire, and with his chariots like the whirlwind, to render his anger with fury, and his rebuke with flames of fire. For by fire will Jehovah plead, and by his sword with all flesh, and the slain of Jehovah shall be many. They that consecrate themselves and purify themselves, that they may enter the gardens, behind one in the midst, that eat swine's flesh, and the abominations, and the mouse, shall be consumed together ; the utterance is of Jehovah.

5.

[18.] But I will punish their words and their thoughts. The time cometh when I will gather all nations and tongues, and they shall come and see my glory. Then will I work a sign upon them, and will send those that escape of them unto the nations, to Tarshish, to Pul and Lud, that draw the bow, to Tubal and Javan, even to the sea-coasts afar off which have not heard my fame, neither have seen my glory, and they shall declare my glory among the nations. And they shall bring all your brethren for an oblation unto Jehovah, out of all nations, upon horses and in chariots and in litters, and upon mules and upon dromedaries, to my holy mountain, even to Jerusalem, saith Jehovah, as the children of Israel bring the oblation in a clean vessel to the house of Jehovah; and some of them also will I add to the priests and to the Levites, saith Jehovah. For like as the new heavens and the new earth, which I will make, stand continually before me, saith Jehovah, so shall continue your seed and your name. And from new moon to new moon, and from sabbath to sabbath, shall all flesh come to worship before me, saith Jehovah. And they shall go forth and look upon the carcases of the men that rebelled against me, for their worm shall not die, neither shall their fire be quenched; and they shall be an abhorring unto all flesh.

Par. 1 *Thus saith Jehovah,* &c. The passage may be thus paraphrased: ' Even if the Jewish polytheists, or the insincere worshippers of the spiritual God, should desire to co-operate with the prophet in building a temple to Jehovah, their assistance will be rejected The maker of all things in heaven and earth is not in need of any local habitation, and only condescends to accept any outward forms of worship, when they are the natural expression of devout humility ' Thus we regard the passage as describing a purely imaginary case, and not (as Hitzig) a project at any time debated among Jewish exiles If the latter had actually contemplated the erection of a Babylonian temple, similar to that afterwards erected by the Jews in Egypt (see note on xix. 18, p 111), the prophet would have given vent to his indignation in less ambiguous language Our view seems to be confirmed by the parallel passage in Ps l 8–15, which, though it can scarcely have been composed by the author of Isa. xl-lxvi, as Hitzig, in his Commentary on the Psalms, conjectures, must at any rate have been written subsequently to the reformation of Josiah.

He that killeth an ox is as if he slew a man. That is, the ceremonial acts of formal worshippers are an abomination to Jehovah Comp. 1 Sam xv. 23, ' For disobedience is like a sin of witchcraft, and stubbornness is like the worship of idols and teraphim.'

As if he offered swine's blood. The rigour with which devout Israelites observed the prohibition of swine's flesh is strikingly shewn by the narratives in the Second Book of Maccabees See 2 Maccab. vi, vii.

I will choose their contumelies. That is, misfortune shall pursue them, as it were, with the wanton malice of an ill-trained child. Comp. iii. 4 (p. 8), 'I will make boys their rulers, and contumely shall rule over them.'

Par. 2. *That cast you out*, i.e. that exclude you from their society. Comp. lxv. 5.

A crashing of thunder from the city, a crashing from the temple! Here the prophet changes his point of view. Those who believe the promises of Jehovah embodied in this prophecy are represented as having returned to Palestine. The splendour of the New Jerusalem (see chap. iii, p. 211) is so marvellous as to attract visitors from all countries, including those Jews who had remained behind in Babylonia (compare verses 18 and 24). But while the latter are yet on the way, they are destroyed by a direct interposition of Jehovah. This appears to be the most natural meaning, and is in perfect harmony with the Babylonian origin of these chapters. Those who, like Dr. Payne Smith, regard this passage as presupposing the existence of the temple of Solomon, have to answer the objection that verse 1 presupposes that the temple needed to be rebuilt.

Should I bring to the birth, and not cause to bring forth? That is, should I, who announced the liberation of the Jews and their return to Palestine, fail to carry out my promises in the most glorious manner? Compare the different anticipations of another Jewish prophet in Babylon, couched in very similar metaphorical language, xxvi. 18 (p. 127).

Par. 3. *All ye that love her*, i.e. all who have preserved a patriotic attachment to the land of their forefathers.

From the udder of her glory. See 'Notes and Criticisms,' pp. 40-42.

Par. 4. *They that consecrate themselves*, i e those who prepare themselves by lustrations to take part in idolatrous mysteries.

Behind one in the midst. The meaning of these obscure words seems irrecoverably lost. Some have compared the phrase 'to go after, i e to worship, Jehovah,' and suppose an allusion to an image or symbolic representation of some heathen deity, placed in the centre of the sacred grove or garden. 'One' might be used contemptuously, or in the sense of 'unique,' as in Song of Sol vi. 9. Others interpret the words to mean, 'after the pattern of a hierophant in the midst of the throng of worshippers, or, in the midst of the house, i.e. in the court.' Others, following the Targum of Jonathan, suppose the phrase to be elliptical, and interpret, 'one after the other.' We are not inclined to accept any of these explanations. Possibly the passage is corrupt, or some of the words, necessary to complete the sense, were dropped in the typical MS. or

MSS from which the received text was taken, or even intruded accidentally into a neighbouring column of the same roll.

The abominations, i. e. the flesh of reptiles, such as the mouse, Lev. xi. 11, 29.

Par. 5. *But I will punish their words,* &c. Literally, ' But I—their words and their thoughts—it cometh to gather.' The construction is left imperfect to indicate the speaker's indignation.

When I will gather all nations and tongues. The object of this great concourse of visitors from all nations is stated to be ' that they may see the glory of Jehovah,' i. e. the splendour of the revived kingdom of Israel. Instead, however, of being admitted within the sacred borders, they are punished for their previous hostility by a mysterious destruction. This way of describing the final judgment seems peculiar to our prophet. Other prophetical writers represent it as being provoked by a combined heathen assault upon Jerusalem. See Joel iii. 11-14 ; Zech. xiv, Ezek. xxxviii, xxxix.

Then will I work a sign upon them. According to some the sign consists in the concession of priestly functions to Gentile converts, as a reward for their zeal in forwarding the return of the exiles. This, however, is inconsistent with the doctrine of Israel's spiritual supremacy announced in lxi. 6. 'The sign' must therefore be the destruction of Jehovah's enemies ; it is a vague but suggestive expression, and well calculated to prepare the mind of the reader for the awful description with which the prophetic volume closes.

Those that escape of them, i. e. those who are spared in the great judgment.

Pul. Pul is a secondary form of Put, which in three other Biblical passages (Jer. xlvi 9, Ezek. xxvii 10, xxx. 5) is coupled with Lud or the Ludim. For the interchange of *l* and *t*, see Gen. xxx. 20 (Heb.). The most probable conjecture as to the origin of Put is that of G. Ebers, who connects the word with *Pu(n)t*, the name given on the Egyptian monuments to the Arabian peninsula, though properly belonging only to the nomad Arab tribes. The Arabs of the north, as the inscriptions prove were for a long time tributary to Egypt. See ' Egypt and the Books of Moses,' by Dr. G. Ebers, vol. i. pp. 63-71.

Lud. This is connected, by the writer just mentioned, with the word *Rut,* which is found on the Egyptian monuments, and denotes the Egyptian citizens, as opposed to slaves and foreigners. See ' Egypt and the Books of Moses,' vol. i pp 96-98.

Tubal, i. e. the Tibareni, a branch of ' that Scythic or Turanian people, who spread themselves in very early times over the entire region lying between the Mediterranean and India, the Persian Gulf and the Caucasus.' Sir H. Rawlinson, in Rawlinson's ' Herodotus,' vol. i p. 652.

Javan, i. e. the Greeks of Ionia and the coast of the Euxine Sea. Comp. Joel iii 6, where the Phœnicians are denounced for having sold Jewish captives to 'the sons of the Javanites,' and Obad. 20, where 'captives of Jerusalem' are mentioned as living 'in Sepharad,' i e probably either Sardis or Sparta

And they shall bring all your brethren, &c. Comp lx 9, and the parallel passage in Zeph iii 10, 'From beyond the rivers of Ethiopia shall they bring my worshippers, even the company of my dispersed for mine oblation'

As the children of Israel bring the oblation. Here, as throughout this paragraph, except verse 22, the prophet places himself mentally in the new Jerusalem, where the temple and its ritual have been re-established 'The oblation' is, literally, 'the meat-offering,' which consisted of fine flour seasoned with salt, and mixed with frankincense and oil, Lev. ii. 1.

Some of them also will I add to the priests and to the Levites That is, Jehovah will no longer confine the service of the temple to the tribe of Levi, nor even to the Jews from Babylonia, to whom the promise in lxi 6 was addressed, but will open it to some at least of the Jews of the Dispersion. Many of the latter were doubtless descended from families of the old northern kingdom, and, by their admission to so sacred an office as the priesthood, the religious schism of Jeroboam would be finally healed, and the prophecy of Hos iii 5 fulfilled.

Stand continually before me, i e. are the subject of my continual attention Comp. xlix. 16, 'Thy walls are continually before me.'

And from new moon to new moon, &c. Comp the parallel passage, Zech xiv 16, where a part of the heathen are, as in our prophecy, represented as being spared by Jehovah, and converted to the true religion 'Then shall every one that is left of all the nations which came against Jerusalem go up from year to year to worship the King, Jehovah of Hosts, and to keep the feast of tabernacles.'

And they shall go forth. It is instructive to compare the various prophetic representations respecting the great final judgment, which was announced to usher in the Messianic era. According to Joel (iii 2, 12, written about 870 B.C), this was to take place in 'the valley of Jehoshaphat,' i. e not the narrow glen so called, through which the brook Kedron runs, but some imaginary valley of far vaster dimensions, corresponding to those of the new Jerusalem, which receives from the prophet the symbolic name, Jehoshaphat, or 'Jehovah judgeth.' According to an anonymous prophet, shortly before the first siege of Jerusalem B.C. 599 (Zech xiv. 12), the army of the heathen invaders of Palestine should 'consume away while they stood upon their feet' before the walls of Jerusalem. According to Ezekiel (xxxix 4, 11, written about 574) Gog and his savage hordes, representing the heathen world, should fall by pestilence and by fire from heaven on 'the mountains of Israel, and be buried in the plain on the east of the Dead Sea.   According to the anonymous author of the apocryphal Book of Enoch (xxvi, xxvii, liv, lvi, written, according to Dillmann, about 110 B.C.), the final judgment was to take place by fire and sword in a valley near 'the centre of the earth,' which, as the context shews, is synonymous with mount Zion, so that the valley referred to can be no other than that of Hinnom, whence the Gehenna of the New Testament.

All these various accounts agree with the prophecy before us in representing the punishment of the heathen to result from a direct Divine interposition, and all, except that of Ezekiel, in placing the theatre of the judgment in the neighbourhood of Jerusalem   All of them, too, are marked in some degree by the infirmity of human passion, which, until the rise of Christianity, prevented the possessors of spiritual religion from making due allowance for the unavoidable ignorance of their opponents.   Still it may be well to remind the student that the terrible fate of the heathen, which our prophet describes so calmly, and in such glaring colours, would be justified by him on the ground that the religious state of the sufferers was one of wilful disobedience to the King of kings. In fact, those who might attach themselves to the Jewish exiles on their return home from Babylonia, were welcomed by the prophet (lvi. 3-8, pp. 197, 198) in language, which seems almost evangelical in the depth of its tenderness   But the discrepancies of these prophetic descriptions are not less instructive than their points of resemblance.   The anonymous prophecy in Zechariah mentions pestilence and the sword as the agencies by which the heathen are to be consumed ; Ezekiel, the prophecy before us, and the Book of Enoch, speak of fire descending from heaven.   Ezekiel, too, as we stated above, differs from the rest in the theatre which he assigns to the judgment of the heathen and their burial. Joel, the prophecy in Zechariah, and Ezekiel, merely describe the earthly fate of Jehovah's enemies, but the author of Isa. xl-lxvi, vaguely and mysteriously, and the author of the Book of Enoch, in terms distinct and unmistakeable, announce the prolongation of the torments of the unbelievers even after bodily dissolution.   In other words, the final triumph of the kingdom of God was held with almost equal firmness by all the prophets, but the form which this doctrine assumed varied with the circumstances of the time.   In particular, the representation of the punishment of the wicked as everlasting, in the Book of Enoch, marks the reaction of spiritual religion against the alien influences of Hellenism.

For their worm shall not die, &c.   That is, the phantoms in Hades shall have some dim consciousness of the vengeance that is being wreaked on their earthly bodies.   Comp. xiv. 20, 21 (p. 139), Job xiv. 22; Judith xvi 17; Mark ix. 43-48.

SUPPLEMENTARY NOTES.

Page 6. *In the days to come.* The expression thus rendered is somewhat vague and indefinite. It may signify either 'in the latter part of the present period,' or 'at its conclusion.' To render with the Authorised Version 'in the last days' is certainly wrong, for the Messianic period, to which the description before us relates, is represented by all the prophets as one of unending felicity. A very similar phrase occurs in xxx. 8 (par. 3, p 70), 'that it may serve to a time to come for a testimony,' literally, 'to a day to come'

P. 39. Note on *To behold my face.* The view here adopted is not the one generally received among modern critics, Gesenius, Ewald, Hitzig, and Delitzsch being all opposed to it. We are therefore glad to be able now to confirm it by the authority of the eminent Semitic scholar, Dr. Noldeke See 'Gottingische gelehrte Anzeigen,' 1869, p 2008, and comp. Geiger's 'Urschrift,' pp 337–339

P. 40 Note on *The oaks.* The most recent authority on the trees of Scripture, Mr H B Tristram, states that terebinths are common in the south and east of Palestine (See his 'Natural History of the Bible,' Art. Terebinths.) But the isolation in which he allows that they are found, and the fact that they are neither shady nor evergreen, induce us to adhere to the view already expressed.

P 44 (Prophecy respecting Moab.) A few words may be added on the geographical notices in this prophecy Most of the towns mentioned had, in remote antiquity, passed out of the possession of the Moabites into that of the Amorites. They were afterwards captured by the Israelites (Num. xxi. 21–32), though the Moabites may from time to time have reasserted their territorial rights. See Judges iii 12; 1 Sam. xxii. 3. The victories of David (2 Sam. viii. 2) no doubt restored the land north of the Arnon to the occupancy of the Israelites, yet we learn from this prophecy that at some later period the Moabites had once more expelled the Israelites from the debated region. Two additional facts may probably be gathered from the inscription recently discovered on the site of the ancient Dibon, viz. (1) that Omri found the Moabites again in possession of the north side of the Arnon, from which, however, he seems to have expelled them, and (2) that Mesha, king of Moab, recovered and fortified the towns which Omri had destroyed. These statements may be supplemented from the Second Book of Kings (xiv. 25), which records that Jeroboam II, king of Israel, 'restored the coast of Israel from the region about Hamath to the sea of the plain,' i e. recovered, amongst other territories, those which had been wrested from his predecessors by the Moabites.

None of these facts, however, can be used in illustration of the age of Isa xv, xvi, for nearly a century must have elapsed between the revolt of Mesha and the victories of Jeroboam II   From data of a different kind supplied by the prophecy itself we have been enabled to refer it with some confidence to the beginning of the reign of Uzziah, who came to the throne of Judah in the fifteenth year of Jeroboam II (2 Kings xiv. 17), i.e. in all probability before the re-conquest by the Israelites of the country on the east of the Jordan   (Our reason for the latter assumption is that, considering the weakness to which the northern kingdom had been reduced by the Syrian invasions, fifteen years are not too much to allow for the gradual improvement in its fortunes, which culminated in the capture of Hamath and Damascus)

P. 44   *Baith and Dibon are gone up the high places*   M Neubauer and M. Derenbourg propose to read, *'ālāh béth-habbāmōth vedibon*, 'Beth-Bamoth and Dibon went up (to weep).'   The name Beth-Bamoth occurs in the inscription of king Mesha

P. 45. *A lion*, or, lions, i.e. probably the Assyrians, who began to influence the fortunes of Palestine as early as the time of Ahab.   See M. Oppert's ' Histoire des Empires de Chaldée et d'Assyrie,' p 140, whence it appears that Ahab contributed 10,000 men to the army of Benhadad II, which was defeated by Shalmaneser III in his third campaign.

P. 46 *Reached unto Jazer   .   passed over the sea.*   That is, the Moabitish vineyards extended as far north as Jazer, in the former territory of Gad, as far east as the wilderness, and as far south as the Dead Sea

Ibid *Yet when Moab spendeth his strength in vain.*   The tenacity with which the Moabites adhered to the worship of their god Chemosh is illustrated by many passages of the inscription of king Mesha.   The subjection of Moab to Israel is said to be caused by the wrath of their god, and the victories of Mesha are connected (line 14) with an oracle given by Chemosh to the king, Go and take Nebo from Israel.

P 56. (Prophecy respecting Tyre.)   To avoid distracting the attention of the reader from the contents of this prophecy, we have retained the conventional name of Shalmaneser, as that of the besieger of Tyre   For several reasons, however (see note on ' Sargon,' p. 91), it seems necessary to suppose that Shalmaneser is a mistake of the later Jewish historians, including Josephus, the real name of the successor of Tiglath-Pileser II being Sargon. The passage from Menander's 'Tyrian Annals,' quoted by Josephus, omits to mention the name of the king of Assyria.

Since writing the above Introduction, Mr A. H. Sayce, of Queen's College, Oxford, has informed us of a passage in one of the inscriptions of Sargon (Brit Mus Coll vol. 1. pl 36, line 21), where the 'partitioner of the wide-spread country of Bit-Khumriya (House of Omri = Samaria)' declares that he 'has destroyed the city of Tsurru (Tyre)' We doubt, however, whether this boast can be considered to outweigh the opposite testimony of Menander. That Tyre, however, like other Phœnician cities, became tributary to Assyria in Sargon's reign is probable enough

P. 59 Note on *Thou shalt have no rest*. The foe, from whose pursuit the Tyrians should be in danger, is still of course the king of Assyria. In the inscription quoted above, Sargon claims further to have 'laid his yoke upon the land of the Yavnai (the Greeks).' And so in the eighth plate at the end of M. Botta's letters· 'From the land of Yavnana, which is in the midst of the sea, towards the setting of the sun, to the borders of Egypt and the Moschi, the widespread land of Phœnicia, the country of the Hittites to its full extent . . . I levied tribute, and appointed my governors to have rule over them'

P. 70. *The help of Egypt is idle and in vain*. Mr. G. Smith illustrates this by an event which took place shortly after the date of the prophecy, when Yaman, one of the rival kings of Ashdod, was betrayed into the hands of the Assyrians by the king of Egypt and Ethiopia.

P. 86. Note on *The vain gods*. In illustration of the religious spirit of the Assyrian kings, compare the following quotations from M. Oppert's translation of the 'Annals of Sargon.' ('Les Fastes de Sargon,' Paris, 1863) 'Les dieux Assour, Nebo et Mérodach m'ont conféré la royauté des nations,' (p 4) 'J'assiégai et vainquis Kibaba, préfet de la ville de Kharkar . . . J'y ai institué le culte du dieu Assour, mon maître, (p 6) 'J'assiégai, je pris Asdod *j'enlevai comme captifs les dieux d'Jaman,'* (p. 8.) 'J'ai invoqué Assour, le père des dieux, le plus grand souverain des dieux,' (p. 11.)

P. 88 Note on *There shall come forth a rod*. That Isaiah regarded Hezekiah as the destined Messiah is altogether improbable. But there is a curious saying in the Talmud (Sanhedrin 94) which may deserve mention, to the effect that God originally designed Hezekiah to be the Messiah, as he designed Sennacherib to be Gog Magog, but afterwards renounced the purpose. This and similar passages seem to have originated in a misunderstanding of the hopes once fondly cherished of a certain Hezekiah, the father of that Judah of Galilee

(Acts v. 37), who founded the order of the Zealots. This Hezekiah was, according to Josephus (Archæol. xiv. 9, 2), 'the captain of a troop of brigands,' but in reality the leader in a patriotic resistance to the Roman authority. The wide-spread veneration for his memory is attested by a saying of the great Rabbi Hillel, to the effect that Israel had no future Messiah to expect, since it had already enjoyed his presence in the days of Hezekiah. Similar expectations were afterwards excited by his celebrated grandson, Menahem. See an interesting article in Geiger's 'Judische Zeitschrift,' 1870, pp 35–43.

P. 91 Note on *Sargon* An article on 'Hosea,' in Schenkel's 'Bibel-Lexicon,' contains a defence of the theory distinguishing Sargon from Shalmaneser, by Dr Schrader, the author of a well-timed plea for Assyriology, addressed to Semitic scholars The arguments which he has brought forward, however, are by no means conclusive, as the following remarks, which Mr. A. H. Sayce has been good enough to communicate, sufficiently shew 'The inscription referred to by Dr. Schrader is much too mutilated to be made the basis of any conjectural conclusions All we learn from it is that some time between the first and fifteenth years of Sargon's reign, Samaria was taken, and a large number of its inhabitants deported, and that those who were left continued to pay tribute. Dr. Schrader is hasty in assuming that the name of the Israelite king was not mentioned by Sargon, because Hoshea had been carried captive by Tiglath-Pileser before the final capture of Samaria Hoshea's name may have been once extant in the inscription, and even if this were not the case, it would be nothing unusual, since the Assyrian monarchs are sometimes contented with specifying the submission and the tribute of the tribe or town. Neither is Dr. Schrader justified in assigning the capture of Samaria to the first year of Sargon. There are no marks of time given in the inscription, and we know that Sargon's first campaign was against Khumba-nigas, king of Elam It makes little difference whether or not Sargon was of royal extraction. Certainly Tiglath-Pileser was not. And Sargon actually endeavours to trace back his descent to two ancient Assyrian kings, Bilu-bani and Paldasi. Of a Shalmaneser as predecessor of Sargon, the Assyrian Canon seems to be altogether silent It is true that in one copy of it a line is drawn across the seventeenth year of Tiglath-Pileser, and another across his twenty-second year in a second copy. But these probably have to do with chronological epochs , besides, we are in possession of the annals of the seventeenth year of Tiglath-Pileser. The Canon never fails to give the name of the reigning monarch, with his title attached.'

P. 109 *Shall Egypt be the third to Israel and to Assyria.* Comp. Ps. lxxxvii. 4, 5,

‘ I will declare Rahab and Babylon to be my familiars :
Behold, Philistia, and Tyre, with Ethiopia ;
This man was born there (i. e. is a citizen of Zion).’

P. 235. Note on *And they shall go forth.* The following are the passages of the Book of Enoch referred to (Dillmann’s translation) :

Chap. xxvii. ‘Then I said, Whereunto is this blessed land, which is altogether filled with trees, and this cursed valley between? And Uriel, one of the holy angels, who was by me, answered and said unto me, This cursed valley is for those who are cursed for ever ; here must all those gather together, who utter unseemly words against God, and speak impudently concerning his glory ; here doth one gather them, and this is the place of their punishment. And in the last time shall the spectacle of a righteous judgment be given upon them before the righteous from everlasting to everlasting . . .’

Chap. liv. ‘And I looked up and turned to another region of the earth, and saw there a deep valley with burning fire. And they brought the kings and the mighty ones, and laid them in the deep valley. And there mine eyes saw how men made instruments for them, iron chains of immeasurable weight. And I asked the angel of peace, who was by me, saying, These chain-instruments, for whom are they prepared? And he said unto me, These are being prepared for the bands of Azazel, that they may take them and lay them in the nethermost hell : and with rough stones shall one cover their jaws, as the Lord of spirits hath commanded. Michael and Gabriel, Rufael and Fanuel, shall lay hold of them on that great day ; they shall cast them on that day into the furnace of flaming fire, that the Lord of spirits may take vengeance on them for their unrighteousness, forasmuch as they were subject unto Satan, and have seduced them that dwell on the earth.’ The ‘iron chains’ mentioned in this chapter may serve to illustrate Isa. xxiv. 21 ; Jude 6 ; and 2 Pet. ii. 4.

921319

Printed in Great Britain by
Amazon.co.uk, Ltd.,
Marston Gate.